CyberEthics

Morality and Law in Cyberspace
Second Edition

CyberEthics
Morality and Law in Cyberspace
Second Edition

Richard A. Spinello
Carroll School of Management
Boston College

JONES AND BARTLETT PUBLISHERS
Sudbury, Massachusetts
BOSTON   TORONTO   LONDON   SINGAPORE

World Headquarters
Jones and Bartlett Publishers
40 Tall Pine Drive
Sudbury, MA 01776
978-443-5000
info@jbpub.com
www.jbpub.com

Jones and Bartlett Publishers Canada
2406 Nikanna Road
Mississauga, ON L5C 2W6
CANADA

Jones and Bartlett Publishers International
Barb House, Barb Mews
London W6 7PA
UK

Library of Congress Cataloging-in-Publication Data
Spinello, Richard A.
    CyberEthics : Morality and Law in Cyberspace / Richard A. Spinello.--2nd ed.
       p. cm.
    ISBN 0-7637-0064-9
    1. Internet—Moral and ethical aspects. 2. Computers and civilization.
    3. Law and ethics. I. Title.
    TK5105.875.I57 S68 2002
    303.48'34—dc21

                                                                    2002072214

Production Credits
Editor-in-Chief: J. Michael Stranz
Production Manager: Amy Rose
Senior Marketing Manager: Nathan Schultz
Associate Production Editor: Tara McCormick
Editorial Assistant: Theresa DiDonato
Production Assistant: Karen C. Ferreira
Manufacturing and Inventory Coordinator: Amy Bacus
Cover Design: Philip Regan
Composition: Chiron, Inc.
Printing and Binding: Malloy, Inc.
Cover Printing: Malloy, Inc.

Printed in the United States of America
06 05 04 03   10 9 8 7 6 5 4 3 2

In memory of my grandmothers,
Guiseppa Padrevita and Olga Spinello

In memory of my grandmothers,
Guiseppa Padrevita and Olga Spinello

CONTENTS

PREFACE

Since this book first appeared only a few short years ago, the social and technical landscape of cyberspace has undergone remarkable changes. There are new Internet architectures, such as peer-to-peer systems that make it easier to download digital music and movies. At the same time, there have been extraordinary legal developments—new laws like the Children's Internet Protection Act and various court decisions—defining new constraints for Web surfers. New governance bodies, such as ICANN, have emerged in an effort to impose order on this rapidly expanding network. We have taken all of these developments into account in this second edition.

The growth of the Internet has been one of the most remarkable phenomena of the last century. In the early 1980s, the Internet was known to only a handful of scientists and academics, but it is now being regularly used by over 60 million people, and many predict that it will revolutionize everything from the practice of medicine to education. The Internet is more than merely a communications network. It is at the center of a global information infrastructure that is creating a new social and economic order characterized by global connectivity and the decentralization of authority.

The success of the Internet would not have been possible without the recent development of the World Wide Web, which has made a wide variety of media (such as text, video, and audio) available through a user-friendly interface. The Web has ignited electronic commerce and changed the face of Internet communications. As we move into a new millennium, the Web is beginning to have a dominating influence on our culture as it insinuates itself into many aspects of our daily lives.

This rapid development of the Web and the entire Internet economy is not without its social costs. If it is easier to publish and spread truthful and valuable information, it is also easier to spread libel, falsehoods, and pornographic material. If it is easier to reproduce and share digitized information instantaneously, it is also easier to violate copyright protection. And if it is easier to build personal relationships with consumers, it is also easier to monitor consumers' behavior and invade their personal privacy. Thus, the Internet's vast capabilities can be misused to undermine private property and to mock our traditional sense of moral propriety.

Our primary purpose in this revised edition is to review carefully the social costs and moral problems that have been triggered by the expanded use of this communications and information network. While some of these problems are familiar ones, many are new to the fields of computer ethics and public policy. For example, while much work has been done on the topic of intellectual property, little attention has been paid to the ethical dimension of interconnectivity, that is, the proper use of hyperlinks, metatags, and search engines. In the process of examining these issues, we will identify some of the legal disputes that will most likely become paradigm cases for more complex situations yet to come.

The Internet is also a challenge to legal systems, which have had a difficult time keeping up with this borderless global technology. In the past, the Internet was an unstructured electronic terrain, a frontier with few rules and restrictions. Now that cyberspace has become a widely used forum for our economic transactions and social interactions, many argue that anarchy must yield to some type of order and that new laws must be crafted to restrict and punish asocial users. Some civil libertarians, however, steadfastly resist intrusive government intervention. "Keep your hands off our Net" is one of their favorite slogans. But is that philosophy still tenable or is it just too romantic and antiquated for a commercialized Internet?

If we do agree that the Net needs some type of order, the key question is how that order should be imposed or how the Net should be governed. A framework of laws and regulation is one solution, but there are others, such as greater reliance on self-regulation from below with the help of technology. Why not let technology correct itself? There are, after all, viable Internet architectures that can deal with some of the Internet's social problems perhaps even more effectively than a centrally imposed set of regulations. These two approaches represent the fundamental options for the future of Internet regulation. Should the state, for example, promulgate and enforce laws that ban pornography or should individual users rely on filtering devices to keep it out of their homes? Is the proper model centralized state controls or decentralized individual controls?

In Chapter 2, we will present the case for greater reliance on a decentralized, bottoms-up approach to governing the Internet. Its proponents argue that this approach best fits the Internet's open architecture, along with the logic of this medium. This approach can also overcome some of the administrative difficulties of controlling an international network. It is quite difficult for any nation to exercise local jurisdiction over the information available in cyberspace, but it is often possible for technology itself to constrain behavior, without the need for the heavy hand of government. According to this perspective, the role for government involvement in regulating the Internet should be as modest as possible. There may be externalities or market imperfections that cannot be handled by technology, such as monopolistic behavior that threatens the Internet economy. Such situations may warrant strong government intervention, but in most cases Internet stakeholders should be allowed to govern themselves.

On the other hand, there are many perils in depending upon self-regulation, especially when we empower the regulator with sound technology. There could be excesses, such as the privatization of unfair copyright regulations or irresponsible content control. This has led many scholars and analysts to call for more comprehensive, top-down regulations that will ensure that the Internet is governed with regularity and fairness. Their viewpoint will also be presented in Chapter 2.

Thus, our second purpose in this book is to stimulate the reader's reflection on the broad issue of Internet regulation. How one resolves this fundamental question will provide an important context for addressing the formidable social problems triggered by the explosive growth of the Internet.

In order to accomplish both of these objectives, we will first lay out some theoretical groundwork drawn from the writings of contemporary legal scholars like Larry Lessig of Stanford and philosophers like Kant, Finnis, and Foucault. We then focus on four broad areas: content control and free speech, intellectual property, privacy, and security. For each of these critical areas, we consider the common ethical and public policy problems that have arisen and how technology or law would propose to solve some of those problems.

The first of these four topics concerns the fringes of Internet communication, such as pornography, hate speech, online threats, and spam (unsolicited commercial e-mail). We will review the history of public policy decisions about the problem of pornography and treat in some depth the suitability of automated content controls. Are these controls technically feasible and can they be used in a way that is morally acceptable to the relevant stakeholders?

We then review the new breed of intellectual property issues provoked by the steady commercialism of the Internet and the proliferation of Web sites. Much of our attention here will be on digital music and the predicament of companies like Napster, but we will also discuss ownership of domain names, the "right" to link to other Web sites, the propriety of framing, the appropriate use of metatags, and the growing reliance on trusted systems.

Perhaps the most notorious and widely publicized social problem is the ominous threat that the Internet poses to personal privacy. The Internet seems to have the potential to further erode our personal privacy and to make our lives as consumers and employees more transparent than ever before. What, if anything, should be done about online databases overflowing with personal information? The covert gathering of information from consumers visiting Web sites, the use of "cookies," and the strict monitoring of employees' Internet interactions are other problematic concerns. Here again we will explore whether certain protective technologies can be part of the solution.

Finally, we treat the critical area of security with a primary focus on the perennial problem of trespass in cyberspace. We will dwell on what constitutes trespass and why "trespass to chattels" has become a favorite cause of action for Internet lawyers. We will also discuss the use of encryption as a means of ensuring that transmitted data is confidential and secure. The encryption controversy epitomizes the struggle between government control and individual rights that is shaping many of the public policy debates about the Internet. Should users be able to encrypt data without giving the government back-door access? Or is this too big a threat to national security? In addition to a cursory overview of the federal government's policies on encryption, we will analyze this matter from a moral framework in order to expose this dilemma to a slightly different perspective. We will conclude with an overview of security issues and electronic commerce.

It should be apparent by now that this book is a bit more narrowly focused than traditional books about computer or information ethics, since the topics are limited to the particular moral problems that emerge in the realm of cyberspace. However, if one considers the rapid evolution of the Internet and the great potential of Web communications, what is presented here represents the new generation of moral issues that will occupy computer ethicists, lawyers, and public policy makers for many years to come.

Also, throughout the book we implicitly embrace the philosophy of *technological realism*, which sees technology as a powerful agent for change and forward progress in society. But unlike more utopian views, this position does not ignore the dangers and deterministic tendencies of technology, along with its potential to cause harm and undermine basic human rights and values.

However, corporations and individuals, though heavily influenced by information technology, are not powerless to exercise some control over the underlying code of cyberspace. Such control will require prudent decision-making, which will help ensure that computer and network technologies are used wisely and cautiously, in a way that enhances the human condition and the opportunity for human flourishing. It will also demand that all information technologies, including those targeted at the social problems of cyberspace, be implemented with respect for standards of justice and fairness.

Like most traditional books on ethics, this one is optimistic about the tenacity of the human spirit and the depth of moral conviction even in cyberspace. The technology determinists believe that the forces of technology have already won the war, but the realists contend that the struggle continues on and that the final outcome is still in doubt.

▶ The Web Site

This book is accompanied by a Web site, www.jbpub.com/cyberethics. While books are static entities, Web sites are dynamic, and this Web site will be consistently updated and modified to reflect the changes and developments in this field. We strongly encourage both faculty and students to make use of this important resource.

The Web site contains valuable links to other Web sites, which will facilitate further research for the topics and subtopics covered in this book. These links also provide additional background material for some of the cases that are included at the end of each chapter. In addition, this Web site contains elaborate exercises for each chapter, along with suggested topics for "white papers" on some of the controversial themes covered in the text. Instructors will find sample syllabi and suggestions for organizing a course around this book and the topic of Internet ethics. Finally, the Web site will provide an opportunity for instructors and students to give feedback to the author or to contact the author with questions or comments.

The book and its Web site are meant to be used jointly in order to enhance the academic experience of studying cyberspace ethics. One complements the other. It is our hope that both those who use this book in the classroom and the general reader will consult the Web site for its up-to-date supplementary material and its other supportive features. It is designed to make this exploration of the Internet and the ethical issues that surface there as instructive and rewarding as possible.

▶ Acknowledgements

In this book I have incorporated a small amount of material from several articles or papers that I published elsewhere: a portion of the material on spam was derived from "Ethical Reflections on the Problem of Spam" originally published in *Ethics and Information Technology* (vol. 1, no. 4); several paragraphs of the discussion on James Boyle's theory of intellectual property also originally appeared in *Ethics and Information Technology* (vol. 1, no. 2); and some of the discussion on e-mail privacy rights was part of a paper entitled "Electronic Mail and Panoptic Power in the Workplace," delivered at The Fifth Annual International Conference Promoting Business Ethics at DePaul University (October, 1998).

I am most grateful to Boston College for giving me a sabbatical; the free time has allowed me to complete this book along with several other related projects. I am indebted to Joyce O'Connor in the Carroll School of Management for her assistance in helping me handle some of the mechanics involved in publishing this manuscript. Many thanks also to several individuals at Jones and Bartlett, especially Michael Stranz, Theresa DiDonato, Karen Ferreira, and Amy Rose, for their help in bringing this second edition out so quickly. Finally, I owe a great debt of gratitude to my wife, Susan T. Brinton, for her patience and continued tolerance for the lonely life of an author.

Richard A. Spinello

CHAPTER ONE

The Internet and Ethical Values

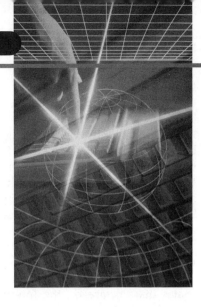

The end [of ethics] is action, not knowledge.

Aristotle[1]

▶ Introduction

More than three decades have passed since the first communications were transmitted over a fledgling global network that would later be called the Internet. At the time few would have predicted the Internet's explosive growth and persistent encroachment on our personal and professional lives. This radically decentralized network has been described in lofty terms as empowering and democratizing. It has lived up to this ideal by creating opportunity for many new voices with extraordinary reach. While the claim that the Internet will revolutionize communications may be hyperbole, there is no doubt that this transforming technology has the potential to magnify the individual's power and fortify democratic processes.

Many governments, however, are clearly threatened by some of this decentralized power and they have sought to impose some centralized controls on this anarchic network. The United States has attempted to regulate speech through the ill-fated Communications Decency Act and to restrict the use of encryption technology through its key recovery schemes. More Draconian regulations have been imposed by countries like China and Saudi Arabia. The Net and its stakeholders have stead-

1

fastly resisted the imposition of such controls, and this has led to many of the tensions and controversies that we will consider throughout this book.

While the control of technology through law and regulation has often been a futile effort, "correcting" technology with other technology has been more effective. The regime of law has had a hard time suppressing the dissemination of pornography on the Internet, but blocking software systems that filter out indecent material have been much more successful. This reflects the Net's paradoxical nature—it does empower individuals and allows them to exercise their rights, such as free speech, more vigorously, but it also makes possible effective technical controls that can undermine those rights.

Although the primary axis of discussion in this book is the ethical issues that surface on the Internet, we must devote attention to these related matters of cybergovernance and public policy. Thus we will explore in some detail the tensions between the radical empowerment that the Net allows and the impulse to tame this technology through laws and other mechanisms.

Since this is a book about ethics, about *acting* well in this new realm of cyberspace, we begin by reviewing some basic concepts that will enrich our moral assessment of these issues. In this introductory chapter, our purpose is to provide a concise overview of the traditional ethical frameworks that can guide our analysis of the moral dilemmas and social problems that arise in cyberspace.

More importantly, we will also elaborate here on the two underlying assumptions of this work: a.) the *directive* and architectonic role of moral ideals and principles in determining responsible behavior in cyberspace, and b.) the capacity of free and responsible human beings to exercise some control over the forces of technology (technological realism). Let us begin with the initial premise concerning the proper role of cyberethics.

▶ Cyberethics and the "Law of the Horse"

An ethical norm such as the imperative to be truthful is just one example of a constraint on our behavior. In the real world there are other constraints, including the laws of civil society or even the social pressures exerted by the communities in which we live and work. There are many forces at work shaping our behavior, but where does ethics fit in?

This same question can be posed about cyberspace. To help us reflect on this matter, we turn to the framework of Larry Lessig. In his highly influential book, *Code and Other Laws of Cyberspace*, Lessig first describes the four constraints that regulate our behavior in real space: laws, norms, the market, and code.

Laws, according to Lessig, are rules or commands imposed by the government that are enforced through *ex post* sanctions. There is, for example, the complicated IRS tax code, a set of laws that dictates the amount of taxes we owe the federal government. If we break these laws, we can be subjected to fines or other penalties levied by the government. Thanks to law's coercive pedagogy, those who get caught violating tax laws are usually quick to reform.

Social norms, on the other hand, are informal expressions of the community. Most communities have a well-defined sense of normalcy, which is reflected in their norms or standards of behavior. Cigar smokers are not usually welcome at most community functions. There may be no laws against cigar smoking in a particular setting, but those who try to smoke cigars will most likely be stigmatized and ostracized by others. When we deviate from these norms, we are behaving in a way that is socially abnormal.

The third regulative force is the market. The market regulates through the price it sets for goods and services (including labor). Unlike norms and laws, market forces are not an expression and they are imposed immediately (not in *ex post* fashion). Unless you hand over $2 at the local Starbucks, you cannot walk away with a cup of their coffee.

The final modality of regulation is known as architecture. The world consists of many physical constraints on our behavior. Some of these are natural (such as the Rocky Mountains), while others are human constructs (such as buildings and bridges). A room without windows imposes certain constraints since no one can see outside. Once again "enforcement" is not *ex post*, but at the same time the physical constraint is imposed. Moreover, this architectural constraint is "self-enforcing" in that it does not require the intermediation of an agent who makes an arrest or who chastises a member of the community. According to Lessig, "the constraints of architecture are self-executing in a way that the constraints of law, norms, and the market are not."[2]

In cyberspace we are subject to the same four constraints. Laws, such as the ones that provide copyright and patent protection, regulate behavior by proscribing certain activities and by imposing *ex post* sanctions for violators. It may be commonplace to copy digital music but this activity breaks the law. There is a lively debate about whether cyberspace requires a unique set of laws or whether the laws that apply to real space will apply here as well, with some adjustments and fine-tuning. Judge Frank Easterbrook has said that just as there is no need for a "law of the horse," there is no need for a "law of cyberspace."[3]

Markets regulate behavior in various ways—advertisers gravitate to more popular Web sites, which in turn enables those sites to enhance services; the pricing policies of the Internet Service Providers determine who can afford access to the Internet; and so forth. It should be noted that the constraints of the market are often different in cyberspace than they are in real space. For instance, pornography is much easier and less expensive to distribute in cyberspace than in real space, and this increases its available supply.

The counterpart of architectural constraint in the physical world is software "code"; that is, programs and protocols that make up the Internet. They too constrain and control our activities. These programs are often referred to as the architectures of cyberspace. For example, code limits access to certain Web sites by demanding a username and password. Software programs have recently appeared that effectively filter out unsolicited commercial e-mail (or spam). There are no federal laws to contain the rogue, antisocial activities of spammers, which rankle many users, but there is code to contain their efforts.

Finally, there are norms that regulate cyberspace behavior, including Internet etiquette and social customs. For example, "flaming," the practice of sending nasty or offensive e-mail messages, is considered bad form on the Internet and those who do it will most likely be disciplined by other members of the Internet community. Those who misrepresent themselves in chat rooms also violate those norms and they too will be reproved if their true identity is revealed. Just as in real space, cyberspace communities rely on shame and social stigma to enforce cultural standards.

But what role does ethics play in this neat regulatory framework? Lessig apparently includes ethical standards in the broad category he calls "norms," but in our view, cultural norms should be segregated from ethical ideals and principles. Cultural norms are nothing more than variable social action guides, completely relative and dependent upon a given social or cultural environment. Their validity is to some extent dependent on custom, prevalent attitudes, public opinion, and a myriad of other factors. Just as customs differ from country to country, the social customs of cyberspace could be quite different from the customs found in real space. Also, these customs will likely undergo some transformation over time as the Internet continues to evolve.

The fundamental principles of ethics, however, are metanorms, since they have universal validity. They remain the same whether we are doing business in Venezuela or interacting in cyberspace. Like cultural norms they are prescriptive, but unlike these norms, they have lasting and durable value since they transcend space and time. Ethics is about (or should be about) intelligible human goods intrinsic to our humanity and the chosen acts that realize those goods. Hence the continuity of ethical principles despite the diversity of cultures.

Our assumption that ethics and customs (or cultural norms) must be kept distinct defies the popular notion of ethical relativism, which often equates the two. A full refutation of that viewpoint is beyond the scope of our discussion here. But consider this reflection of the contemporary philosopher Phillippa Foot:

> Granted that it may be wrong to assume identity of aim between people of different cultures; nevertheless there is a great deal all men have in common. All need affection, the cooperation of others, a place in community, and help in trouble. It isn't true to suppose that human beings can flourish without these things—being isolated, despised or embattled, or without courage or hope. We are not, therefore, simply expressing values that we happen to have if we think of some moral systems as good moral systems and others as bad.[4]

None of this by any means invalidates Lessig's framework. His chief insight is that "code and market and norms and law together regulate in cyberspace as architecture and market and norms and law regulate in real space."[5] Also, according to Lessig, "Laws affect the pace of technological change, but the structures of software can do even more to curtail freedom. In the long run the shackles built by programmers could well constrain us more."[6] This notion that private code can be a more potent constraining force than public law has significant implications. The use of code as a surrogate for law may mean that certain public goods or moral values once protected by law will now be ignored or compromised by those who develop or utilize this code. Moreover, there is a danger that government itself will regulate the architectures of cyberspace in order to make it more controllable. It could, for instance, mandate the traceability of all Internet transactions, and thereby increase the capacity for surveillance or oversight of all interactions in cyberspace. In the hands of the private or public sector, the architectures of cyberspace can have extraordinary regulatory power.

Thus, Lessig's model is quite instructive and we will rely upon it extensively in the pages to come. However, I would argue that the model would be more useful for our purposes if greater attention were given to the role of fixed ethical values as a constraining force. But how do these values fit with the other regulatory forces?

Before we can answer this question we must say something about the nature of those values. The notion that there are transcendent moral values grounded in our common human nature has a deep tradition in the history of philosophy. It is intuitively obvious that there are basic goods that contribute to human well-being or human flourishing. Reason tells us that these goods are beneficial because they perfect us in some way. Although there are several different versions of what these goods might be, they are all substantially similar, as one would expect. James Moor's list of core human goods simply includes life, happiness, and autonomy. According to Moor, happiness means "pleasure and the absence of pain," and autonomy includes those goods that we need to complete our projects (ability, security, knowledge, freedom, opportunity, reason). Individuals may rank these values differently, but all human beings attribute value to these goods or "they would not survive very long."[7]

Similarly, another contemporary philosopher, John Finnis, argues persuasively for the following list of premoral goods: life, knowledge, play, aesthetic experience, sociability, religion, and practical reasonableness (which includes autonomy). According to Finnis, these goods allow us to lead worthwhile lives and to achieve genuine human flourishing. They are opportunities for realizing our full potential as human beings, for being all that we can be. Hence the master principle of morality: one's choices should always be open to human fulfillment, *or*, humanity whether in oneself or in others must be respected. None of our projects or objectives provides sufficient reason for setting aside or ignoring that responsibility.

For both Moor and Finnis, then, the source of moral normativity is these intelligible, authentically *human* goods that adequately explain the reasons for our choices and actions, and overcome the presumption of subjectivism. Moreover, our reason is attracted to these goods by virtue of their intelligible goodness.

The ultimate good, the human flourishing of ourselves and of others, should function as a prescriptive guidepost of enduring value, serving as a basis for crafting laws, developing social institutions, or regulating the Internet. Since this moral ideal is rather lofty, its application to policy-making can be difficult. As a result, we are also guided by intermediate ethical principles, such as the Golden Rule or Kant's categorical imperative, which direct us to respect these basic goods in our fellow human beings.[8] The Golden Rule, for example, states that "whatever you wish that men would do to you do so to them" (Matthew 7:12). From this "love your neighbor as yourself" principle, one can derive more specific core moral values about murder, theft, and so forth. These principles can function as more practical guidelines for moral decision-making, and enable us to pursue the basic human goods in a way that respects our fellow humanity. According to Finnis, our fundamental responsibility is to respect each of these human goods "in each person whose well-being we choose to affect."[9]

We contend, therefore, that these intelligible goods, intrinsic to our humanity and essential for human flourishing, should play an architectonic or *directive role* in the regulation of cyberspace, that is, they should guide and direct the ways in which code, laws, the market, and social norms exercise their regulatory power. The value of human flourishing is the ultimate constraint on our behavior in real space and in cyberspace. Accordingly, we have enhanced Lessig's model as depicted in Figure 1.

In order to illustrate our point about the role of these supreme ethical values and how they can be translated into the actual world of our experience, let us consider the regulatory impact of code. There are responsible and irresponsible ways of developing code that constrains behavior. As we will see in Chapter 3, blocking software systems have become a common way of protecting young children from pornography. Those who write this code have developed proprietary blocking criteria and as a rule they do not reveal these criteria or the specific sites that are blocked. In some cases sex education or health-related sites are filtered out along with the pornography. If this is done inadvertently, the software should be fixed; if it is done deliberately, parents should be informed that the scope of the blocking criteria is broader than just pornography. One could certainly make the case that parents should know what the blocking criteria are in order to make an informed judgement about the suitability of this software. Failure to reveal this information is tantamount to disrespecting parental autonomy. As a result, one could argue that when the criteria are concealed, or obscured for some ulterior agenda, the code is not being developed in a responsible manner that is consistent with the core good of autonomy.

I am not suggesting that this is a clear-cut matter or that moral principles can provide all the answers to proper cyberspace regulations. And I am not making a judgment about whether law or code is the more effective constraint for cyberporn. I am simply claiming that those who write these programs or formulate laws to regulate cyberspace should rely on ethics as a guide. Code writers must be responsible and prudent enough to incorporate into the new architectures of cyberspace structures that preserve basic moral values such as autonomy and privacy. Further, government regulations of cyberspace must not yield to temptations to impose excessive controls. Regulators too must be guided by high moral

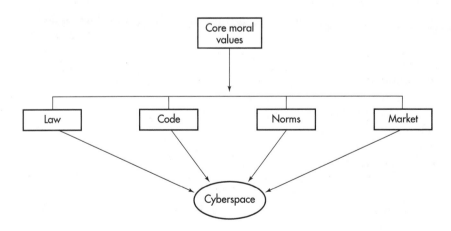

FIGURE 1 Constraints of Cyberspace Activities (Adapted from Professor Lessig's framework)

standards and respect for basic human values such as freedom and privacy. The code itself is a powerful sovereign force, and unless it is developed and regulated appropriately, it will surely threaten the preservation of those values.

The role of morality should now be quite evident: *it must be the ultimate regulator of cyberspace that sets the boundaries for an individual's actions and an organization's policies.* It should direct and harmonize the forces of law, code, the market, and social norms so that interactions and dealings there will be measured, fair, and just.

▶ An Iron Cage or a Gateway to Utopia?

While most of us agree that some constraints will need to be imposed on the technologies of networking and computing that have come to pervade the home and workplace, there is legitimate skepticism about anyone's ability to control the ultimate evolution and effects of these technologies. Are our attempts to regulate cyberspace merely a chimera? Are we too trammeled by the forces of technology, or still capable of exercising sovereignty over the code that constitutes the inner workings of the Internet?

As we observed in the preface, some philosophers have long regarded technology as a dark and oppressive force that menaces our individuality and authenticity. These technology determinists see technology as an independent and dehumanizing force beyond humanity's capacity to control it. The French philosopher Jacques Ellul presents a disturbing vision of technology in his seminal work, *The Technological Society.* His central argument is that *technique* has become a dominant and untranscendable human value. He defines technique as *"the totality of methods rationally arrived at and having absolute efficiency* (for a given stage of development) in *every* field of human activity."[10] According to Ellul, technique is beyond our control; it has become autonomous and "fashioned an omnivorous world which obeys its own laws and which has renounced all tradition."[11] For Ellul, modern technology has irreversibly shaped the way we live, work, and interact in this world.

Ellul has not been alone in advancing such a pessimistic outlook on technology. Max Weber coined the term "iron cage" to connote how technology locks us into certain ways of being or patterns of behavior. And Martin Heidegger saw technology not merely as a tool that we can manipulate but as a way of "being in the world" that deeply affects how we relate to that world. But is it really so that technology forces us into this "iron cage," and into a more fragmented, narrow-minded society dominated by a crude instrumental rationality?

In contrast to the bleak outlook of Ellul and Heidegger, we find technology neutralists who argue that technology is a neutral force, completely dependent on human aims and objectives. According to this viewpoint, technologies are free of bias and do not promote one type of behavior over another. Technology *is* only a tool, and it does not compromise our human freedom or determine our destiny in any appreciable way—it is up to us whether this powerful force is used for good or ill purposes.

Some go even farther and embrace technological utopianism, which regards certain technologies as making possible an ideal world with improved lifestyles and workplaces. This optimistic philosophy assumes that humanity can eradicate many of technology's adverse effects and manipulate this tool effectively to improve the human condition.

The philosophy of technological neutralism (or for that matter utopianism) seems problematic for several reasons. Technology does condition our choices with certain "givens," which are virtually impossible to fully overcome. Langdon Winner describes this as a process of reverse adaptation or "the adjustment of human ends to match the character of the available means."[12]

However, in our view it is also an exaggeration to claim that computer and network technology locks us into a virtual but inescapable iron cage. The middle ground between these extreme positions is known as *technological realism*, which holds that "although technology has a force of its own, it is not independent of political and social forces."[13] Technological realism acknowledges that technology has reconfigured our political and social reality and that it does influence human behavior in particular ways. To some extent, this notion is echoed in Lessig's work. He argues that we sometimes fail to see how code is an instrument of social and political control. Code is not neutral. Most often, embedded within code are certain value decisions that define the set of options for policy problems.

Nonetheless, while technology is determinative to some degree of how we live and work, we still have the capacity to redirect it or to subdue it when necessary. In effect, we can still shape and dictate how certain technological innovations will be deployed and restrained, particularly when there is a conflict with the common good or core human goods. Our human freedom is undoubtedly attenuated by technology's might and its atomizing tendencies, but it is not completely effaced. We can still choose to implement systems and develop code in ways that protect fundamental human rights, such as autonomy or privacy. We can be liberated from the thralldom of privacy-invasive code by developing new code that enhances privacy.

In this postmodern age such a position may seem simplistic and outdated. While we recognize that human choices may sometimes be socially constructed, there is still room for conscious, deliberate choice. The human self is a moral agent responsible for its actions and responsible for making decisions about the deployment of various technologies.

Beyond any doubt, technology and its counterpart of instrumental rationality are dominant forces in this society that exert enormous pressures upon us to make choices and behave in certain ways. But as Charles Taylor points out, one can find throughout history pockets of concerted opposition to oppressive technologies. Further, the chances for such successful resistance are greatly enhanced when there is some common understanding about a particular threat or imperilment, such as the threat to our ecology that occupied us during the 1970s. Perhaps the same common consciousness will emerge about the threat to personal privacy, and this will provide yet another impetus for human choice to trump the dominating forces of information technology. While we should not be overly optimistic about our freedom and our capacity for resisting the seductive thrall of technology, we must recognize that we still have *some* degree of freedom in this world. Thus, we agree with Taylor's assessment: "We are not, indeed, locked in. But there is a slope, an incline in things that is all too easy to slide down."[14]

How then do we avoid this fatal slide? This brings us to our next topic of discussion in this introduction—the importance of cultivating and sustaining a moral point of view as one deliberates the responsible deployment of information technology protocols.

▶ Ethical Frameworks and the Digital Frontier

We avoid this slide and its accompanying perils only if we conscientiously adopt the moral point of view as we evaluate technological capabilities and make decisions about the ground rules of the digital frontier. How can we characterize this moral point of view? According to Kenneth Goodpaster, it can be seen "as a mental and emotional standpoint from which all persons have a special dignity or worth, from which the Golden Rule derives its worth, and from which words like *ought* and *duty* derive their meaning."[15] This is quite consistent with our earlier claim that the fundamental moral imperative is the promotion of human flourishing both in ourselves and in others.

Several distinct types of ethical reasoning have been associated with the moral point of view, and they provide us with the basic principles that serve as a moral yardstick or "compass" that can assist us in making normative judgements. Our discussion here will be quite concise, but for the interested reader it can certainly be amplified by many other books on ethical theory or on applied ethics.[16] We will consider several models of ethical reasoning based on moral frameworks emphasizing the maximization of social utility, natural rights, contract rights, and moral duties.

The fact that there are several different theories embodying the moral point of view does not contradict our assumption regarding the core human goods that form the basis of a unifying moral framework. All of these theories would recognize such goods in one form or another. Kant would embrace the principle that we must respect humanity in all our choices and actions, though he might define humanity differently from Finnis. Rights-based theories discuss core human goods in terms of protection of human rights such as the rights to life, liberty, and the pursuit of happiness. The utilitarian approach puts a great deal of emphasis on happiness and, although it may have a hard time standing on its own, it can be complemented by other theories to form a more comprehensive framework.

All of these theories are worth our careful consideration. Each of them represents a valuable perspective from which complex moral issues can be assessed and reflected upon. They help us to engage in the critical moral analysis necessitated by the thorny dilemmas that are beginning to surface all over the Internet.

Before we discuss these theories, it is worth pointing out that modern ethical frameworks fall under two broad categories: *teleological* or *deontological*. The word *teleological* derives from the Greek term *telos,* which means goal or end. These theories argue that the rightness or wrongness of an action depends upon whether or not it brings about the end in question (such as happiness). *Deontological* theories, on the other hand, consider actions to be intrinsically right or wrong—their rightness or wrongness does not depend in any way on the consequences that they effect. These frameworks emphasize duty and obligation (*deon* is the Greek word for duty or basic moral rights).

Utilitarianism

The theory of utilitarianism is a teleological theory, and it is by far the most popular version of consequentialism, which argues that optimizing the consequences of one's choices is the fundamental principle of ethics. Classic utilitarianism was developed by two British philosophers, Jeremy Bentham [1748–1832] and John Stuart Mill [1806–1873]. According to this theory, the right course of action is to promote the general good. This general good can also be described in terms of "utility," and this principle of utility is the foundation of morality and the ultimate criterion of right and wrong. The term *utility* simply refers to the net benefits (or good) created by an action. According to Frankena, utilitarianism is the view that "the sole ultimate standard of right, wrong and obligation is the *principle of utility* or *beneficence,* which says quite strictly that the moral end to be sought in all that we do is *the greatest possible balance of good over evil* (or the least possible balance of evil over good)."[17] Thus an action or policy is right if it will produce the greatest net benefits or the lowest net costs (assuming that all of the alternatives impose some net cost).

It should be emphasized that utilitarianism is quite different from ethical egoism. An action is right not if it produces utility for the person performing that action but for *all* parties affected by the action. With this in mind we might reformulate the moral principle of utilitarianism as follows: *Persons ought to act in a way that promotes the maximum net expectable utility, that is, the greatest net benefits or the lowest net costs, for the broadest community affected by their actions.*

On a practical level, utilitarianism requires us to make moral decisions by means of a rational, objective cost/benefit analysis. In most ethical dilemmas there are several possible alternatives or courses of action. Once one has sorted out the most viable and sensible alternatives, each one is evaluated in terms of its costs and benefits (both direct and indirect). Based on this analysis, one chooses the alternative that produces the greatest net expectable utility, that is, the one with the greatest net benefits (or the lowest net costs) for the widest community affected by that alternative.

A concrete example will illustrate how cost/benefit analysis might work. Let us assume that a corporation has to make a policy decision about random inspection of the electronic mail of its employees. This might be done as a routine part of a performance review, or as a means of checking to make sure that workers are using e-mail only for work-related purposes and are not involved in any untoward activities. This practice is perfectly legal, but some managers may wonder if it's really the right thing to do, since it seems to violate the privacy rights of employees. Rightness in the utilitarian ethical model is determined by consequences that become transparent in a cost/benefit analysis. In this case the managers might reduce their various choices to three options: e-mail messages are not inspected on a routine basis and are kept confidential (unless some sort of malfeasance or criminal activity is suspected); e-mail messages will be inspected regularly by managers, but employees will be informed of this policy and reminded of it every time they log in to the e-mail system, so that there is no expectation of privacy; and e-mail will be regularly but surreptitiously perused by managers with employees uninformed of the company policy. Which of these alternatives promotes the general good, that is, produces the greatest net expectable utility?

The matrix in Figure 2 will give you some idea of how this analysis might work out. It becomes clear from this exercise that it's difficult to calculate *objectively* the diffuse consequences of our actions or policies and to weight them appropriately. And herein lies a major obstacle in using this approach. Nonetheless, there is value in performing this type of analysis, since it induces us to consider the broad consequences of our actions and to take into account the *human* as well as the economic costs of implementing various technologies.

	Costs	Benefits
(1) Confidential e-mail	Lack of control over employees; difficult to prevent misuses of e-mail; e-mail could be used for various personal reasons without company knowledge.	Maintains morale and an environment of trust and respect for workers; protects personal privacy rights.
(2) Inspect e-mail messages with employees informed of policy	Violates privacy rights; diminishes trust and impairs morale; workers less likely to use e-mail if communications are not confidential and instead rely on less efficient modes of communication.	Prevents misuse along with inappropriate comments about superiors and fellow workers via e-mail; workers know the risks of using e-mail; they are less likely to use e-mail for personal purposes.
(3) Inspect e-mail messages surreptitiously	Same as option (2) but even more loss of trust and morale if company policy is uncovered.	Better chance to catch employees doing something wrong, such as transmitting trade secrets; perfectly legal.

FIGURE 2 Illustrative Cost/Benefit Analysis

Although this theory does have certain strengths, it is also seriously flawed in some ways. Depending upon the context, utilitarianism could be used to justify the infliction of pain on a small number of individuals for the sake of the happiness or benefits of the majority. There are no intrinsically unjust or immoral acts for the utilitarian, and this poses a problem. What happens when human rights conflict with utility? Can those rights be suppressed on occasion for the general good? There is nothing in utilitarianism that would prevent this from happening as long as a cogent and objective case is made that the benefits of doing so exceed the costs. The primary problem then is that this theory lacks the proper sensitivity to the vital ideals of justice and human rights.

Contract Rights (Contractarianism)

Another mode of reasoning that exemplifies the moral point of view is rights-based analysis, which is sometimes called contractarianism. Contractarianism looks at moral issues from the viewpoint of the human rights that may be at stake. A "right" is simply an entitlement or a claim to something. For instance, thanks to the Fourth Amendment, American citizens are entitled to protection from unwarranted search and seizures in the privacy of their homes. In contrast to the utilitarian view, the consequences of an action are morally irrelevant for those who support contractarianism. Rights are unequivocally enjoyed by all citizens, and the rights of the minority cannot be suspended or abolished even if that abolition will maximize social welfare.

An important distinction needs to be made between positive and negative rights. Possession of a negative right implies that one is free from external interference in one's affairs. Examples of negative rights include the right to free speech, the right to property, and the right to privacy. Since all citizens have a right to privacy in their homes, the state cannot interfere in their affairs by tapping their phone calls unless it has demonstrated a strong probability that laws are being broken.

A positive right, on the other hand, implies a requirement that the holders of this right be provided with whatever they need to pursue their legitimate interests. The rights to medical care and education are examples of positive rights. In the United States, the right to universal health care is rather dubious, but the right to education is unequivocal. Therefore, the state has a duty to educate children through the twelfth grade. If everyone had a "right" to Internet access there would be a correlative duty on the part of the government to provide that access for those who could not afford it.

Rights can be philosophically grounded in several ways. Some traditional philosophers such as Locke and Rousseau and the contemporary social philosopher John Rawls' claim that we have basic rights by virtue of an implicit social contract between the individual and civil society. Individuals agree to a contract outside of the organized civil society, which stipulates the fundamental principles of their association, including their rights and duties. Rights are one side of a quid pro quo—we are guaranteed certain rights (for example, life, liberty and the pursuit of happiness) as long as we obey the laws and regulations of civil society. This contract is not real but hypothetical. According to Kelbley, "we are not discussing facts but an ideal which rational individuals can embrace as a standard to measure the moral nature of social institutions and efforts at reform."[18]

According to this perspective, moral reasoning should be governed by respect for these individual rights and by a philosophy of fairness. As Ken Goodpaster observes, "fairness is explained as a condition that prevails when all individuals are accorded equal respect as participants in social arrangements."[19] In short, then, this rights-based approach to ethics focuses on the need to respect an individual's legal, moral, and contractual rights as the basis of justice and fairness.

The problem with most rights-based theories is that they do not provide adequate criteria for resolving practical disputes when rights are in conflict. For example, those who send *spam* (unsolicited commercial e-mail) over the Internet claim that they are exercising their right to free speech, but many recipients argue that spam is intrusive and even a form of trespass. Hence they claim that the transmission of spam is an invasion of their property rights. The real difficulty is how we adjudicate this conflict and determine which right takes priority. Rights-based theories are not always helpful in making this determination.

Natural Rights

One wonders, of course, how firm the ground is beneath this social contract. Is there some other way to validate basic human rights that is not contingent on such a contract? The tradition of natural law philosophy supposes that all human beings have fundamental natural rights that are grounded in their common human nature. Hence it seems to provide a stronger basis for rights than a hypothetical social contract. The natural law/natural rights tradition has been neglected in most books on business and information technology ethics, perhaps because of its impracticality or because it is enmeshed with Roman Catholic tradition and the systematic philosophy of St. Thomas Aquinas. MacIntyre, however, makes the case that the natural law ethic is superior to the "theories of those imprisoned within modernity [that] can provide only ideological rationalizations [such as] modern consequentialism and modern contractarianism."[20]

This theory stresses that human fulfillment or human flourishing is the final goal of existence—one's ultimate purpose in life is to realize his/her potential as a human person to the fullest extent possible. Hence it allows us to evaluate information management practices and policies from a unique vantage point: do those policies and practices adequately respect and foster human well-being and contribute to or impede human flourishing?

John Finnis, among others, has attempted to develop an updated natural law ethic that remains faithful to the broad lines of natural law theory as developed in the philosophy of St. Thomas Aquinas. Recall his claim that there are seven irreducible premoral goods that are the key to our flourishing as humans: life and health, knowledge, play, aesthetic experience, sociability (or friendship), religion, and practical reasonableness. Each one of us participates in these basic goods, though we may participate in some goods more than others, and we do so in order to achieve "fullness of life." Practical reasonableness, which includes the value of autonomy, is the most important of these goods since it shapes one's participation in the other basic goods. One requirement of practical reasonableness is that it is unreasonable to choose directly against any basic value, "whether in oneself or in one's fellow human beings."[21]

But how do we get from these basic human goods to specific moral norms and human rights? Like Aquinas, Finnis argues for a rational connection between laws and rights. If someone has a natural right, he or she has that right by virtue of natural law; on the other hand if a person has a legal right, it is by virtue of positive law. Natural laws are deduced from those basic premoral human goods. For example, human life is a basic human good and therefore certain acts, such as the taking of innocent life, are forbidden as a matter of natural law. Finnis states this natural law (or absolute moral norm) as follows: "every act which is intended, whether as end or means, to kill an innocent human being and every act done by a private person which is intended to kill any human being" is prohibited.[22] This precludes necessary acts of self-defense. From this natural law we can deduce the natural right to life. And from the premoral good of knowledge (and truth) we can deduce the moral imperative of veracity and "the right not to be positively lied to in any situation in which factual communication is reasonably expected."[23]

Natural law theory even in the hands of contemporary philosophers like Finnis remains abstract, but it does provide a valuable vantage point to judge ethical conundrums in cyberspace. The value of this approach is its unwavering fidelity to the role of basic human goods such as life, health, and truth in ethical inquiry. It compels us to consider whether certain policies or actions are consistent with human flourishing, that is, with the realization of these core human goods identified by Finnis. Or do they contradict the rights that flow from the overarching duty not to choose deliberately against any basic human good? It is difficult to argue, for instance, that deceptive spamming promotes any basic human good; by undermining the truth in factual Internet communications, this form of spam deserves to be classified as morally reprehensible. The natural law framework allows us to appreciate why this is so wrong by focusing on its true negative impact.

Although Finnis has tried to disengage his natural rights framework from the cumbersome metaphysics of Aquinas, his critics claim that he does not succeed. They contend that his list of premoral goods is arbitrary and that for natural law to work, an underlying ontology is essential. According to this critique, it is unclear how Finnis justifies his list of the basic forms of the good. Finnis contends that they are basic goods that reasonable persons would accept upon serious reflection. According to Lisska, however, "One intuits the basic goods and it just happens that set of goods correspond to human well-being. But what establishes the causal relationship?"[24] This is obviously a complicated issue that cannot be further explored here, but it is worth pointing out that Finnis does offer a substantial rationale for each of these goods, and this helps buttress the objectivity and plausibility of his position.

Moral Duty (Pluralism)

The final framework is based not on moral law or rights, but on duty. The moral philosophy of Immanuel Kant (1724-1804), which can be found in his short but difficult masterpiece on ethics, *Foundations of the Metaphysics of Morals,* is representative of this approach. It assumes that the moral point of view is best expressed by discerning and carrying out one's moral duty. This duty-based, deontological ethical framework is sometimes referred to as *pluralism*.

Kant believed that consequences of an action are morally irrelevant: "an action performed from duty does not have its moral worth in the purpose which is to be achieved through it but in the maxim by which it is determined."[25] According to Kant, actions only have moral worth when they are done for the sake of duty. But what is our duty and how is it derived? In Kant's systematic philosophy our moral duty is simple: to follow the moral law that, like the laws of science or physics, must be rational. Also, like all rational laws, the moral law must be universal, since universality represents the common character of rationality and law. This universal moral law is expressed as the categorical imperative: "I should never act except in such a way that I can also will that my maxim should become a universal law."[26] The imperative is categorical because it does not allow for any exceptions.

A *maxim*, as referred to in Kant's categorical imperative, is an implied general principle or rule underlying a particular action. If, for example, I usually break my promises, then I act according to the private maxim that promise-breaking is morally acceptable when it is in my best interests to do so. But can one take this maxim and transform it into a universal moral law? As a universal law, this particular maxim would be expressed as follows: "It is permissible for everyone to break promises when it is in their best interests to do so." Such a law, however, is invalid since it entails both a pragmatic and a logical contradiction. There is a pragmatic (or practical) contradiction because the maxim is self-defeating if it is universalized. According to Korsgaard, "your action would become ineffectual for the achievement of your purpose if everyone (tried to) use it for that purpose."[27] Consider this example. An individual borrows some money from a friend and he promises to pay her back. However, he has no intention of keeping that promise. But this objective, that is, getting some money from her without repaying it, cannot be achieved by making a false promise in a world where this maxim has been universalized. As Korsgaard puts it, "The efficacy of the false promise as a means of securing money depends on the fact that not everyone uses promises that way."[28]

Universal promise-breaking also implies a logical contradiction (like a square circle) since if everyone broke promises, the entire institution of promising would collapse; there would be no such thing as a "promise" because in such a climate, anyone making a promise would lack credibility. A world of universalized promise-breaking is inconceivable. Thus, in view of the contradictions involved in universalizing promise-breaking, we have a perfect duty to keep all of our promises.

Kant strongly implies that perfect duties, that is duties that we are always obliged to follow such as telling the truth or keeping a promise, entail both a logical and pragmatic contradiction. Violations of imperfect duties, however, are pragmatic contradictions.[29] Korsgaard explains that "perfect duties of virtue arise because we must refrain from particular actions *against* humanity in our own person or that of another."[30] Imperfect duties, on the other hand, are duties to develop one's talents where the individual has the latitude to fulfill this duty using many different means.

Kant's categorical imperative is his ultimate ethical principle. It is the acid test of whether an action is right or wrong. According to Kant, then, any self-contradictory universalized maxims are morally forbidden. The categorical imperative functions as a guide, a "moral compass" that gives us a reliable way of determining a correct and consistent course of action. According to Bowie, "the test of the categorical imperative becomes a principle of fair play—one of the essential features of fair play is that one should not make an exception of oneself."[31]

Also, from the categorical imperative we can derive other duties such as the duty to keep contracts, to tell the truth, to avoid injury to others, and so forth. Kant would maintain that each of these duties is also categorical, admitting of no exceptions, since the maxim underlying such an exception cannot be universalized.

How might we apply Kant's theory to the rather mundane ethical dilemmas that arise in cyberspace? Let us return once again to the problem of spam. Spamming clearly violates the spirit of Kant's categorical imperative, which requires us to perform only those actions that can be universalized. In this case, we must imagine what would happen if all organizations and vendors that had an interest in online advertising adopted a policy of spamming, that is, transmitting volumes of bulk e-mail through cyberspace on a regular basis. Beyond any doubt, the global e-mail system and even the Internet itself would rapidly become dysfunctional. Spamming, then, is not a coherently universalizable practice.

At the heart of Kant's ethical system is the notion that there are rational constraints on what we can do. We may want to engage in some action (such as sending millions of unsolicited e-mail messages) but we are inconsistent and hence unethical unless we accept the implications of everyone doing the same thing. According to Kant, it is unethical to make arbitrary exceptions for ourselves, which is exactly what the spammers are *implicitly* doing. In the simplest terms, the categorical imperative suggests the following question: what if everybody did what you are doing? In this case, if everybody practiced spamming, the end result would be a calamity for the Internet.

Before concluding this discussion on Kant, it is worth citing his second formulation of the categorical imperative: "Act in such a way that you treat humanity, whether in your own person or in the person of another, always at the same time as an end and never simply as a means."[32] For

Kant as well as for other moralists (such as Finnis), the principle of humanity as an end-in-itself serves as a limiting condition of every person's freedom of action. We cannot exploit other human beings and treat them exclusively as a means to our ends or purposes. This could happen, for example, through actions that deceive one's fellow human beings or actions that force them to do things against their will. Korsgaard writes,

> According to [Kant's] Formula of Humanity, coercion and deception are the most fundamental forms of wrongdoing to others—the roots of all evil. Coercion and deception violate the conditions of possible assent, and all actions which depend for their nature and efficacy on their coercive or deceptive character are ones that others cannot assent to . . . Physical coercion treats someone's person as a tool; lying treats someone's reason as a tool.[33]

If we follow this categorical imperative, we will ensure that the worth of our projects and objectives does not supercede the worth of other human beings. This principle can also be summed up in the notion of *respect*. One way to express universal morality is in terms of the general principle of respect for other human beings, who deserve that respect because of their dignity as free and rational persons.

One of the problems with Kant's moral philosophy is its rigidity. There are no exceptions to the moral laws derived from the absolute categorical imperative. Hence lying is *always* wrong even though we can envision situations where telling a lie (e.g., to save a human life) is a reasonable and proper course of action. In cases like this there is an apparent conflict of moral laws (the law to tell the truth and the law to save a life in jeopardy), and we have no alternative but to admit an exception to one of them. As A. C. Ewing points out,

> In cases where two laws conflict, it is hard to see how we can rationally decide between them except by considering the goodness or badness of the consequences. However important it is to tell the truth and however evil to lie, there are surely cases where much greater evils can still be averted by a lie, and is lying wrong then?[34]

Ewing's argument that it is difficult to avoid an appeal to consequences when two laws conflict poses problems for Kant's moral philosophy, despite its powerful appeal.

An alternative duty-based philosophy proposed by contemporary English philosopher William D. Ross (1877–1940) attempts to obviate the difficulties posed by Kant's inflexibility. Ross argues in his book *The Right and the Good* that we are obliged to follow several basic *prima facie* duties, which each of us can intuit through simple reflection. These duties are *prima facie* in the sense that they are conditional and not absolute. This means that under normal circumstances, we must follow a particular duty, but in those unusual situations where duties conflict with one another, one duty may be overridden by another duty that is judged to be superior, at least under these specific circumstances. According to Ross, moral rules or principles are not categorical as they are for Kant, so they can have exceptions. Thus, a moral principle can be sacrificed or overridden, but only for another moral principle, not just for arbitrary, selfish, or even utilitarian reasons.

According to Ross, the seven *prima facie* moral duties that are binding on all moral agents are the following:

1. One ought to keep promises and tell the truth (*fidelity*).
2. One ought to right the wrongs that one has inflicted on others (*reparation*).
3. One ought to distribute goods justly (*justice*).
4. One ought to improve the lot of others with respect to virtue, intelligence, and happiness (*beneficence*).
5. One ought to improve oneself with respect to virtue and intelligence (*self-improvement*).
6. One ought to exhibit gratitude when appropriate (*gratitude*).
7. One ought to avoid injury to others (*noninjury*).

Ross makes no effort to provide any substantial rationalization or theoretical grounding of these duties. We might just say that they are common rules of morality, obvious to all rational humans because they have the general effect of reducing harm or evil to others.

The Achilles' heel of Ross's theory can be isolated by examining two specific problems: (1) his list of duties seems arbitrary since it is not metaphysically or even philosophically grounded, and (2) the list seems incomplete—where, for example, is the duty not to steal property from another? It may be included under the duty to avoid injury to others, but that is not altogether clear. Moreover, is it really true that all human beings (even those in different cultures) simply "intuit" these same principles? Finally, *The Right and the Good* provides little help for resolving situations where two prima facie duties do conflict. Ross offers few concrete criteria for determining when one obligation is more stringent and compelling than another.

Despite these shortcomings, however, Ross's framework, like the others we have considered, is not without some merit. A focus on one's moral duty (or even conflicting duties) in a particular situation is a worthy starting point for moral reasoning about some intricate dilemma. Further, for many moral conundrums, a sincere and rational person can develop sound, objective reasons for determining which duty should take priority.

▶Postscript on Moral Theory

As we have seen, none of these theories are without flaws or contradictions, but they do represent viable avenues for reasoning about moral issues, especially when those issues go beyond the level of moral common sense. They also have certain elements in common, particularly an orientation to "the other"—along with the need to consider the interests and perspectives of the affected parties when assessing alternative action plans. And they all stand in opposition to the dangerous and myopic philosophy of ethical egoism, which is blind to the rights and aspirations of others.

Before concluding this material on ethical theory, we can summarize how it can be applied to some of the moral quandaries that arise in the electronic frontier of cyberspace. The following matrix provides a concise framework for putting these three basic theories into action:

Theory Type	Operative Questions
Consequentialism/Utilitarianism	Which action or policy generates the best overall consequences or the greatest net expectable utility for all affected parties?
Duty-Based Morality	Can the maxim underlying the course of action being considered be universalized? Is the principle of fair play being violated? If there appears to be conflicting duties, which is the stronger duty?
Rights-Based Morality	Which action or policy best protects the human and legal rights of the individuals involved? Does the proposed action or policy impede the basic requirements of human flourishing?

Despite the potential for conflict, these three general theories should be seen as complementary. In most cases, these three frameworks will converge on the same solution to an ethical quandary. At other times, they will suggest different solutions to the problem and one must decide which framework should "trump" or override the others. Should we respect the rights of some group or individual even though following that alternative will be less beneficial to all affected parties than other alternatives? Resolving such questions will require careful and objective reasoning, but responsible behavior will sometimes require that this difficult, extra step be taken. To be sure, the Internet will present unique ethical challenges that could never have been envisioned by Kant or Mill, but these frameworks still provide a general way of coming to terms with these tough questions.

Because each of these theories does have certain shortcomings, some attempts have been made to combine the central elements of two or more frameworks. One such attempt is James Moor's model of *just consequentialism*. Moor, recognizing the deficiencies of pure consequentialism, argues that it must be tempered by considerations of justice. The starting point for moral reasoning is the safeguarding of human rights, including life, happiness, and autonomy. As we have argued throughout this chapter, our actions and policies should protect those rights, and this imperative extends to policies for the use of information technology. Sometimes, however, harmful consequences are unavoidable, and this leads to conflicts of action or policy. For example, we should not inflict harm on others, but what if someone is threatening my life? Moor refers us to Bernard Gert's book, *Morality*, which "provides us with a notion of moral impartiality that offers a good approach to justice that is useful in resolving these conflicts."[35] Justice demands impartiality so it is unjust for someone to adopt a policy he would not allow others to adopt. Moor uses the example of adopting a policy of installing defective computer chips. If the general policy is that any company can manufacture defective goods that could be quite harmful to people, no rational person would accept such a policy, since he would put himself at risk.

Gert's test of impartiality involves two steps: (1) determine the applicable moral rule in a given situation; (2) consider whether that rule should be publicly allowed, i.e., what would be the consequences if everybody followed this rule? Gert refers to this impartiality as the "blindfold of justice," which does not remove general knowledge of consequences, but does remove knowledge of whom will benefit and whom will be hurt by one's choices. This blindfold of justice or impartiality test is the constraint on consequentalism. If this test is applied to computing policies, "some policies will be regarded as unjust by all rational, impartial people, some policies will be regarded as just by all rational, impartial people, and some will be in dispute."[36]

Once we have subjected a policy to the impartiality test and have determined that it is not unjust, we can then determine which of the just policies (or perhaps those in dispute) optimizes the consequences. For example, if we are considering two policies designed to promote privacy on the Internet that are both just, we should choose the one with the best outcome where the benefits most clearly outweigh the costs.

Just consequentalism therefore has some distinct advantages. It enables us to analyze moral dilemmas through the lens of consequences but with adequate attention given to issues of justice and human rights, which cannot be sacrificed even for the sake of maximizing the beneficial consequences for the affected communities.

▶ Normative Principles

For those who find theory too abstract to apply to complex dilemmas, another approach, which has become known as *principilism*, is available. Principilism is commonly used in biomedical ethics and has become popularized through the work of Beauchamp and Childress.[37] These intermediate principles are derived from and compatible with all of the theories articulated here. They constitute *prima facie* duties that are always in force but may conflict on occasion. The four principles proposed by Beauchamp and Childress are autonomy, nonmaleficence, beneficence, and justice. Those who advocate this approach also prescribe certain prudential requirements that determine when one *prima facie* principle should be given more weight than another. These include : "being sure that there is a realistic prospect of achieving the moral objective one has chosen to honor; no alternative course of action is possible that would honor both conflicting obligations; and we minimize the effects of infringing on the *prima facie* duty."[38]

Here is a brief sketch of these four principles:

The Principle of Autonomy

Kant and other philosophers have consistently argued that a defining element of personhood is one's capacity to be autonomous or self-determining. According to Gary Doppelt, "the Kantian conception of personhood ties the moral identity of persons to the supreme value of their rational capacities for normative self-determination."[39] All rational persons have two key moral powers or capacities: (1) they possess the ability to develop and revise a rational plan to pursue their conception of the good life, and (2) they also possess the capacity to respect this same capacity of self-determination in others. Thus, autonomy is not only a necessary condition of moral responsibility, it is also through the exercise of autonomy that individuals shape their destiny according to their notion of the best sort of life worth living. When someone is deprived of their autonomy, their plans are interfered with and they are not treated with the respect that they deserve. Of course, respect for autonomy must be balanced against other moral considerations and claims.

The Principle of Nonmaleficence

The principle of nonmaleficence can best be summarized in the moral injunction "above all, do no harm." According to this core principle, one ought to avoid unnecessary harm or injury to others whenever possible.

This negative injunction against doing injury to others is sometimes called the "moral minimum." However one may choose to develop a moral code of conduct, this injunction must be given a preeminent status. Most moral systems go well beyond this minimum requirement, as we have seen in the theories already discussed, but that does not detract from the central importance of this principle. According to Jon Gunneman and his coauthors,

> We know of no societies, from the literature of anthropology or comparative ethics, whose moral codes do not contain some injunction against harming others. The specific notion of *harm* or *social injury* may vary, as well as the mode of correction and restitution but the injunctions are present.[40]

The Principle of Beneficence

Beneficence is a positive duty that has been formulated in many ways. In the simplest terms, it means that we should act in such a way that we advance the welfare of other people when we are able to do so. In other words, we have a duty to help others. But what does this really mean? When am I duty-bound to help another person or even an institution? It is obvious that we cannot help everyone or intervene in every situation when someone is in need. Hence some criteria are necessary for determining when such a moral obligation arises. In general, it can be argued that we have a duty to help others under the following conditions:

- The need is serious or urgent.

- We have knowledge or awareness of the situation.

- We have the capability to provide assistance ("ought assumes can" is the operative principle).

If, for instance, one is an Olympic swimmer and sees someone drowning at the beach, one has an obligation to attempt a rescue of that person, especially if this is the only recourse and there is little risk to one's own life. This principle has some relevance when we evaluate society's questionable duty of beneficence to provide universal Internet service.

The Principle of Justice

Although theories of justice have their differences, most have in common adherence to this basic formal principle: "Similar cases ought to be treated in similar ways." Above all else, justice requires fair treatment and impartiality. This is a formal procedural principle of justice and needs to be supplemented by the criteria for determining similar cases. This leads into theories of distributive justice that attempt to formulate an underlying principle for how we should distribute the benefits and burdens of social life. Some theories emphasize equality, that is, all goods should be distributed equally. John Rawls, for example, adopts an egalitarian approach, though he does argue that an unequal distribution of goods is acceptable when it works for the advantage of everyone, especially the least advantaged (the difference principle).[41] Other theories emphasize contribution and effort as formulated in this maxim: Benefits or resources should be distributed according to the contribution each individual makes to the furtherance of society's goals. And still another theory of justice, which has typically been associated with socialism, argues for justice based on need: "From each according to his ability, to each according to his needs."[42]

Our purpose here is not to defend one of these theories against the other, but to illustrate that moral judgements should be based in part on the formal principle of justice and take into account some standard regarding how the benefits and burdens should be fairly distributed within a group or society at large.

There is no reason that these intermediate moral principles cannot be applied to some of the controversial problems that we will consider in this book. They are certainly general enough to have applicability in the field of computer and Internet ethics as well as bioethics. A person who makes choices and develops policies attentive to the core human goods and to these more practical principles that promote those goods would surely be acting with the care and prudence that is consistent with the moral point of view.

Discussion Questions

1. Do you agree with the philosophy of technological realism?
2. Discuss the basic elements of Lessig's framework. What does he mean when he says that in cyberspace "the code is the law?"
3. Explain and critically analyze the essentials of Kant's moral theory.
4. Explain the difference between teleological and deontological theories.

References

1. Aristotle, *Nicomachean Ethics*, I, 3: 1095a6.
2. Larry Lessig, *Code and Other Laws of Cyberspace* (New York: Basic Books, 1999), p. 236.
3. See Frank Easterbrook, "Cyberspace and the Law of the Horse," 207, *University of Chicago Law Forum*, 1996.

4. Phillippa Foot, "Moral Relativism," Lindley Lecture, Department of Philosophy, University of Kansas, 1979.
5. Larry Lessig, "The Laws of Cyberspace;" available at: http://cyberlaw.stanford.edu/lessig.
6. Larry Lessig, "Tyranny in the Infrastructure," Wired, 5.07, 1997, p. 96.
7. Jim Moor, "Just Consequentialism and Computing," in R. Spinello and H. Tavani, eds., Readings in Cyberethics (Sudbury, MA: Jones and Bartlett), p. 100.
8. This concept will be discussed later in the chapter. For Finnis, Kant's principle is acceptable as long as we acknowledge Kant's inadequate conception of humanity, which is reduced to its rational nature.
9. John Finnis, Fundamentals of Ethics (Washington, DC: Georgetown University Press, 1983), p. 125. The discussion here on basic human goods is largely based on the insights set forth by Finnis in this important book.
10. Jacques Ellul, The Technological Society, trans. John Wilkinson (New York: Vintage Books, 1964), p. xxv.
11. Ellul, p. 14.
12. Langdon Winner, Autonomous Technology: Technics-out-of Control as a Theme of Political Thought (Cambridge: MIT Press, 1977), p. 229.
13. Priscilla Regan, Legislating Privacy (Chapel Hill: University of North Carolina Press, 1995), p. 12.
14. Charles Taylor, The Ethics of Authenticity (Cambridge: Harvard University Press, 1991), p. 101.
15. Kenneth Goodpaster, "Some Avenues for Ethical Analysis in Management," in John Matthews et al., Policies and Persons (New York: McGraw-Hill, 1985), p. 495.
16. See, for example, James Rachels, The Elements of Moral Philosophy (New York: Random House, 1986); William K. Frankena, Ethics (Englewood Cliffs, NJ: Prentice-Hall, 1963); Steven Cahn and Peter Markie, Ethics: History, Theory, and Contemporary Issues, 2nd ed. (New York: Oxford University Press, 2002).
17. William Frankena, Ethics (Englewood Cliffs, NJ: Prentice-Hall, 1963), p. 29.
18. Charles Kelbley, "Freedom from the Good," in Freedom and Value, ed. R. Johann (New York: Fordham University Press, 1975), p. 173.
19. Goodpaster, p. 497.
20. Alasdair MacIntyre, Three Rival Versions of Moral Enquiry: Encyclopaedia, Genealogy, Tradition (Notre Dame: University of Notre Dame Press, 1990), p. 194.
21. John Finnis, Natural Law and Natural Rights (New York: Oxford University Press, 1980), p. 225.
22. John Finnis, Aquinas (Oxford: Oxford University Press, 1998), p. 141.
23. Finnis, Natural Law and Natural Rights, p. 225.
24. Anthony Lisska, Aquinas' Theory of Natural Law (New York: Oxford University Press, 1996), p. 161.
25. Immanuel Kant, Foundations of the Metaphysics of Morals (Indianapolis: Bobbs Merrill, 1959), p. 16.
26. Ibid., p. 18.
27. Christine Korsgaard, Creating the Kingdom of Ends (Cambridge: Cambridge University Press, 1996), p. 78.
28. Ibid., p. 92.
29. Norman Bowie, Business Ethics: A Kantian Perspective (Oxford: Blackwell Publishers, 1999), p. 26.
30. Korsgaard, p. 21.
31. Bowie, p. 17.
32. Kant, p. 36.
33. Korsgaard, p. 194.

34. A. C. Ewing, *Ethics* (New York: Free Press, 1965), p. 58.
35. James Moor, "Just Consequentialism and Computing," p. 101.
36. Ibid.
37. Thomas Beauchamp and J.F. Childress, *Principles of Biomedical Ethics*, 4th ed. (New York: Oxford University Press, 1994).
38. Mark Kaczeski, "Casuistry and the Four Principles Approach," in *Encyclopedia of Applied Ethics*, ed. Ruth Chadwick (San Diego, CA: Academic Press, 1998), V. 1, p. 430.
39. Gary Doppelt, "Beyond Liberalism and Communitarianism: A Critical Theory of Social Justice," *Philosophy and Social Criticism*, V. 14: 3/4 (1988), p. 278.
40. Jon Gunneman et al., *The Ethical Investor* (New Haven: Yale University Press, 1972), p. 20.
41. John Rawls, *A Theory of Justice* (Cambridge: Harvard University Press, 1971), pp. 85–90.
42. Karl Marx, *Critique of the Gotha Program* (London: Lawrence and Werhart, Ltd., 1938), p. 14.

CHAPTER TWO

Regulating and Governing the Internet

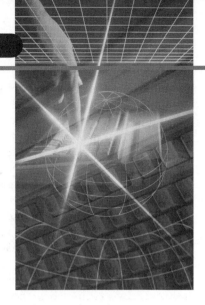

▶ Introduction

Although there has been much written about the perils of overexposing children and teenagers to the Internet, a 1997 headline in *The New York Times* sounded especially ominous: "A Seductive Drug Culture Flourishes on the Internet." The article explained how the Internet is now rife with Web sites that endorse illegal drugs or provide explicit instructions for making, growing, and consuming such drugs. Many of these Web sites make drugs sound exciting and alluring, and never even hint about the risks of addiction. Also, the problem is compounded because "the Internet lacks a quality control mechanism to separate fact from hyperbole or from outright falsehood, even in discussions that may ultimately encourage an activity that remains illegal for Americans of all ages."[1]

This is a disturbing but certainly not surprising development, and for some it does not augur well for the future of this ubiquitous technology. But from its earliest origins, a free-wheeling spirit has dominated the rules of discourse in cyberspace. According to Jonathan Katz, "it is the freest community in America."[2] Hence one of the most formidable issues faced by public policy-makers throughout the world is whether or not to impose some limits on this free and unencumbered flow of information in cyberspace—to restrict, for example, the dissemination of pornography or perhaps to ban Web sites that promote illicit drug use. Even if a decision were made to do so, implementation of that decision would be quite challenging given the jurisdictional problems of dealing with a technology with a vast global reach.

The debate about pornography on the Internet or about Web sites advocating illicit activities reflects deeper questions about how the Internet should be regulated or governed. While the Internet's anarchy and lack of structure has led to some excesses, many users are loath to see that anarchy replaced by tighter, centralized controls. Most civil libertarians, for example, contend that the Internet thrives precisely because there is no central governing authority. Consequently, they favor the continuation of decentralization and self-governance instead of any form of government intervention, believing that traditional forms of regulation would interfere with electronic interactions and the free flow of ideas. They argue that the Internet should be able to develop its own unique political structure, set appropriate standards, and even handle its own disputes.

Civil libertarians, however, are slowly losing this struggle. During the last several years there have been many regulations imposed on the Net. The Europeans have been particularly active with their extensive data protection policies and a new international treaty on cybercrime. As these regulations proliferate, the haze of ambiguity in cyberspace will begin to dissolve.

Nonetheless, the residual confusion and anarchy can still expose some businesses to legal landmines and potentially costly liabilities. Take the case of the Blue Note jazz club in Greenwich Village versus the Blue Note nightclub in Missouri. While the Blue Note club in New York has a federal trademark for its name, the Blue Note in Missouri obtained "the right to use the trade name locally in Missouri—what is known in trademark law as a 'geographical carve-out.'" But when this Blue Note designed its own Web page, the Blue Note in New York protested, claiming that its trademark had been violated by the Missouri club's worldwide presence on the Internet. As a result of this and similar cases, the legal system is still trying to decide whether business on the Internet "falls under the laws of some, all, or any of the jurisdictions from which that Internet site can be reached."[3]

Can governments begin to resolve the numerous jurisdictional problems created by the Internet? What will happen when different sovereignties begin to assert their authority in cyberspace? Will increased regulation stifle the Internet's innovative spirit? Are there alternatives to a cyberspace burdened by more and more rules and restrictions?

Before plunging into a discussion of these complex questions, it is instructive to review the history and technology of the Internet, and so we will devote a portion of this chapter for that purpose. It is important to understand the architectures of the Internet in order to appreciate the various possibilities for regulation and government intervention. This overview will include a cursory treatment of electronic commerce and the most popular online business models. It is also instructive at this point to consider the separate but related issue of governance, that is, managing routine tasks such as the assignment of domain names. This process too has triggered ethical controversies that will be considered in later chapters.

Our primary purpose in this chapter, however, is to discuss the appropriate regulatory response to the social problems that are emerging in the online world. Can market forces handle these problems or is government intervention essential? What about the possibility of a more decentralized, bottoms-up approach? Perhaps the optimal approach is finding the right interaction of policy and technology.

This discussion will set the stage for the more in-depth treatment of speech, property, privacy, and security in the remaining chapters. For each of these broad issues it will be necessary to evaluate how underlying technologies change our ability to establish and enforce policy.

▶ A Short History of the Internet

This summary of the Internet's creation is not a mere indulgence in nostalgia. We investigate the past in order to understand the present—by looking at the Internet's technological evolution, we can better appreciate its present architecture and perhaps uncover some clues about its future.

The origin of the Internet's basic architecture can be traced back to the search for a "survivable communications" system. During the late 1950s, the U.S. Defense Department was concerned about the need for a failure-resistant communications method. In 1961, Paul Baran developed such a method, which has become known as *packet switching*. Baran admits that "the origin of packet switching itself is very much Cold War."[4] Packet switching (originally called *message switching*) works by breaking up a message into small blocks of data; each of these packets is "labeled with its origin and destination and is then passed from node to node through the network."[5] Each packet can take a different route from the sender to the recipient. This technology was also being separately developed by Donald Davies, a British expert on computer security who was the first to use the term *packet* in reference to data communications. Davies also built an experimental packet switching network in the mid-1960s.

The first large scale packet switching network that was developed based on the insights of Baran and Davies was the work of the Advanced Research Projects Agency (ARPA), a research agency of the Defense Department, which financed high technology research. In the late 1960s this agency provided generous grants to universities and corporations in order to establish a communications network between major research centers in the United States, including universities such as MIT and Stanford. It recruited Lawrence Roberts of MIT's Lincoln Laboratory to oversee the construction of the ARPANET, the first incarnation of what is now known as the Internet.

The basic infrastructure of the ARPANET consisted of several time-sharing host computers, packet switching interface message processors (IMPs), and leased telephone lines. The host computers were already in place at the universities and research centers that would be part of the network and the telephone lines were being provided by AT&T. The IMPs were needed to perform key network functions such as sending and receiving data, error-checking, and message routing. The responsibility for building these systems was delegated to Bolt, Beranek, and Newman (BBN), a research and consulting firm in Cambridge, Massachusetts.

By the end of 1971, the primitive ARPANET was up and running. Its primary goal was supposed to be resource sharing, that is, enabling connected sites to share hardware processing power, software, and data. But the network's users soon discovered another function: electronic mail. Instead of using the network primarily to leverage remote hardware resources, users began sending huge volumes of mail. As a result, this popular application soon began to dominate traffic on this fledgling network. According to Abbate, "Network users challenged the initial assumptions, voting with their packets by sending a huge volume of electronic mail but making relatively little use of remote hardware and software. Through grassroots innovations and thousands of individual choices, the old idea of resource sharing that had propelled the ARPANET project forward was gradually replaced by the idea of the network as a means of bringing people together."[6]

In the early 1980s, this system was subdivided into two networks, the ARPANET and Milnet. Furthermore, connections were developed so that users could communicate between the two networks. The interaction between these networks came to be known as the "Internet." The term "Internet" was actually first used in a research paper written by Cerf and Kahn in 1974; that paper described a "network of networks" that would eventually link together computers all over the world. In the late 1980s, the National Science Foundation network (NSFNET), which relied on five supercomputers to link university and government researchers from across the world, replaced the ARPANET. The NSFNET began to encompass many other lower level networks such as those developed by academic institutions, and gradually the Internet as we know it today, a maze of interconnected networks, was born.

In these early days the Federal Government generously subsidized the Internet, and as a consequence, there were restrictions on any commercial use. The Internet was the exclusive domain of government researchers, scientists, university professors, and others who used it primarily to share their research findings or other academic information.

But the NSF no longer subsidizes the Internet, which has assumed a strong commercial character during the last decade. During the early 1990s, the Internet quickly became available to corporate users, while e-mail providers such as MCI and CompuServe opened up e-mail gateways. By 1993, 29 percent of the host computers connected to the Internet belonged to corporations. Commercial use now accounts for the vast majority of all Internet traffic. Management of the network has been transferred to private telecommunications carriers that manage the backbone, that is, the large physical networks that interconnect with each other. Thus, the network's future vitality depends to some extent on the cooperation and good will of these telecom providers.

The global diffusion of Internet usage during this period has been an extraordinary phenomenon. In 1983 there were a mere 500 host computers (i.e., computers with unique Internet Protocol addresses) connected to the Internet, but by the end of 2001, there were over 175 million registered host computers connected. Although the rapid development of the global Internet has been extraordinary, there is still a disparity between developed and developing countries. However, in some countries that is also beginning to change. In China there were 36.3 million Internet users in 2001, but that number is expected to grow to 152 million by 2005.[7]

This global connectivity provided by the Internet is perhaps its most attractive feature. It brings together millions of people and thousands of organizations all over the world, and has helped to achieve what *The Economist* calls "the death of distance," that is, the overcoming of geographic proximity as a barrier for conducting business.

▶ The Internet's Current Architecture

How does this all work? As intimated, there is actually little physical substance to the Internet. There are a number of dedicated computers at key connection junctures, but "like a parasite, the Internet uses the multibillion dollar telephone network as its hosts and lets them carry most of the cost."[8] Data is fluidly transferred over this network by means of a network protocol called TCP/IP. The TCP/IP protocol allows for complete interoperability on the Internet so that computers can communicate with one another even if they have different operating systems or different versions of applications software. TCP/IP therefore makes the network virtually transparent to end users no matter what hardware system they are using, and it allows the Internet to function as a single, unified network.

TCP/IP consist of two elements. The first is the IP or Internet Protocol, which establishes a unique numeric address (four numbers in the form nnn.nnn.nnn.nnn ranging from 0 to 255) for each system connected to the Internet. IP is a means of labeling data so that it can be sent to the proper destination in the most efficient way possible. If a user connects to the Internet through an Internet Service Provider, that user is normally assigned a temporary IP address, but a user who connects from a local area network (LAN) in an organization is more likely to have a permanent IP address.

The second piece, TCP, or Transmission Control Protocol, enables network communication over the Internet. As discussed, the data is broken up into pieces called packets, with the first part of each packet containing the address of where it should go. The packets are then sent to their destination by a system of routers, or servers on the Internet that keep track of Internet addresses. These packets can take completely different routes to reach their goal. Once all the packets arrive, thanks to TCP, the message or data will be reconstructed based on the sequence numbers in the headers to each packet and directed to the appropriate application.

The Internet's physical infrastructure is comprised of many large, interconnected networks that are known as Network Service Providers (NSPs). NSPs include IBM, SprintNet, and PSINet as well as several others. According to Hafner, these backbone providers "adhere to what are known as peering arrangements, which are essentially agreements to exchange traffic at no charge."[9] Each NSP connects to three network access points, and at those points packet traffic may be transferred from one NSP backbone to another. NSPs also sell bandwidth to smaller network providers and to ISPs.

Routers, also known as *packet switches*, perform much of the work in getting data transmitted over the Net to its ultimate destination. When a packet arrives at a router, the router looks at the IP address and checks the routing table, and if the table contains the network included in the IP address, the message is sent to that network. If not, the message is sent along on a default route (usually to the next router in the backbone hierarchy). If the address is in another NSP, the router connected to the NSP backbone will send the message to the correct backbone, where it will be sent along by other routers until it reaches the correct address.[10]

As we survey the Internet's technical and social evolution, the most distinctive features of its network architecture should be apparent. Perhaps the Internet's most important characteristic is its *openness*. Thanks to an open-ended network architecture, the Internet, has supported an extraordinary level of innovation: e-mail, bulletin boards, and instant messaging are just some of the many applications this technology has enabled. According to Castells, "the openness of the Internet's architecture was the source of its main strength: its self-evolving development, as users became producers of the technology and shapers of the whole network."[11]

Second, the Internet is *asynchronous*—unlike telephone communication there is no need for coordination between the sender and recipient of a message. An e-mail message, for example, can be sent to a mailbox that can be accessed at any time by its owner. Third, the Internet permits a *many-to-many format of communications*[12]: many users can interact with many other users through electronic mail, bulletin boards, Web sites, and other vehicles. Unlike traditional media such as newspapers, the Net is interactive since those users can speak back. Fourth, the Internet is a *distributed* network instead of a centralized one, whereby data can take any number of routes to its final destination. There is no center to the Internet, that is, there is no central server or single controlling authority, since information travels from one location to another without being transmitted through a central hub. This gives users more control over the flow of information. Since it is a decentralized, packet-based network, it is more difficult to censor that information. Also, this resilient design makes the Internet's structure more durable. As Hafner points out, "that deceptively simple [packet-switching] principle has, time and again, saved the network from failure."[13] In the summer of 2001, for example, a train fire in Baltimore damaged a critical fiber optic loop, but Internet data easily circumvented the problem. Finally, the Internet is highly *scalable,* that is, it is not directly affected when new computer links are added or deleted. Hence it allows for much more flexible expansion or contraction than many other proprietary network technologies. Its basic architecture encourages universal access and participation.

The Internet, then, should really be conceptualized as a flexible and open infrastructure. It is designed to maximize interoperability, that is, to be completely independent of software programs, hardware platforms, and other protocols. As a result, it is well-suited to new applications and can easily accommodate revolutionary developments in both software and hardware. Because of its malleability, however, it is naive to assume that the Internet of today will be the Internet of the future. The architectures of cyberspace could conceivably undergo a major transformation in the next few years. As we pointed out in Chapter 1, if the state chose to influence those architectures by mandating digital identity or otherwise controlling access through the Internet Service Providers, cyberspace could become a very different place.

▶ The World Wide Web

The most recent surge in the Internet's popularity can be attributed to the emergence of the World Wide Web. The Web is a collection of multimedia documents that can be easily accessed through the Internet. The

Web was developed at the European Particle Physics Lab as a means of exchanging data about high-energy physics among physicists scattered throughout the world. This group developed a standard known as HTML or Hypertext Markup Language, which supports a procedure whereby "tags" or triggers are attached to a word or phrase that links it to another HTML document located anywhere on the Internet. The documents created by HTML are stored on computers known as Web servers and can include straight text, visual images, streaming video, and audio clips. Documents belong to a Web site that has a specific address such as "www.bc.edu." The last three letters represent a top level identification (for example, "edu" stands for education and "com" stands for a commercial enterprise), while the middle part of the name designates the actual site (bc = Boston College).

Net browsers such as Navigator provided by Netscape or Microsoft's Internet Explorer enable users to surf or "explore" the Web rather effortlessly. They are highly versatile navigational tools that permit users to access, display, and print documents; they also give users the ability to link to other documents at any location on the Web. Hyperlinks can create a maze of interconnected documents and Web sites that can sometimes confuse users, but also greatly expand opportunities for research and investigation. Browsers are supplemented by networked utilities such as Real Networks' Real Player, which gives users access to streaming audio and video content.

The Web has transformed the Internet into a user-friendly medium since the Web page is an intuitively obvious interface for even the most novice user. More significantly, according to Samuelson and Varian, "the back-end protocols for authoring and distributing Web pages (HTML and HTTP) were easy to understand and use as well, facilitating the rapid deployment of Web servers."[14] The diversity and heterogeneity of Web sites is evidence that this assessment is accurate.

Despite its brief history, the World Wide Web itself has already become a vast, tangled network. Web sites were first deployed at major universities and research centers, but now proliferate throughout cyberspace at schools, hospitals, corporations, and many other organizations. According to the Commerce Department, 143 million Americans, or 54 percent of the population, used the Web in 2001.[15] Even individuals or small businesses have established their own Web pages. These Web pages will undoubtedly be the vehicle for the further acceleration of electronic commerce and many other network-based activities such as online education, news reporting, or fund raising.

The plethora of Web sites has created a density of information that can make it difficult for users to locate a particular site. Search engines such as those provided by Yahoo or Google can help in this process, but even they are sometimes ineffectual in the face of such voluminous data. Part of the problem, of course, is that the Web is just too large and too volatile to index properly, but these search engines have made great strides in this regard.

Regardless of the difficulties that users encounter trying to navigate their way through cyberspace, the Web continues to rapidly gain in popularity. It is regarded as an encyclopedic source of information that is almost infinitely extensible. As more and more users develop their own sites, it has helped bring about the democratization of information predicted by many Internet visionaries.

Finally there are predictions that by 2005 we will witness the birth of a more sophisticated next-generation Web, thanks once again to the work of Berners-Lee and his colleagues. This is being called the Semantic Web, since it will be able to understand human languages, thanks in part to the extensive use of XML, a language that can tag words and phrases so that computers will know what they mean. For example, if a *bot* (a robot) travels to a site and sees an 11:05 A.M. departure time, the bot does not know what 11:05 means unless it is accompanied by a tag <departure time>. The ultimate objective is to transform the Web into a giant intellect so that "every computer connected to the Internet would have access to all the knowledge that humankind has accumulated in science, business, and the arts since we began painting the walls of caves 30,000 years ago."[16]

▶ Electronic Commerce

Electronic commerce or *e-commerce*, refers to trade that occurs on the Internet. Thanks to the infamous dot.com debacle in 2000, the euphoria about e-commerce has faded, as we have come to appreciate that many e-commerce ventures were no more than phantom edifices. But no one is dismissing the likelihood that this global network will be a main thoroughfare of commerce in the near future. What are some of the general benefits of e-commerce? First, it eliminates the constraints of time and space and thereby provides extraordinary convenience for consumers. As noted, the Net is a fundamentally asynchronous technology so users can do their browsing and shopping at any time. Second, the Internet is a low-cost communications technology so it can greatly reduce overhead and transaction costs. According to Mandel and Hof, "the Internet is a tool that dramatically lowers the cost of communication, [and] that means it can radically alter any industry or activity that depends heavily on the flow of information."[17] It is, of course, much less expensive to operate one virtual bookstore (Amazon.com) than a chain of physical stores. And the more digitizable the product, the lower the cost structure, since those products do not require an infrastructure for distribution. Thus, it is more advantageous for a company such as Charles Schwab to sell securities online than it is for Amazon.com to sell books, since the online broker does not have to worry about warehousing a physical product and delivering that product to its customers.

A third advantage of online commerce is the ability to customize sales and advertising to each individual consumer. A Web shopper's every move in cyberspace can be traced, and this allows vendors to compile a profile of a consumer's preferences. According to *The Economist*, "With this feedback, online merchants can further differentiate themselves from their physical world competitors by customizing their shop or service for each customer."[18] For example, the online book dealer Amazon uses collaborative-filtering technology, which enables it to analyze a customer's purchases and to suggest other books the customer might like based on what people with similar purchase histories have bought.

The e-business landscape is complicated, but it is useful to follow Applegate's helpful distinctions. She categorizes some companies as digital infrastructure providers, including IBM, Cisco, AT&T, and Microsoft, since they provide the servers or physical networks that make electronic commerce possible. In a second category she includes companies that operate in the Internet's distribution channel: focused distributors and portals. Focused distributors provide products and services primarily on the Web while portals serve as gateways to the Net.[19] Under the category of focused distributors, there are four basic digital business models: business-to-consumer (B2C), consumer-to-business (C2B), business-to-business (B2B), and consumer-to-consumer (C2C).

The business-to-consumer (B2C) model involves direct sales to consumers and includes online retailers such as Amazon.com and Staples.com. With several hundred million people already online, the potential here is obviously enormous. For the consumer, the big attraction is convenience—with a single click of the mouse an order for clothes, books, fine wine, or office supplies can be placed at a Web site. For the retailer, a key advantage is lower costs. Hence the B2C model allows for quick scalability of one's business. Only one Web site is needed to service customers from all over the world. There may be a high initial investment for an elaborate computer system, but unlike traditional retailers, there is no need to continually invest in new stores and other physical assets in order to increase revenues.

The consumer-to-business (C2B) model is epitomized by Priceline, the company that allows customers to name their price for various objects such as airline tickets or hotel rooms. According to Priceline's founder, Jay Walker, "In the traditional model of commerce, a seller advertises a unit of supply in the marketplace at a specified price, and a buyer takes it or leaves it. Priceline turns that model around. We allow a buyer to advertise a unit of demand to a group of sellers. The sellers can then decide whether to fulfill that demand or not. In effect, we provide a mechanism for collecting and forwarding units of demand to interested sellers."[20]

The third model is consumer-to-consumer, or C2C, and the prime example is eBay, the online auction service that acts as an intermediary for customers who want to auction off various goods to other customers. The eBay operation illustrates how online commerce can function with extraordinary efficiency. The buyers and sellers do all the work: sellers pay a fee to eBay for the opportunity to auction their wares, and when the auction ends, the seller and buyer negotiate over the payment and shipping. For its role as an intermediary, eBay normally receives between 7 and 18 percent of the sale price. Since its customers do most of the work and take most of the risk, some have concluded that eBay is the perfect virtual business.

Finally, business-to-business (B2B) refers to electronic commerce between two organizations and includes procurement, inventory management, sales service and support, and so forth. Perhaps the greatest potential in the B2B market is the remarkable growth of trading sites, which range in complexity from online catalogs to public exchanges where buyers and sellers come together to exchange goods. Ventro, formerly known as Chemdex, was a public exchange for the medical equipment industry. These public exchanges are open to a much larger group of buyers than a private network, and this greatly enhances the potential market for both the sellers and buyers.

In addition to focused distributors, we find portals. Horizontal portals such as Yahoo in America and Star Media in Latin America function as gateways to the Internet by providing a single point of access from which users can connect to various Web sites. Vertical portals such as Quicken.com, in the area of financial services, provide "deep content" in one area. The boundaries between portals and focused distributors have become increasingly murky. According to Applegate, many portals now "serve not only as gateways but also as destinations where people stop and conduct business."[21]

Despite the success of companies like Amazon.com, eBay, and Yahoo, some consumers are still reluctant to embrace electronic commerce. Some fear becoming the victims of fraud or scams that are easier to execute thanks to the anonymous nature of Internet transactions. Others are concerned about the tenuous security of the Internet and worry that the price of convenience may be a loss of privacy. The accretion of social trust has not happened at a fast enough pace, but it will be accelerated by "trustworthy" systems that are secure and respectful of privacy rights. These systems will go a long way to inspire more confidence in Web-based transactions.

Although electronic commerce Web sites have made the greatest progress in the United States, they are also proliferating in many other countries, such as China. The Chinese government has encouraged the private sectors to develop Web-based businesses, and entrepreneurs are responding enthusiastically. As these sites gain in popularity, they could transform China's outdated retail business and enable manufacturers to automate purchases from suppliers. According to Einhorn, "the global implications of this are enormous—as Web-based e-commerce spreads, traders around the world could link directly with suppliers and retailers across China."[22] Chinese language portals such as sina.com and china.com are also emerging to serve as gateways to the Net for Chinese citizens.

The Internet can never return to its halcyon days when it was frequented only by technology buffs and academic researchers who formed an intimate and knowledgeable online community. As electronic commerce continues to consume the Net, it will face a new set of social problems that could never have been envisioned by its founders. We turn now to a few remarks about the downside of the Internet phenomenon.

▶ Social Problems and Social Costs

The Internet's popularity and commercialization has led to some familiar social problems and frictions in cyberspace. The erosion of privacy, the emergence of perverted forms of speech, and the illegitimate copying of music and video files represent just some of these problems. At the same time, e-commerce vendors have been victimized by fraud and attacks by hackers. In the remaining chapters of this book, we will diagnose and analyze these social harms, and review some equitable resolutions.

At this stage, however, it would be instructive to consider broad philosophical differences for dealing with these difficulties. In Lessig's terms, is the optimum solution to be found in law, the market, code, or social norms? It is naive to think that any one of these four modalities of regulation can single-handedly resolve a problem such as illicit copying in cyberspace. For complex problems, the proper solution will undoubtedly be found in the interplay of law, code, and the market. The question becomes, which of these forces should have primacy? Which one should generally take the lead in controlling the Net? One's answer to this query will depend on one's faith in the market forces or on ideological assumptions about the efficacy of government regulation.

In economic terms, some of these frictions in cyberspace can be described as social costs or negative externalities. The economist Ronald Coase explains that social costs are generated by "those actions of business firms which have harmful effects on others."[23] Some of the social harms we have been discussing can be viewed from this perspective, that is, as harmful byproducts of certain Internet transactions. For example, the erosion of privacy, which often results when information is exchanged between two parties, or the transmission of disruptive forms of speech like spam, would fall into this category. Social costs represent failures of the market system or market imperfections, since they are costs borne involuntarily by others that are not reflected in the price of the good whose production created those costs. In the case of privacy, the sale of personally identifiable data to third parties is an externality, because the cost (loss of privacy) is imposed on the individual whose data is sold, and hence that cost is ignored by the seller. When regarded from an economist's viewpoint, the issue becomes one of weighing the economic benefits of the sale of this data against the social costs of privacy erosion.

Or consider the problem of unsolicited electronic e-mail known as spam. The production and distribution costs of spam messages advertising some product or service are minimal, but the real costs are shifted to other parties in cyberspace, such as Internet Service Providers that are forced to store and deliver these messages. Because the true costs of spam are not internalized by its "producers," spam is overproduced, resulting in a lack of *allocative efficiency,* or efficiency in the allocation of society's economic resources.

But what should be done about these market failures, these externalities that now plague cyberspace just as they plague real space? Let us review several ideologies for how best to deal with market imperfections and those social harms we find accumulating on the Net.

The Invisible Hand

The vast majority of users agree that spam is a menace, but when it comes to doing something about spam, opinions diverge. Do we need government intervention and public policies to contain the flood of junk mail and restore economic efficiency? Economists such as Ronald Coase of the Chicago School are skeptical of the government and tend to put more faith in the invisible hand of the marketplace to solve problems like spam. According to this school of thought, the impersonal forces of the market can often do a better job of fixing market imperfections than the vested interests of other marketplace participants (such as government regulators). Much of Coase's work has drawn attention to the limitations of government regulation as an ideal solution to the problem of negative externalities. The government's regulatory agencies often do not understand the industries they are trying to regulate, a problem that could be exacerbated in contexts where sophisticated technologies are involved. Coase and others have also frequently noted the inefficiencies of large, centralized bureaucracies and the persistence of organizational inertia. Finally, there is always the potential for capture, a process whereby those being regulated influence regulators so that they no longer act in the public interest. According to Coase, there are "few more unpleasant sights than an unholy alliance between the regulators and the regulated industry to solve the problem of competition by suppressing it."[24]

What Coase and others favor as an alternative is greater reliance on the marketplace. Consider, for example, the problem of privacy erosion in cyberspace. We can certainly enact laws to deal with this problem but maybe the markets will effect a more efficient, welfare-enhancing solution. Those who favor this approach presume that market pressures will force vendors to respect privacy rights at a level consistent with the needs and interests of consumers. According to Reidenberg, the U.S. approach to privacy relies in part on just such a market-based solution, since data protection in the U.S. is a "question of economic power rather than political right."[25]

But the marketplace has often proved to be an inadequate forum for addressing social problems. The market's reaction to those problems is often reactive and inequitable. Lessig, for one, sees the invisible hand threatening "liberty and openness" in cyberspace.[26] Economists like Pigou have categorically rejected the viability of market-based solutions to these externality problems: "No 'invisible hand' can be relied upon to produce a good arrangement of the whole from a combination of separate treatments of the parts. It is, therefore, necessary that an authority of wider reach should intervene and should tackle [society's] collective problems. . . ."[27] According to this view, the marketplace will always function as an important constraint on behavior, but it should not take priority over other regulatory forces such as law, norms, and code.

Regulating the Net: The Visible Hand

As Pigou suggested, the alternative to the market as primary regulator is the greater reliance on policy constraints imposed by government. But can the Net be regulated—is it really "regulable" in the same way that the physical world can be subjected to rules and regulations of local sovereigns? Can the unrestricted freedom of cyberspace be reigned in by government forces?

The Internet defies regulation for several key reasons. First, its distributed architecture and resilient design makes the Net hard to control. Packet switching technology has meant that it's not so easy to stop the flow of information. As John Gilmore puts it, "Information can take so many alternative routes when one of the nodes of the network is removed that the Net is almost immortally flexible . . . . The Net interprets censorship as damage and routes around it."[28] The Internet's lack of a physical center means that it has no moral center that can be held accountable for information flowing over the network.

Second, there is the Internet's content, digital information, 1s and 0s that can be transmitted through cyberspace with ease and stored on the recipient's hard drive. As Negroponte observed, "The information superhighway is about the global movement of weightless bits at the speed of light."[29] All forms of information, including images and voice, can be digitized, and a digital file, which is nothing more than a stream of bits, is especially difficult to contain. One consequence of this has been the destabilization of copyright law in cyberspace, thanks in part to the technologies developed by companies like Napster.

Finally, governments that seek to control or regulate the Net face an array of jurisdictional conundrums. As we have seen, a fundamental problem with a particular sovereignty imposing its will on the Internet is that laws and regulations are based on geography—they have force only within a certain territorial area, for example, a state, a county, or a nation. As one jurist put it: "All law is *prima facie* territorial."[30] Moreover, since the Internet is a borderless global technology, it is almost impossible for any country to enforce the laws or restrictions it seeks to impose on this sprawling region of cyberspace. If the United States decides to outlaw pornography, it can probably only enforce this restriction among U.S. purveyors of pornography. It cannot restrict vendors located in Europe or the Caribbean from making pornography available on the Internet for everyone to see. It can, of course, put the burden on Internet providers and hold them liable for transmitting the illicit material no matter where its source is located. But this seems to be an unfair and unworkable solution since it is expensive and difficult for ISPs to detect and properly filter out all communications with pornographic elements.

Despite these obstacles, local sovereignties will not be deterred from regulating the Net. At the broadest level there are several forms of Internet regulation; that is, structural regulations of the information infrastructure, regulation of e-commerce, and regulation of content. For example, a particular sovereignty might be concerned with preserving open and equitable access on the Internet but give free reign to content providers along with the focused distributors and portals that are engaged in e-commerce.

Governments that do seek to regulate e-commerce might do so by regulating privacy through establishing data protection standards or by insisting on certain security standards for a Web site. The European Union Privacy Directive, for example, lays out strict privacy rules for companies doing business within the European Union. In the United States, however, the preferred solution has been self-regulation.

Lastly, sovereignties can impose restrictions and guidelines on the content on the Internet and the Web. Several countries, such as the United

States and Singapore, have attempted to adopt what Venturelli calls a "nationalist or cultural model," which calls for the regulation of content to conform to a country's cultural or moral principles.[31] Singapore has been particularly repressive in its approach to regulating the Internet by imposing severe penalties on Internet providers for transmitting pornographic or seditious material. The Singaporean government has periodically searched the files of these providers and levied heavy fines when violations have been uncovered. In the United States, most attempts to regulate content have so far run afoul of the First Amendment.

All sovereignties must make these decisions about the scope of Internet regulations. Should they aspire to develop structural regulations that protect the infrastructure and mandate universal access. Or should they focus on content controls? Once the appropriate scope is defined, sovereignties must decide whether they should apply existing laws or craft new ones. For example, should the U.S. apply existing intellectual property laws to the Web, or is it necessary to develop new ones that will apply to digital content? According to Samuelson, "Although some commentators have suggested that copyright law is outmoded in the Internet environment, the general view in the U.S. and the EU is that copyright law can be applied and adapted to protect expressive works in digital form."[32]

Some countries, unfortunately, have been overly aggressive in Internet regulations. Despite its encouragement of Web-based business, the Chinese government remains exceedingly anxious about the Internet, and they have made it quite clear that "by linking with the Internet, we do not mean the absolute freedom of information."[33] Chinese officials use a firewall to block access to pornographic and other objectionable Web sites, such as those operated by human rights groups. China's iron grip on political discourse has been tested by Internet access, but this country has responded with its usual heavy-handed and repressive tactics.

Finally, there are perils in having each national jurisdiction impose its own laws on the Net. Different privacy laws, for example, could disrupt the flow of e-commerce or impede other information exchanges. If this borderless global technology is to be properly regulated, shouldn't there be a set of international standards? There has been some effort made to harmonize laws pertaining to the Internet. Consider, for example, the World Intellectual Property Organization (WIPO) Copyright Treaty, which stipulates how copyright laws will be applied to digital works. In addition, other countries besides the European Union have begun to embrace its Privacy Directive. Argentina, Australia, Canada, Switzerland, and New Zealand have either adopted the E.U. Directive or they are working on a set of rules that are heavily influenced by that directive.[34] Some in the United States see this trend towards convergence as a threat to national sovereignty, but others believe that a simple global standard is the only way to ensure that privacy rights are recognized and enforced throughout the world.

While harmonization is sound in theory, it will be immensely difficult to accomplish in practice thanks to deeply embedded cultural and legal differences between most countries. Given this difficulty, Samuelson recommends that nations should instead strive for "policy interoperability" instead of full harmonization, that is, "agreeing on goals a policy should achieve, while recognizing that nations may adopt somewhat different policy means to implement goals."[35]

▶ A "Bottoms-Up" Approach: The Sovereignty of Code

In the previous chapter, we alluded to the Net's empowerment of the individual through its code. Thanks to strong encryption programs, it is more difficult for the state to conduct surveillance on confidential electronic communications. Similarly, filtering technologies give individuals the power to limit content or to format the information they wish to receive. Electronic anonymity also frustrates lawmakers' efforts to hold individuals accountable for their online actions. The Net is empowering the individual by the means of technology. It appears to be shifting control from the state to the individual, and this has been a source of great consternation for many government leaders.

The individual's empowerment through code makes possible a more bottoms-up approach to regulation that some users and civil libertarians favor. But can a case be made for letting the Internet organize and moderate itself as much as possible? According to David Post, "there are some problems on the Internet best solved by these messy, disordered, semi-chaotic, unplanned, decentralized systems . . . and the costs that necessarily accompany such unplanned disorder may sometimes be worth bearing."[36] This messy bottoms-up approach described by Post is not a panacea for the Internet's various externalities, but it may be an adequate means of regulating conduct and addressing *some* aspects of the social problems described in the chapters ahead.

There are surely benefits that accompany a decentralized scheme of regulation with users relying on code to curtail certain social harms. In some ways this approach seems preferable to the regulatory regime of government. It's nonintrusive, simpler, less expensive, and gives users the ultimate choice about what they want to see or not see. Bottoms-up constraints also avoid the expensive government infrastructure that inevitably accompanies a regulatory scheme. In addition, the decentralization philosophy fits with the cultural shift now taking place in countries like the United States, where citizens are increasingly antibureaucratic.

Instead of reliance on bureaucracy and public policy to solve society's ills, they favor individual empowerment and local control whenever possible.

As we observed in Chapter 1, however, some legal scholars have made the case that technical solutions implemented by private parties can sometimes be more restrictive than actions taken by a democratic state. As Seth Finkelstein writes, "because of a perspective that might be rendered 'government action bad, private action good' there's great unwillingness to think about complicated social systems, or private parties acting as agents of censorship."[37]

In his critique of filtering systems such as PICS, Lessig has made similar observations. PICS, which stands for Platform for Internet Content Selection, is a labeling standard that provides a way of labeling and blocking online material. It can be used by parents or schools to block access to Web sites with pornographic material or virulent hate speech. According to Lessig, the widespread deployment of this technology can yield a "tyranny of the code" as those in positions of local authority impose their own standards on unsuspecting users.[38]

The power and potential of blocking software like PICS has not been lost on civil libertarians who have begun to better appreciate how these technologies can undermine the free flow of information far more effectively than government-imposed censorship. The threat to freedom may be more subtle and dispersed, but the end result is still the same sort of social domination, now effected by private parties, which the Net was designed to prevent.

The French philosopher Michel Foucault appreciated the import of this difference as well. In his writings on the nature of power, he differentiated between explicit state commands emanating from the sovereign power and a more covert and implicit exercise of domination. The latter normally has taken the form of surveillance, but it can take other forms as well. According to Foucault, "We have the emergence or rather the invention of a new mechanism of power possessed of a highly specific procedural technique. It is a type of power which is constantly exercised by means of surveillance rather than in a discontinuous manner by means of a system of levies or obligations distributed over time."[39] This clearly echoes Lessig's concern about the "tyranny of the code," a tyranny that can come from different and non-obvious sources.

We are left then with a provocative but seminal question—should control and regulation of the Internet for the most part be left in the hands of private parties and the corrective technologies that they create and distribute in the marketplace? Or should we embrace a more top-down approach? Should the Internet be regulated more directly in order to contain its social costs without the collateral damage that can accompany the bottoms-up approach? Are the sinews of Internet stability best found in the rational laws and regulations emanating from a sovereign power or an international body? Or are they found in the architectures of the Net responsibly deployed by individuals?

▶ Internet Governance

Although there is some disagreement on how the Internet should be regulated through government intervention, no one questions the need for some type of governance and technical coordination. No matter how opposed one is to regulatory oversight, the Net cannot survive without this type of coordination. There must be governing bodies that handle ordinary and routine technical matters, such as the determination of technical standards and the management of domain names and IP addresses. For our purposes, the term "governance" will refer to managing these matters rather than regulating the Net through content controls or other mechanisms.

Two major policy groups that provide such governance are the World Wide Web Consortium, an international standards setting body, and the Internet Engineering Task Force (IETF), which develops technical standards such as communications protocols. According to *The Economist*, a culture of "cautious deliberation" prevails within the IETF, which strives to be democratic in its decision-making processes. Anybody can join the IETF and any member can propose a standard "and so start a process that is formal enough to ensure that all get a hearing, but light enough to avoid bureaucracy."[40]

The Domain Name System (DNS) also needs coordination. The DNS maps the domain names of organizations such as eBay to the actual numeric Internet Protocol address (e.g., 709.14.3.26). The DNS is a hierarchical system divided into separate domains. When a domain name is invoked by a browser, the request is forwarded to the DNS server, which is normally operated by an Internet Service Provider, and that server locates the databases for each subdomain. If the domain name is www.loyola.edu, the DNS server will first locate the server for ".edu," which is the Top Level Domain (TLD); it will then find the server for "loyola," the Second Level Domain, and so forth. Using this method, the web page is found and transmitted back to the recipient.

This system was formerly administered by a small private company called Network Solutions International (NSI), which charged $50 for the registration of a domain name and usually awarded the name on a first-come, first-served basis. As the Internet became commercialized, there was escalating disenchantment with the NSI arrangement. As a result, after some political maneuvering, the domain name system is now in the hands of ICANN (Internet Corporation for Assigned Names and Numbers). ICANN is an international, nonprofit organization with full responsibility for the Domain Name System. ICANN itself does not actually distribute domain names. That task is delegated to domain name registrars such as VeriSign. ICANN determines the policies for domain name distribution, and it has the final say for selecting firms that qualify as registrars.

Domain names were introduced to impose some order on the Net, and originally there were six TLDs: .com, .net, .org, .edu, .gov, and .mil. ICANN has recently decided to create several new top level domains such as .aero. (air transport companies), .coop (cooperatives), .biz (business), .museum (museums), .name (individuals), .pro (professionals such as lawyers), and .info (non-restricted use). The purpose of these new extensions is to handle the overusage of popular TLDs such as .com and .org. It remains to be seen whether these new extensions (like .biz) will be embraced by the public and become as popular as the original TLDs such as .com.

To its credit, ICANN has acted swiftly and deliberately to deal with the issue of cybersquatting and other domain name disputes. In October, 1999, it established the Uniform Dispute Resolution Policy (UDRP) for adjudicating such disputes and protecting legitimate trademarks. That policy will be discussed in more detail in Chapter 4 in the context of the treatment of trademark law and the Lanham Act.

ICANN is currently governed by a board of 18 members; nine of those members are elected by the at-large membership. Critics of ICANN contend that despite its claims to represent an international constituency, ICANN is dominated by Americans. Moreover, they insist that its structures are not democratic enough and that it does not give average users enough say in its governing procedures. Whether these criticisms will undermine ICANN's authority is anyone's guess at this point, but its supporters say that ICANN has the potential to emerge as a model of consensus-building and international cooperation demanded by the global Internet community.

▶ Net Regulation and Ethics

At this stage of the Internet's rapid evolution, it would be presumptuous to predict which, if any, of the regulatory approaches described here might actually prevail. There will undoubtedly be some mixture of bottoms-up controls combined with top-down regulations. The real question is how expansive a role the government will end up playing in regulating the Internet. There is a case to be made that this role should be substantial given the importance of cyberspace for the future of commerce and for many other social interactions. There is also understandable wariness about the unpredictability of trusting the Internet to regulate itself. Without the government's sustained efforts to ensure a level playing field, companies like Microsoft and America-OnLine Time Warner could exert undue influence on e-commerce and monopolize essential facilities. Also, supporters of more extensive government regulations raise legitimate concerns about the poor results of efforts in the United States to handle online privacy through self-regulation.

However, if the state does intend to expand its regulatory role in the recalcitrant region of cyberspace, it will continue to confront at least two formidable challenges. First, it will be frustrated in trying to apply territorially based laws to a global entity. For example, the French government has sued the American company Yahoo for displaying Nazi memorabilia (which is illegal in France) but U.S. courts are unlikely to enforce any foreign judgment, especially where free speech issues are at stake. Second, the state must contend with code that has radically empowered the individual. Individuals have at their disposal programs like anonymizer.com, which can block IP-address tracking, along with peer-to-peer architectures that make it almost impossible to stop illicit copying of copyrighted content. These obstacles *appear* to have weakened the state's sovereignty and given the individual the upper hand.

It is premature, however, to dismiss the power of the state and to toll the death knell for its sovereignty. As Michel Foucault writes, "wherever there is power, there is resistance."[41] The state will certainly resist this state of affairs and seek to retrieve its lost dominance and diminished sovereignty. It may, for instance, use its vast power to more tightly control Internet Service Providers or to demand that other private surrogates carry out its regulatory regime. Public policy makers also recognize the power of code as a constraint in cyberspace and might be willing to mandate the use of certain codes (such as filtering and IP-address tracking) to counteract the difficulties of regulating cyberspace through fiat alone. As Lessig observes, the state will work to increase the very *regulability* of cyberspace by exercising control over its code.[42]

What we are left with, then, is a power struggle between a frustrated state and a newly empowered Internet community. At the epicenter of that struggle is the code of cyberspace. In many respects, the code is a far more effective constraint than law, norms, or the marketplace. One can envision many possibilities on both sides for using that code to gain control. For example, the architectures of the Internet currently facilitate electronic anonymity, but the state could respond by requiring that ISPs use code that mandates digital identity and the traceability of all Internet transactions.

What makes this struggle so perilous is the facility with which the code of the Internet can be manipulated. Andrew Shapiro describes the Internet's capacity for empowering individual users as the "control revolution." He argues that the state's resistance to that revolution will "become more refined as governments become more adept at influencing code without running afoul of constitutional limitations or public opposition."[43]

The code is such a powerful regulator in the hands of the state or individuals because of its *malleability* and *obscurity*, its flexible ability to regulate or shape behavior gradually and inconspicuously. Code does not always constrain or influence behavior openly and directly in a way that is transparent to those it affects. This contrasts sharply with the constraint of law, since the process of crafting laws through democratic procedures is subject to considerable public scrutiny.

Hence the paramount importance of ethics in all of this. While we do not take a stand on the preferability of a bottoms-up or a top-down regulatory philosophy, we contend that whatever approach becomes dominant, there must be careful attention paid to core human values such as autonomy, privacy, and liberty. Informal social controls abetted by technology may have the potential to provide effective and fair-minded regulations of cyberspace conduct, but only if the developers and users of code are committed to responsible behavior. This will help to minimize any negative effects on human rights that these corrective technologies (such as filtering) can bring about if they are carelessly deployed.

Likewise, a top-down legislative process must be guided by these same core values. Governments must not overreact to the control revolution with restrictive laws or bypass the democratic process and manipulate Internet architectures to curtail basic human freedoms and rights merely for the sake of greater order and stability in cyberspace. They too must behave responsibly in their attempts to regulate cyberspace.

As we argued in the previous chapter, what is of primary and utmost significance is the preservation in cyberspace of those transcendent human goods and moral values, which are so basic for the realization of human flourishing. *Moral values must be the ultimate regulator of cyberspace, not the code of engineers.* This orientation will help ensure that abuses of the code will be kept to a minimum. If Internet stakeholders, including public policy makers, software developers, educators, and corporate executives, act prudently and responsibly, they will be vigilant and conscientious about respecting these values. As a result, they will find themselves guided by a moral wisdom that encourages care for others and a sense of measure concerning the public affairs of the Internet. This will also help to achieve a reasonable equilibrium between the state and other Internet stakeholders.

In the next several chapters we will discuss what constitutes responsible approaches to cyberspace regulation. In the course of that discussion, we will consider how code can be responsibly designed, developed, and utilized. We also will focus on how the core moral values can be applied to some of the troubling dilemmas now emerging in cyberspace. To be sure, the application of those values is not an exact science and there will often be room for reasonable people to disagree. But if there is a shared conviction that the Internet must be governed by these broad moral standards, it will be easier to equitably resolve these inevitable conflicts.

Discussion Questions

1. Discuss the pros and cons of extensive government regulation of the Internet either by a local sovereign government or by an international body specifically constituted for this purpose.
2. Evaluate the "bottoms-up" approach to regulation as it was presented in this chapter.
3. In what ways does the structure and present architecture of the Internet affect the choice of an optimal regulatory structure?
4. What is ICANN and what does it do?

References

1. Christopher Wren, "Drug Culture Flourishes on the Internet," *The New York Times*, June 20, 1997, p. A19.
2. Jonathan Katz, "Birth of Digital Nation," *Wired*, April 1997, p. 186.
3. Geanna Rosenberg, "Trying to Resolve Jurisdictional Rules on the Internet," *The New York Times*, April 14, 1997, p. D1.
4. Stewart Brand, "Interview with Paul Baran (Founding Father)," *Wired*, March, 2001, pp. 145–153.
5. Janet Abbate, *Inventing the Internet* (Cambridge, MA: MIT Press, 1999), p. 11.
6. Ibid., p. 111.
7. Carol Sliwa, "China: The Web's Next Frontier," *Computerworld*, May 28, 2001, p. 1.
8. "The Accidental Superhighway: A Survey of the Internet," *The Economist*, July 1, 1995, p. 6.
9. Katie Hafner, "The Internet's Invisible Hand," *The New York Times*, January 10, 2002, p. E1.
10. This discussion is adapted from Rus Shuler, "How Does the Internet Work," available at http://rus1.home.mindspring.com/whitepapers.
11. Manuel Castells, *The Internet Galaxy* (New York: Oxford University Press, 2001), p. 28.
12. Jonathan Zittrain, "The Rise and Fall of Sysopdom,"10 *Harvard Journal of Law and Technology* 495 (1997).
13. Hafner, p. E5.
14. Pamela Samuelson and Hal Varian, "The 'New Economy' and Information Technology Policy," Working Paper, University of California, Berkeley, July 18, 2001.
15. Yochi Dreazen, "U.S. Says Web Use Has Risen to 54% of the Population," *The Wall Street Journal*, February 4, 2002, p. B4.
16. Otis Port, "The Next Web," *Business Week*, March 4, 2002, p. 97.
17. Michael Mandel and Robert Hof, "Rethinking the Internet," *Business Week*, March 26, 2001, pp. 116–117.
18. "Survey of Electronic Commerce," *The Economist*, May 10, 1997, p. 6.
19. Lynda Applegate, "E-Business Models," in *Information Technology and the Future of the Enterprise*, edited by G. Dickson and G. DeSanctis (Upper Saddle River, NJ: Prentice-Hall, 2001), pp. 49–101.

20. N. Carr, "Redesigning Business," *Harvard Business Review*, November-December, 1999, p. 19.

21. Applegate, p. 64.

22. Bruce Einhorn, "China's Web Masters," *Business Week*, August 2, 1999, p. 49.

23. Ronald Coase, "The Problem of Social Cost," *The Journal of Law and Economics*, 3, 1960, p. 1.

24. Ronald Coase, "The Theory of Public Utility Pricing and its Application," *Bell Journal of Economics and Management Science*, 1, 1970, p. 125.

25. Joel Reidenberg, "Privacy Protection and the Interdependence of Law, Technology, and Self-Regulation," *Cahiers du C.R.I.D.*, 2002.

26. Lessig, *Code and Other Laws in Cyberspace*, p. 60.

27. A.C. Pigou, *The Economics of Welfare* (London: Macmillan, Ltd., 1962), p. 195.

28. Howard Rheingold, *The Virtual Community: Homesteading on the Electronic Frontier* (Reading, MA: Addison-Wesley, 1993), p. 7.

29. Nicholas Negroponte, *Being Digital* (New York: Knopf, 1995), p. 12.

30. *America Banana Co. v. United Fruit Co.* 213 U.S. 347, 357 (1909).

31. Shalini Venturelli, "Information Liberalization in the European Union," in *National Information Infrastructure Initiatives*, edited by Brian Kahin and Ernest Wilson (Cambridge, MA: The MIT Press, 1997), pp. 457–489.

32. Pamela Samuelson, "Five Challenges for Regulating the Global Information Society," paper presented at Communications Regulation in the Global Information Society Conference, University of Warwick, June, 1999.

33. Tony Walker, "China's Wave of Internet Surfers," *The Financial Times*, June 24, 1995.

34. Patrick Thibodeau, "Europe's Privacy Laws May Become Global Standard," *Computerworld*, March 12, 2001, p. 77.

35. Samuelson, "Five Challenges."

36. David G. Post, "Of Horses, Black Holes, and Decentralized Law-Making in Cyberspace," paper delivered at Private Censorship/Perfect Choice Conference at Yale Law School, April 9–11, 1999.

37. Seth Finkelstein, "Internet Blocking Programs and Privatized Censorship," *The Ethical Spectacle*, August, 1998, available at: http://www.spectacle.org/896/finkel.html.

38. Lessig, "Tyranny in the Infrastructure," p. 96.

39. Michel Foucault, *Power and Knowledge: Selected Interviews and Other Writings*, trans. C. Gordon (New York: Random House, 1980), p. 111.

40. "Regulating the Internet—The Consensus Machine," *The Economist*, June 10, 2000, p. 73.

41. Michel Foucault, *The History of Sexuality, Volume I*, trans. R. Hurley (New York: Vintage Books, 1978), p. 95.

42. Lessig, "The Laws of Cyberspace," p. 11.

43. Andrew Shapiro, *The Control Revolution* (New York: Century Foundation Books, 1999), p. 73.

Free Speech and Content Control in Cyberspace

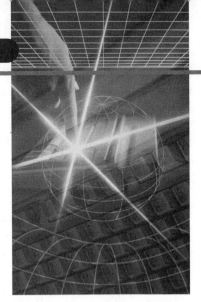

▶ Introduction

The Internet has clearly expanded the potential for individuals to exercise their First Amendment right to freedom of expression. The Net has become a democratizing force by creating many new voices and by facilitating the redistribution of information. Users can operate their own bulletin boards, publish electronic newsletters, or establish a home page on the Web. According to Michael Godwin, the Net "puts the full power of 'freedom of the press' into each individual's hands."[1] Or as the Supreme Court eloquently wrote in its *Reno v. ACLU* decision, the Internet enables an ordinary citizen to become "a pamphleteer, . . . a town crier with a voice that resonates farther than it could from any soapbox."[2]

But some forms of speech, like pornography and hate speech, are offensive. They provoke a great sense of unease, along with calls for limited content controls. Many resist this notion, however, insisting that the state should not interfere with unfettered access to online content.

As a result, the issue of free speech and content controls in cyberspace has emerged as arguably the most contentious moral problem of the nascent Information Age. Human rights such as free speech have taken a place of special prominence in the past century. In some respects these basic rights now collide with the states' inclination to reign in this revolutionary power enjoyed by Internet users. While the United States has sought to suppress online pornography, the target of some European countries such as France and Germany has been mean-spirited hate speech.

In addition, speech is at the root of most other major ethical and public policy problems in cyberspace, including privacy, intellectual property, and security. These three issues will be discussed in the next three chapters where the free speech theme will continue to have considerable saliency, but it is useful at this point to consider how these issues are interconnected.

Restrictions on the free flow of information to protect privacy (such as the mandatory opt-in requirement in Europe) constrain the communication of information and therefore could be interpreted as a commercial speech issue. This assumes, of course, that the collection and sharing of personally identifiable data is a form of "speech." While it is true that "there is reason to question whether the traditional modes of First Amendment review should apply . . . to regulation of commercial processing of information," the issue is surely open for debate.[3] Intellectual property rights can also be construed as restrictions on free speech. If someone has property rights to a trademark, others cannot use that form of expression freely and openly. One way in which users seek to secure their data is encryption, but encryption in the wrong hands could be a threat to national security, and hence many argue that encryption needs to be subject to government control. But shouldn't the right to free speech include the right to protect it from cybersnoopers by means of encryption? And isn't encryption source code itself a form of speech that deserves constitutional protection? Thus, many of the intractable and publicized difficulties in cyberspace can be reduced to the following question: *what is the appropriate scope of free expression for organizations and individuals?*

Many of those who pioneered Internet technology have consistently asserted that the right to free expression in cyberspace should have as broad a scope as possible. They argue for a free-spirited web and for unrestricted access to all forms of speech in cyberspace. For many years there was also considerable reluctance on the part of the government to restrict or filter any form of information on the network for fear of stifling an atmosphere that thrives on the free and open exchange of ideas.

But the increased use of the Internet, especially among more vulnerable segments of the population such as young children, has forced some public policy makers to rethink this laissez-faire approach. In the United States, the result has been several frantic and futile attempts to control Internet content through poorly crafted legislation. Other countries have also entered the fray, seeking to impose their own restrictions.

In this chapter, we will focus primarily on those problematic forms of free expression, well known to anyone who has surfed the Web, that inspire the ire of regulators. They include pornography, hate speech, virtual threats, and even the nuisance speech known as spam. In the context of this discussion, we will consider whether the libertarian ethic favoring broad free speech rights still has validity despite the proliferation of so much offensive content. A central theme will also be the social implications that arise when local sovereigns seek to regulate content based on ideology.

▶Speech and Internet Architecture

As we saw in the previous chapter, content controls and censorship are alien to the original design of the Internet. Thanks to the TCP/IP protocol, the Internet has been architected to transmit packaged bits of information indiscriminately from one location to another. And, of course, bits are just bits. Routers and intermediate servers that support this transmission pay no attention to content—they simply forward along a compressed string of anonymous 1s and 0s.

Furthermore, these bits are being transported to an IP address that could be anywhere in the world. Territorial borders and boundaries are irrelevant. The Internet is oblivious to geography as it mechanically transmits digital data to the destination denoted by the numeric IP address. Hence the Internet's ability to "cross borders, break down barriers, and destroy distance" is often singled out as one of its most remarkable features.[4]

It becomes clear that this distinctive architecture of the Net is wholly consistent with an expansive and robust conception of free speech rights. This network has been designed so that anyone can send any form of digital content to any location throughout the world without interference. The Net's code supports and protects a highly libertarian ethos that gives primacy to the individual speaker.

It is also significant, of course, that this architectural design has its roots in America, where the Net was invented and nurtured for many years. It is not surprising that Americans committed to broad free speech ideals would construct a network that embodies this philosophy. As Lessig remarks, "We have exported to the world, through the architecture of the Internet, a First Amendment *in code* more extreme than our own First Amendment *in law*" (emphasis in original).[5]

But what code "giveth," code can take away. Code is not fixed and immutable, and neither is the nature of cyberspace. Filters, firewalls, and geolocation software, which can differentiate between users of different countries, are beginning to complicate the Net's original, simple architecture. As the Net's architecture changes, it no longer appears to be beyond the control of local sovereigns and regulatory forces. Code itself can breathe new life into territorial sovereignty. Perhaps all of this has the force of inevitability, but is it a good idea? Should the Net too have borders? As we ponder this question, let us turn to how the United States has sought to control content by outlawing bits of data that are pornographic.

▶ Pornography in Cyberspace

Before we discuss the United States Congress' recent efforts to regulate speech on the Net, we should be clear about the legal standards pertaining to pornographic and obscene speech. Obscene speech is completely unprotected by the First Amendment, and is banned for everyone. In *Miller v. California* (1973), the Supreme Court established a three-part test to determine whether or not speech falls in this category of obscenity. To meet this test, speech had to satisfy the following conditions: 1) it depicts sexual (or excretory) acts explicitly prohibited by state law; 2) the depiction of sexual acts must be "patently offensive" and appeal to prurient interests as judged by a reasonable person using community standards; 3) it has no serious literary, artistic, social, political, or scientific value. Child pornography that depicts children engaged in sexual activity is also illegal under all circumstances.

Pornography, that is, sexually explicit speech excluding obscene speech and child pornography, can be regulated and banned, but only for minors. The relevant legal case is *Ginsberg v. New York,* which upheld New York's law banning the sale of speech "harmful to minors" to anyone under the age of 17. The law in dispute in the Ginsberg case defined "harmful to minors" as follows: "that quality of any description or representation, in whatever form, of nudity, sexual conduct, sexual excitement, or sado-masochistic abuse, when it: (1) predominantly appeals to the prurient, shameful, or morbid interests of minors, and (2) is patently offensive to prevailing standards in the adult community as a whole with respect to what is suitable for minors, and (3) is utterly without redeeming social importance for minors."[6] Although state legislatures have applied this case differently to their statutes prohibiting the sale of material harmful to minors, these criteria can serve as a general guide to what we classify as "Ginsberg" speech, which is considered off limits to children under the age of seventeen.

The Communications Decency Act (CDA)

The ubiquity of both forms of pornography on the Internet is a challenge for lawmakers. As the quantity of communications grows in the realm of cyberspace, there is a much greater likelihood that people will become exposed to forms of speech or images that are offensive and potentially harmful. If you are seeking information about the President of the United

States and accidentally retrieve the Web site www.whitehouse.com instead of www.whitehouse.gov, you will see what we mean. By some estimates, the Internet currently has about 280,000 sites that cater to various forms of pornography, and some sources report that there is an average of an additional 500 sites coming online everyday. Hence the understandable temptation of governments to regulate and control free expression on the Internet in order to contain the negative effects of unfettered free speech on this medium. The Communications Decency Act (CDA) represented one such futile, and some say misguided, attempt at such regulation.

One impetus behind the CDA was a flawed 1995 Carnegie Mellon study published in the Georgetown Law Review, which surveyed 917,410 computer images and found that 83.5 percent of all computerized photographs available on the Internet were pornographic. The Carnegie Mellon researchers also confirmed that online pornography was not only ubiquitous but it was also quite profitable for its many purveyors. Those images were not just of naked women, but involved pedophilia and paraphilia (images of bondage and sadomasochism). The results of this alarming study were reported in a famous 1995 *Time* magazine cover story entitled "Cyberporn." According to the *Time* article, "The appearance of material like this on a public network accessible to men, women, and children around the world raises issues too important to ignore—or to oversimplify."[7]

The sensational *Time* article outraged an impressionable American public and greatly heightened interest in the CDA. The bill's sponsor, Senator Exon, cited the Carnegie study as proof that passage of this legislation was essential. There was strong evidence, however, that parts of the study were spurious. Marty Rimm, a Carnegie Mellon undergraduate, was the study's lead researcher and author. The bulk of Rimm's data came from 68 bulletin board services (BBSs), some of which were adult BBSs, and yet Rimm certainly gave the impression that his study was based upon and applied to the whole "information superhighway." According to Michael Godwin, "to generalize from commercial porn BBSs to the 'information superhighway' would be like generalizing from Times Square adult bookstores to the print medium."[8]

Nonetheless, thanks in part to the publicity generated by this study's findings and the *Time* cover story, The Communications Decency Act was passed by Congress and signed into law by President Clinton in 1996. Congress was especially worried about the direct negative effects of easily accessible pornographic material on children. It recognized that this medium erected few obstacles between gross and explicit material and curious children navigating their way through cyberspace. Congress also referred to a secondary effect: the ready availability of pornographic material might make parents less inclined to allow Internet usage in their households and this would diminish the Internet's utility.

The CDA included several key provisions that restricted the distribution of sexually explicit material to children. It imposed criminal penalties on anyone who "initiates the transmission of any communication which is . . . indecent, knowing that the recipient of the communication is under 18 years of age." It also criminalized the display of patently offensive sexual material "in a manner available to a person under 18 years of age."[9]

Defenders of the CDA contended that this was an appropriate way of channeling pornographic or "Ginsberg" speech on the Internet away from children. It did not seek to ban adults from viewing such speech. Rather, it was an attempt to zone the Internet just as we zone physical environments. According to one supportive brief: "The CDA is simply a zoning ordinance for the Internet, drawn with sensitivity to the constitutional parameters the Court has refined for such regulation. The Act grants categorical defenses to those who reasonably safeguard indecent material from innocent children—who have no constitutional right to see it—channeling such material to zones of the Internet to which adults are welcome but to which minors do not have ready access."[10] What this brief is referring to is an "out" for Internet speakers provided by the CDA: if they took "reasonably effective" measures to screen out children, they could transmit indecent material.

Support for the CDA was thin, however, and it was quickly overwhelmed by strident and concerted opposition. An alliance of Internet users, Internet Service Providers, and civil libertarian groups challenged the legislation as a blatant violation of the First Amendment right of free speech. This coalition was spearheaded by the American Civil Liberties Union (ACLU) and the case became known as *ACLU v. Reno*.

There were obvious problems with the CDA that the plaintiffs in that lawsuit immediately seized upon. The most egregious weakness was that this law might cast the net of censorship too far by possibly including works of art and literature and maybe even health-related or sex education information. The category of indecent speech was not well-defined by Congress, and could include forms of speech that went beyond Ginsberg speech. The law was also vague. What did it mean to take "reasonably effective" measures to screen out children? According to Lessig, "The architectures that existed at the time for screening out children were relatively crude, and in some cases, quite expensive. It was unclear whether, to satisfy the statute, they had to be extremely effective or just reasonably effective given the state of the technology."[11]

Also, of course, even if the CDA were enacted, it would have a limited impact on the availability of pornography in cyberspace. It could not control sexual content on the Internet originating in other countries nor could it halt pornography placed on the Internet by anonymous re-mailers, which are usually located off shore and beyond the pale of U.S. regulators. The bottom line is that because the Internet is a global network, localized content restrictions enacted by a single national government to protect children from indecent material would not be fully effectual.

A panel of federal judges in Philadelphia ruled unanimously that the CDA was a violation of the First and Fifth Amendments. The three judge panel concluded that "just as the strength of the Internet is chaos, so the strength of our liberty depends upon the chaos and cacophony of the un-fettered speech the First Amendment protects."[12] The Justice Department appealed the case, which now became known as *Reno v. ACLU*, but to no avail. The Supreme Court agreed with the lower Court's ruling, and in June, 1997, declared that this federal law was unconstitutional. The Court was especially concerned about the vagueness of this content-based reg-ulation of speech. According to the majority opinion written by Justice Stevens, "We are persuaded that the CDA lacks the precision that the First Amendment requires when a statute regulates the content of speech. In order to deny minors access to potentially harmful speech, the CDA effectively suppresses a large amount of speech that adults have a consti-tutional right to receive and to address to one another."[13] Stevens also held that the free expression on the Internet is entitled to the highest level of First Amendment protection. This is in contrast to the more limited protections for other more pervasive media such as radio and broadcast and cable television, where the Court has allowed government-imposed censorship. In making this important distinction, the Court assumes that computer users have to actively seek out offensive material whereas they are more likely to encounter it accidentally on television or radio if it were so available.

Child Online Protection Act (COPA)

Most of those involved in the defeat of the Communications Decency Act realized that the issue would not soon go away. Congress, still supported by public opinion, was sure to try again. In October, 1998, they did try again, passing an omnibus budget package that included the Child Online Protection Act (COPA), a successor to the original CDA, which became known in legal circles as "CDA II." The law was signed by Pres-ident Clinton and, like its predecessor, was immediately challenged by the ACLU. CDA II would make it illegal for the operators of commercial Web sites to make sexually explicit materials harmful to minors available to those under 17 years of age. Commercial Web site operators would be required to collect an identification code such as a credit card number as proof of age before allowing viewers access to such material.

The ACLU and other opponents claimed that the law would lead to excessive self-censorship. CDA II would have a negative impact on the ability of these commercial Web sites to reach an adult audience. According to Max Hailperin, "There is no question that the COPA impairs commercial speakers ability to cheaply, easily, and broadly communicate material to adults that is constitutionally protected as to the adults (nonobscene), though harmful to minors."[14] The law is more narrowly focused than CDA I, since it applies only to material on the World Wide Web, covers only "commercial" communications, and restricts only material that is "harmful to minors." Such material would lack "serious literary, artistic, political or scientific value" for those under the age of 17. COPA also relies on the three-part obscenity test laid out in *Miller v. California* to establish the definition of what is harmful to minors. But the law's critics contend that it is still worded too broadly. Those critics worried about what would happen if the law were arbitrarily or carelessly applied. Would some sites offering sexual education information, for instance, be accused of violating the law? Also, it could be plausibly argued that there is a problem in requiring adults to present an ID in order to exercise their right to access speech that is protected by the First Amendment.

In February 1999, a Philadelphia federal judge issued a preliminary injunction against COPA, preventing it from going into effect. This judge accepted the argument that the law would lead to self-censorship and that "such a chilling effect could result in the censoring of constitutionally protected speech, which constitutes an irreparable harm to the plaintiffs."[15] The Third Circuit Court of Appeals affirmed this decision, arguing that COPA's use of "contemporary community standards" to identify material harmful to minors was "overbroad." The case, *Aschcroft v. ACLU et al.*, was then appealed to the Supreme Court. In May 2002, the Supreme Court justices held that COPA's reliance on "community standards" did not by itself render COPA overbroad for First Amendment purposes. Consequently the Justices remanded the decision to the Third Circuit so that it could reconsider the constitutionality of this statute.

Children's Internet Protection Act (CHIPA)

Despite these defeats, Congress did not abandon its efforts to contain the spread of pornography in cyberspace. This time the legislative effort was led by Senator John McCain, who worked ardently to pass the Children's Internet Protection Act (CHIPA). This bill was signed into law on December 21st, 2000 by President Clinton and it took effect in April, 2001. It represents a decisive change in the government's strategy. This time the government is hoping to rely on private surrogates, libraries, and schools to regulate speech harmful to minors through the use of filters that block out objectionable content. This law is linked to the federal government's e-rate program, which provides an opportunity for schools and libraries to be reimbursed for the costs of connecting to the Internet or to be subsidized for other telecommunications expenses. The law mandates that computer terminals used by all library patrons (i.e., adults and children) must have filters that block Internet access to visual images that are obscene or involve any sort of child pornography. In addition, according to Kaplan, "For library computer terminals used by children under 17, libraries have to screen out these two categories of material plus a third one: visual material that is 'harmful to minors,' such as sexually-explicit images without social or educational value that are obscene for children but legally protected for adults."[16] Public schools seeking e-rate funds must implement the same type of filtering scheme. The blocking mechanism may be overridden for bona fide research purposes.

Like its predecessors, CHIPA was immediately challenged by libraries, educational leaders, and civil libertarians. In April 2001, a group of libraries and library associations (including Multnomah County Public Library, the Connecticut Library Association, the Maine Library Association, and the Santa Cruz Public Library Joint Powers Authority) filed a lawsuit against this legislation. This suit, *Multnomah Public Library et al. v. U.S.*, was filed in the United States District Court for the Eastern District of Pennsylvania where other prominent free speech cases have been heard. The suit argues that CHIPA is unconstitutional: "By forcing public libraries to install such technology, CHIPA will suppress ideas and viewpoints that are constitutionally protected from reaching willing patrons. CHIPA thus imposes a prior restraint on protected speech in violation of the Constitution."[17] The suit also contends that CHIPA is "arbitrary and irrational because existing technology fails to block access to much speech that Congress intended to block, and thus will not protect library patrons from objectionable content."[18] Blocking mechanisms simply cannot block *all* speech that is obscene, child pornographic, and harmful to minors.

Like COPA, CHIPA's fate is in the hands of the courts. But this legislation begins to reframe the debate about the government role in regulating the Internet, since the government has shifted its strategy from direct to indirect regulation, relying on private surrogates to do the work of curbing pornography. Should the government be offering private parties a *quid pro quo* for their role in censoring the Internet, because more direct regulatory efforts seem to be unconstitutional? The *Multnomah* case also explicitly raises the efficacy of using filtering technology (or code) to resolve the pornography problem. Is the lawsuit's negative appraisal of code accurate or can code be a viable part of the solution? With that question in mind, we turn to a more in depth discussion of the employment of filtering architectures in cyberspace.

▶Automating Content Controls

At the heart of the debate about the CDA and content regulation is the basic question raised in the previous chapter about how the Internet should be regulated. Should government impose the kind of central controls embodied in legislation such as the CDA and COPA? Or should the Internet be managed and controlled primarily through a more bottoms-up, user-oriented approach with individuals empowered to develop their own solutions to offensive speech tailored to their own needs and value systems? To put this problematic in Lessig's terms, what is the optimal interaction of law and code?

Thanks to the rulings against CDA and COPA, the burden of content control has begun to shift to parents and local organizations like schools and libraries. Even if COPA is found to be constitutional, the issue of filtering will not vanish, since COPA will probably not have jurisdiction over foreign Web sites. But the exercise of this bottoms-up exertion of power has caused some anxiety due to the potential for abuses. To what extent should local communities and institutions (e.g., schools, prisons, libraries, etc.) assume direct responsibility for controlling content on the Internet? Aside from the demands of CHIPA, libraries must consider whether it is appropriate to use filtering software to protect young patrons from pornography on the Internet. Is this a useful and prudent way to uphold local community or institutional standards? Or does this sort of censorship compromise a library's traditional commitment to the free flow of ideas?

There are two broad areas of concern about the use of content controls that need elaboration. The first area concerns the social and moral probity of censorship itself even when it is directed at the young. There is a growing tendency to recognize a broad spectrum of rights even for children, and to criticize parents, educators, and politicians who are more interested in imposing their value systems on others than in protecting vulnerable children. Jonathan Katz and other advocates of children's rights oppose censorship even within a private household unless it is part of a mutually agreed upon social contract between parent and child. According to Katz, "Parents who thoughtlessly ban access to online culture or lyrics they don't like or understand, or who exaggerate and distort the dangers of violent and pornographic imagery, are acting out of arrogance, imposing brute authority."[19] Rather, Katz contends, young people have a right to the culture which they are creating and shaping. The ACLU seems to concur with this position and it too advocates against censorship as a violation of childrens' rights.

Lurking in the background of this debate is the question of whether children have a First Amendment right to access indecent materials. There is no consensus about this among legal scholars, but if children do have such a right, it would be much more difficult to justify filtering out indecent materials in libraries or educational institutions. One school of thought about this issue is that a child's free speech rights should be proportionate to his or her age. The older the child, the more questionable are restrictions on indecent material.

The second area of concern pertains to the suitability of the blocking methods and other automated controls used to accomplish this censorship. Popular blocking programs include Cyber Patrol, N2H2 Internet Filtering, Websense Enterprise, and SmartFilter. These programs generally function by using categories of objectionable speech. Categories might include Adult/Sexually Explicit, Nudity, Pornography, and so forth. Websense Enterprise uses 75 categories, but that seems to be higher than the norm.[20] Once the categories are established, filtering companies use automated systems (such as an intelligent robot) to examine Web sites and determine candidates for each category. Thus an automated program might visit the penthouse.com Web site and based on keywords at the site and other factors classify it as "Adults Only/Pornography." For the most part the categorization is made without human intervention, but sometimes human reviewers might make the final determination. The extent of human intervention in this process varies from company to company. If a parent installs a filtering program like N2H2 with categories such as "Adults Only/Pornography" activated, anyone trying to access the penthouse.com site will be prevented from doing so by the software.

There are two apparent problems with the use of blocking software. The first problem is the unreliability and lack of precision that typifies most of these products—there are no perfect or foolproof devices for filtering out obscene material. Sometimes automated programs make mistakes and this leads to overblocking, that is, filtering out sites that do not fit a particular category. For example, a report on SmartFilter exposed apparent overblocking, pointing out that "it blocked WrestlePages (The best source for wrestling news); MotoWorld.com, a motorcycle sport magazine produced by ESPN; and Affirmation: Gay and Lesbian Mormons, a support site."[21] On other occasions the problem could be underblocking, failing to find a pornographic site and leaving it off the list. Given the density and volatility of content on the Web, this lack of precision should not be particularly surprising. Whether these incongruities can be overcome by better software products or greater reliance on human review is a matter of some dispute.

Another problem is that these blocking programs are not always transparent, and they can be used to enforce a code of political correctness unbeknownst to parents or librarians who choose to install them. Sites that discuss AIDS, homosexuality, and related topics have been blocked by certain filtering programs, either deliberately or accidentally. Often these programs are not explicit or forthright about their blocking criteria, which greatly compounds this problem.

PICS, which stands for Platform for Internet Content Selection, is another architecture that filters speech. It was developed by the World Wide Web Consortium and appears to be gaining in popularity. PICS is a protocol for rating and filtering content on the Net. It divides the task of filtering into two activities: *labeling,* which involves rating the content of a site, and then *filtering* the content based on those labels. PICS provides a standard format and supports multiple labeling schemes or rating services. Internet content providers can embed a label within their own Web site or third parties could rate that Web site independently. In either case a common labeling vocabulary is available for use. In some cases, of course, authors will be disinclined to label their own Web sites. Neo-Nazi sites, for example, typically do not have labels embedded within them. But the Simon Wiesanthal Center, a nonprofit organization which combats anti-Semitism, could rate those Web sites based on the presence of anti-Semitic content and hate speech.

Users would be free to pick their filtering software along with an appropriate rating system. Once the content is rated, users must have software that can read those labels in order to determine which sites are to be blocked. Both the Netscape and Internet Explorer browsers support PICS, and the popular search engine Alta Vista has the capability to restrict search results to acceptable sites based on PICS ratings. Thus, if parents were concerned about protecting their children from pornography, they might choose the rating system of the Christian Coalition and purchase a browser such as Netscape, which incorporates a PICS-compatible filter.

The use of this labeling infrastructure has already generated significant controversy. PICS certainly has its supporters who argue that this voluntary system is far superior to one imposed by the government. They assert that filtering software devolves responsibility to the level where it should be in a pluralistic society, that is, with parents, schools, and local communities.

Civil libertarians and many responsible professionals, on the other hand, object strenuously to the use of rating systems like PICS, claiming that they can transform the Internet into a virtual censorship machine. For Lessig, among others, PICS epitomizes all that is wrong with the constraints imposed by code: "Blocking software is bad enough—but in my view, PICS is the devil," he says.[22]

These critics worry that because rating is so labor-intensive, a few rating systems will dominate and exclude questionable or controversial material thanks to subjective judgments made by the raters. Restrictions inscribed into computer code end up having the force of law without the checks and balances provided by the legal system. With programs like PICS, we will be handing over regulation of the Internet to private enterprises that can develop tendentious labeling schemes and thereby utilize filtering technologies to further their own particular political or social agendas.

This is indeed a striking example of how code is becoming a substitute for law as a constraint on cyberspace behavior. Thanks to the nullification of the CDA, Internet stakeholders in increasing numbers will resort to software that may be far more effective than the law in suppressing pornographic material.

While some of the criticism directed at PICS and automated content control is exaggerated, the difficulties identified here should not be underestimated. At the same time, a more imperceptible problem with filtering systems is that they can be used to tailor and personalize one's perception of reality, to control one's environment in a detrimental way that narrows one's perspectives and experience. According to Cass Sunstein, "Each person could design his own communications universe. Each person could see those things that he wanted to see, and only those things."[23]

Finally, a potential disadvantage of PICS and filtering software is that the filter can be imposed at any level in the vertical hierarchy that controls the accessibility of Internet services. It can be invoked at the individual user level, the corporate or institutional level, the ISP level, or even the state level. It can be used by the Chinese to limit public discourse about democracy just as easily as it can be utilized by parents to keep pornographic Web sites far from the curious gaze of their children. For example, in Saudi Arabia, all Internet traffic is funnelled through a main server in Riyadh and unwelcome content is not allowed through. If a Saudi user seeks access to a Web site on the prohibited list, the following message is displayed: "Access to the requested URL is denied!"

While we take no position on the merits of PICS, we do contend that users who embrace this method of dealing with cyberporn should deploy this software responsibly in order to minimize any potential for collateral damage. If this code is designed, developed, and used *prudently*, we may find that it has the wherewithal to create the desired effect with limited negative effects on individual liberties or the common good.

What constitutes responsible use of these automated access codes? Let us suggest a few criteria. First, the use of PICS or other automated content controls should be strictly voluntary—parents or schools should be allowed to choose whether to restrict Web content, while authors can choose whether to label their Web sites. In contrast, a mandatory rating and filtering system administered or sponsored by the government would be quite problematic and imprudent. It would impose a uniform solution to what should be seen as a local problem. Second, a Web site that does choose to label must have the integrity to label itself accurately. Third, third parties that rate Web sites must strive to provide fair, accurate, and consistent ratings that are subject to reasonable external scrutiny. They must be flexible enough to judiciously handle appeals from Web sites that maintain that they have been mislabeled. Fourth, there should be an adequate transparency level in blocking software and rating schemes. While some information may be proprietary, labeling services and filtering software companies must be as up front as possible about their labeling philosophy or their list of blocked sites. CyberSitter, for example, which purports to protect children from pornography, has blocked the Web site of the National Organization for Women. This type of blocking is irresponsible unless the company also has a political agenda that it explicitly reveals to its patrons. Finally, PICS should not be adopted as a high level centralized filtering solution. Filtering should only occur at the lowest levels of the hierarchy—it should not be used by search engines, ISPs, or states to censor the Internet; this is especially harmful if it is done in a surreptitious and dogmatic fashion.

Even if automated content controls such as PICS are used responsibly and diligently, their use still raises some troubling questions. Will there be chaos on the Internet as many different private and public groups express opinions about Web sites in the form of content labels? Should there be any restrictions on the provision of such labels? But aren't restrictions on content labels tantamount to restrictions on free speech? And which local institutions should assume the burden of implementing filtering technologies?

We cannot consider all of these question here, but the complex issues involved in the last question clearly emerge in the controversial debate about the use of filtering devices in libraries. Both public and private libraries face a real dilemma: they can either allow unfettered Internet access even to their youngest patrons or use filtering products to protect minors from pornographic material.

Those libraries that favor the first approach argue that the use of filtering devices compromises the library's traditional commitment to the free flow of information and ideas. As we saw in the *Multnomah* case, some of this opposition to these filtering devices originates from the imprecise way in which they function. The public library in New York City subscribes to this philosophy of open access and presently does not employ filtering devices. The Connecticut Library Association has articulated support for "the principle of open, free and unrestricted access to information and ideas, regardless of the format in which they appear."[24]

Further, the American Library Association is opposed to the installation of filters and endorses the idea of unrestricted Internet access for both adults and minors.

Some librarians, however, disagree with the ALA. They maintain that the Internet should be censored and that filtering programs provide a way to support and reinforce local community values. According to Brenda Branch, the director of the Austin Public Library in Texas, "We have a responsibility to uphold the community standard.... We do not put pornographic material in our book collection or video collection, and I also don't feel we should allow pornographic materials in over the Internet."[25]

The public library in Loudon County, Virginia also found it difficult to fully accept the ALA's philosophy of unfettered Internet access. It installed the popular filtering software, X-Stop, a product of Log-On Data Corporation, on its nine computers in order to filter out pornographic Web sites, which, in its view, should not be available to library patrons. While some users and county politicians supported the library's action, others vigorously objected to this censorship. Soon, the Loudon County Public Library found itself embroiled in a testy lawsuit brought by Mainstream Loudon, a local Civil Liberties Union organization, representing Loudon County residents who claimed that the Library's policy infringed upon their right to free speech under the First Amendment.

At issue in this case, known as *Mainstream Loudon et al. v. Loudon County Library,* was whether a public library could adopt a policy "prohibiting the access of library patrons to certain content-based categories of Internet publications."[26] Plaintiffs, who included individuals claiming that Loudon County Library blocked their Web sites, allege that this policy infringed upon their free speech rights under the First Amendment. The library argued that it had a right to limit what it makes available to the public and that restrictions on Internet access do not raise First Amendment issues. The library argued further that its decision to block certain sites was equivalent to an acquisition decision for which the First Amendment has no relevance. The plaintiff, however, saw this differently: "The Library Board's action is more appropriately characterized as a removal decision . . . [and] the First Amendment applies to, and limits, the discretion of a public library to place content-based restrictions on access to constitutionally protected materials within its collection."[27]

The Library further argued that the policy is constitutional because it is the least restrictive method of achieving two key government interests: "1) minimizing access to illegal pornography; and 2) avoidance of creation of a sexually hostile environment."[28] The plaintiffs denied that this policy was the least restrictive means available, arguing that the policy imposes a prior restraint on speech.

In the end, Judge Brinkema ruled for the plaintiff. She rejected Loudon County's arguments and concluded that the policy "includes neither sufficient standards nor adequate procedural safeguards." Her conclusion in this case spells out the copious problems she perceived with the Loudon policy:

> Although defendant is under no obligation to provide Internet access to its patrons, it has chosen to do so and is therefore restricted by the First Amendment in the limitations it is allowed to place on patron access. Defendant has asserted a broad right to censor the expressive activity of the receipt and communication of information through the Internet with a Policy that (1) is not necessary to further any compelling government interest; (2) is not narrowly tailored; (3) restricts access of adult patrons to protected material just because the material is unfit for minors; (4) provides inadequate standards for restricting access; and (5) provides inadequate procedural safeguards to ensure prompt judicial review. Such a Policy offends the guarantee of free speech in the First Amendment and is, therefore, unconstitutional.[29]

Part of the problem with Loudon's approach was that its policy applied to both adults and minors. One compromise and common sense position employed by the Boston Public Library is the installation of filtering devices on children's computers but not on those in the adult areas. But the ALA and the ACLU do not favor this type of zoning approach. As the result of an ACLU lawsuit, the library system in Kern County, California was forced to abandon such a zoning plan and to give all of its patrons, including minors, the right to use a computer without a filter. Moreover, this solution contradicts Article 5 of the ALAs Library Bill of Rights: "A person's right to use a library should not be denied or abridged because of origin, age, background, or views."[30] According to the ALA, this article precludes the use of filters on *any* computer systems within a library.

How should these nettling matters be resolved? Let us assume for the sake of argument that filtering devices and labeling systems (like PICS) do become more precise and accurate. If filtering is more dependable and blocking criteria more transparent, should libraries and other institutions give priority to the value of free expression and the free flow of ideas and information, no matter how distasteful some of that information is, or do they give priority to other community values at the expense of the unimpeded flow of information?

Let us examine both sides of this issue. By following the first option and not regulating the Internet at the local level, we are giving the First Amendment its due—letting all voices be heard, even those that are sometimes rancorous and obscene. One can base this decision on several principles: the rights of children to access indecent material, the notion that censorship should not replace the cultivation of trust, and the education of individuals to act guardedly in cyberspace. Moreover, the occasional abuse of the Internet in a school or library setting should not be a reason to censor the entire network; censorship is a disproportionate response to isolated incidents of abuse.

The argument for reliance on education and trust to solve this problem is a compelling one. Shouldn't schools and libraries attempt to *educate* students and young patrons about Internet use and abuse? As Richard Rosenberg argues, "If the first instinct is to withhold, to restrict, to prevent access, what is the message being promulgated?"[31] If institutions like schools and libraries truly value the ideals of trust, openness, and freedom, imposing censorship on information is a bad idea that mocks those ideals. Also, wouldn't such restrictions start us down a dangerous slide to more pernicious forms of censorship and repression? How and where do we draw the line once we begin to restrict access to Internet content? As a result, many free speech proponents argue that this global medium of expression does deserve the highest level of protection a pluralistic society and its institutions can possibly offer.

There are many other persuasive arguments to be made for keeping the Internet a free and open medium of exchange. There is something satisfying about the Chinese government's impotence to completely control free expression in this medium as they now control other forms of political dissent. The Internet can thereby become a wonderful vehicle for spreading the ideals of democracy. It is surely not the ally of tyrants or the enemies of democracy.

But should *all* information be freely accessible to anyone who wants it? Is this a rational, morally acceptable, and sensible policy? What are the costs of living in a society that virtually absolutizes the right to free speech in cyberspace and makes all forms of speech readily available even to its youngest members?

Since these costs can be quite high, it is critically important to consider the other side of this issue. Many responsible moralists contend that some carefully formulated, *narrow* restrictions on specific types of indecent speech are perfectly appropriate when young children are involved.

They maintain that parents, schools, libraries, and other local institutions have an obligation to promote and safeguard their own values as well as the values of their respective communities. This is part of the more general obligation to help promote public morality and the public order. Freedom and free expression are fundamental human rights, but these and other rights can only be reasonably exercised in a context of mutual respect and common acceptance of certain moral norms, which are often referred to as the public morality. In any civilized society, some of these norms entail sexual behavior and especially the sexual behavior of and towards children. Given the power of sexuality in one's life, the need for carefully integrating sexuality into one's personality, and the unfortunate tendency to regard others as sexual objects of desire (rather than as human persons), there is a convincing reason for fostering a climate where impressionable children can be raised and nurtured without being subjected to images of gross or violent sexual conduct that totally depersonalize sexuality, exalt deviant sexual behavior, and thereby distort the view of responsible sexual behavior. This is clearly an aspect of the common good and public morality and is recognized as such by public officials in diverse societies who have crafted many laws (such as the law against the production of child pornography) to protect minors and to limit the exercise of rights in this area. Hence given the importance of protecting young children as best as we can from psychologically harmful pornographic images, parents and those institutions that function *in loco parentis* should not be timid about carefully controlling Internet content when necessary.[32]

It is never easy to advocate censorship in any form precisely because the right to free expression is so valuable and cherished. But proponents of automated content controls argue that all human rights, including the right to free expression, are limited by each other and by other aspects of the common good or the "public morality." According to this perspective, parents and schools are acting prudently when they choose to *responsibly* implement filtering technologies in order to help preserve and promote the values of respect for others and appropriate sexual conduct that are part of our public morality. Preserving free speech and dealing with sexually explicit material will always be a problem in a free and pluralistic society and this is one way of achieving a proper balance when the psychological health of young children is at stake.

▶ Hate Speech and Online Threats

The rapid expansion of hate speech on the Web raises similar problems and controversies. Groups such as white supremacists and anarchists have Web sites that advocate their particular point of view. Some of these sites are blatantly anti-Semitic, while others are dominated by Holocaust revisionists who claim that the Holocaust never happened. On occasion, these sites can be especially virulent and outrageous, such as the Web site of the Charlemagne Hammerskins. The first scene reveals a man disguised in a ski mask bearing a gun and standing next to a swastika. The site has this ominous warning for its visitors: "Be assured, we still have one-way tickets to Auschwitz."

Some hate Web sites take the form of computer games such as Doom and Castle Wolfenstein that have been constructed to include blacks, Jews, or homosexuals as targets of violence. In one animated game, the Dancing Baby, once a popular television phenomenon, has been depicted as the white power baby. Most recently, in the wake of the September 11th attack in the United States, inflammatory anti-Islamic hate speech has been in vogue at certain Web sites.

Hate speech, unfortunately, is not confined to a few isolated Web sites. According to the Simon Wiesenthal Center, which monitors such sites, "There are more than 2,300 'problematic' Web sites, including more than 500 extremist sites authored by Europeans, but hosted on American servers to avoid stringent anti-hate laws in Europe."[33]

What can be done about this growing subculture of hate on the Internet? The great danger is that the message of hate and bigotry, once confined to reclusive, powerless groups, can now be spread more expeditiously in cyberspace. Unlike obscenity and libel, hate speech is not illegal under U.S. Federal law, and it is fully protected by the First Amendment.

On the other hand, in European countries like Germany and France, anti-Semitic, Nazi-oriented Web sites are illegal along with other forms of hate speech. In Germany the government has required Internet Service Providers to eliminate these sites under the threat of prosecution. Critics of this approach argue that it is beyond the capability of ISPs to control content in such a vast region as the World Wide Web. It is also illegal for Internet companies located in other countries to make available Nazi materials in Germany. American companies have tried to be as accommodating as possible. For example, Amazon.com no longer sells copies of Hitler's autobiography, *Mein Kampf*, to its German customers, that is, customers who access the German language Web site.

Sometimes these strategies for eradicating hate speech have engendered controversy, thanks to the jurisdictional problems that arise when the state seeks to pursue a claim against a foreign Web site. Consider the now celebrated case of Yahoo's encounter with the French legal system, which undoubtedly foreshadows jurisdictional battles that will become common in cyberspace. This occurred when two French antiracist groups filed suit against Yahoo, a major portal company in the U.S., demanding that they remove swastika flags and other Nazi memorabilia from their auctions on the American Web site. French law prohibits the display or sale of objects that represent racism or ethnic hatred, and this includes World War II Nazi memorabilia. Judge Jean-Jacques Gomez ruled in favor of these two groups, concluding that Yahoo had violated French law and offended the "collected memory" of France. Yahoo was ordered to install filtering technology that would block this questionable material for all French users, despite the company's claims that this type of blocking was not technically feasible. Failure to comply would mean a fine of $13,000 per day.

But in the United States in late 2001, a federal judge ruled that the French court's sanctions against Yahoo are unenforceable in the United States, reasoning that "the First Amendment precludes enforcement with the United States of a French order intended to regulate the content of its speech over the Internet."[34] The case, known as *Yahoo v. LICRA*, has been appealed to the U.S. Court of Appeals for the Ninth Circuit.

Despite Yahoo's initial victory, the implications of Judge Gomez's ruling, which holds an American company accountable for breaking French laws, are still significant. What is most troublesome is that this decision might lead other countries to impose restrictive rules on forms of speech that they judge to be offensive. It is impractical and counterproductive, however, for Internet companies like Yahoo to comply with the laws and regulations of many different countries. Civil libertarians such as Alan Davidson of the Center for Democracy and Technology worry that rulings like this will put free speech in jeopardy on the Net. Also, according to Kaplan, "given the potential leverage of a Yahoo-style case on multinational Internet companies, experts say that Judge Gomez has created a powerful tool for the suppression of online speech that a recipient nation finds offensive or dangerous."[35]

Hate speech can also be dealt with through the same constraints used to control pornography, especially law and code. Some sovereignties, like France and Germany, prefer regulation and explicit laws. There is always the problem of regulatory arbitrage, however. Many hate site servers have already relocated to the United States where French and German laws do not apply. An alternative to government regulation is greater dependence on user empowerment through code. Hate speech can be satisfactorily suppressed through *responsible* filtering that does not erroneously exclude legitimate political speech. Given the improbability of a legal solution, parents and certain private and religious institutions might want to seize the initiative to shield young children and sensitive individuals from some of this material such as crude anti-Semitism.

However, even more caution must be exercised in the use of a blocking mechanism for hate speech than for pornography, since there is sometimes a fine distinction between hate speech and unpopular or unorthodox political opinion. A general rule of thumb is that hate speech Web sites would be those that attack, insult, and demean whole segments of the population such as Jews, Arabs, Italians, blacks, whites, gays, and so forth. Many sites will fall in a nebulous gray area, and this will call for conscientiousness and discretion on the part of those charged with labeling those sites.

Sometimes extremist speech that incites hatred can take the form of a threat, and threats are generally not protected by the First Amendment. However, differentiating a threat from constitutionally protected hate speech is no easy matter. Consider the case of the "Nuremberg Files." The Nuremberg Files Web site is the product of the American Coalition of Life Activists (ACLA), a fringe antiabortion group that appears to advocate the use of violent tactics against abortion providers. Doctors who provided abortions were listed on the Web site and declared to be guilty of crimes against humanity. In addition, the names of murdered doctors were crossed out, and the names of those doctors who had been wounded were printed in gray.

The Web site was replete with radical antiabortion statements, and it included links to other antiabortion sites that defended the murder of abortion providers as morally justified. There was also a call for information about abortion providers to assist in "collecting dossiers on abortionists in anticipation that one day we may be able to hold them on trial for crimes against humanity."[36] The site's imagery was also gruesome, with images of dripping blood and aborted fetuses.

Planned Parenthood filed suit against the operators of this site, the American Coalition of Life Activists. They argued that the material on this Web site (along with other activities of the ACLA) violated a 1994 law called the Federal Freedom of Access to Clinics Entrances Act that makes it illegal to use "force or threat of force" against those who provide or seek out abortions. Lawyers representing the ACLA argued that there was no explicit advocacy of violence. In 1999, a jury ruled in favor of the plaintiffs and demanded that the ACLA pay a fine of $100,000 million. However, in March, 2001, the Ninth Circuit Court of Appeals overturned this decision, concluding that this speech was protected by the First Amendment. According to the Appeals Court ruling:

> Defendants can be held liable if they "authorized, ratified or directly threatened" violence. If defendants threatened to commit violent acts, by working alone or with others, then their statements could properly support the verdict. But if their statements merely encouraged unrelated terrorists, then their words are protected by the First Amendment.[37]

Some legal scholars think that this ruling was abetted by recent Supreme Court decisions that have stipulated that threats must be explicit and likely to cause "imminent lawless action." For the three judge panel on this appeals court, the speech found on the Nuremberg Web site, however unappealing and extreme, did not meet this heavy burden.

▶Anonymous Speech

Anonymous communication in cyberspace is enabled largely through the use of anonymous remailers, which strip off the identifying information on an e-mail message and substitute an anonymous code or a random number. By encrypting a message and then routing that message through a series of anonymous remailers, a user can rest assured that his or her message will remain anonymous and confidential. This process is known as *chained remailing*. The process is quite effective because none of the remailers will have the key to read the encrypted message; neither the recipient nor any remailers (except the first) in the chain can identify the sender, and the recipient cannot connect the sender to the message unless every single remailer in the chain cooperates. This would assume that each remailer kept a log of their ingoing and outgoing mail, and that is highly unlikely.

According to Michael Froomkin, this technique of chained remailing is about as close as we can come on the Internet to *untraceable anonymity*, that is, "a communication for which the author is simply not identifiable at all."[38] If someone clandestinely leaves a bunch of political pamphlets in the town square with no identifying marks or signatures, that communication is also characterized by untraceable anonymity. In cyberspace things are a bit more complicated, and even the method of chained remailing is not foolproof: if the anonymous remailers do join together in some sort of conspiracy to reveal someone's identity, there is not much anyone can do to safeguard anonymity.

Do we really need to ensure that digital anonymity is preserved, especially since it is so often a shield for subversive activities? It would be difficult to argue convincingly that anonymity is a core human good, utterly indispensable for human flourishing and happiness. One can surely conceive of people and societies where anonymity is not a factor for their happiness. However, while anonymity may not be a primary good, it is surely a secondary one, since *for some people in some circumstances* a measure of anonymity is quite important for the exercise of their rational life plan and for human flourishing. The proper exercise of freedom and especially free expression does require the support of anonymity in some situations. Unless the speaker or author can choose to remain anonymous, opportunities for free expression become limited for various reasons and that individual may be forced to remain mute on critical matters. Thus, without the benefit of anonymity, the value of freedom is constrained.

We can point to many specific examples in support of the argument that *anonymous free expression* deserves protection. Social intolerance may require some individuals to rely on anonymity to communicate openly about an embarrassing medical condition or an awkward disability. Whistleblowers may be understandably reluctant to come forward with valuable information unless they can remain anonymous. And political dissent, even in a democratic society that prizes free speech, may be impeded unless it can be done anonymously. Anonymity then has an incontestable value in the struggle against repression or even against more routine corporate and government abuses of power. In the conflict in Kosovo, for example, some individuals relied on anonymous programs (such as anonymizer.com) to describe atrocities perpetrated against ethnic Albanians. If the Serbians were able to trace the identity of these individuals, their lives would have been in grave danger.

Thus, while there is some social cost to preserving anonymity in cyberspace, its central importance in human affairs is certainly beyond dispute. It is a positive good, that is, it possesses positive qualities that render it worthy to be valued. At a minimum, it is valued as an instrumental good, as a means of achieving the full actualization of free expression.

Anonymous communication, of course, whether facilitated by remailers or by other means, does have its drawbacks. It can be abused by criminals or terrorists seeking to communicate anonymously in order to plot their crimes. It also permits cowardly users to communicate without civility or to libel someone without accountability and with little likelihood of apprehension by law enforcement authorities. Anonymity can also be useful for revealing trade secrets or violating other intellectual property laws. In general, secrecy and anonymity are not beneficial for society if they are overused or used improperly. According to David Brin, "Anonymity is the darkness behind which most miscreants—from mere troublemakers all the way to mass murderers and would-be tyrants—shelter in order to wreak harm, safe against discovery or redress by those they abuse."[39]

While we admit that too much secrecy is problematic, the answer is not to eliminate all secrecy and make everything public and transparent, which could be the inevitable result of this loss of digital anonymity. Nonetheless, it cannot be denied that anonymity has its disadvantages and that digital anonymity and unrestricted Internet access can be exploited for many forms of mischief. Hence the temptation of governments to sanction the deployment of architectures that will make Internet users more accountable and less able to hide behind the shield of anonymity.

Despite the potential for abuse, however, there are cogent reasons for eschewing the adoption of those architectures and protecting the right to anonymous online speech. A strong case can be put forth that the costs of banning anonymous speech in cyberspace by mandating digital identity for all Internet transactions and interactions are simply too high in an open and democratic society. The loss of anonymity may very well diminish the power of that voice that now resonates so loudly in cyberspace. As a result, regulators must proceed with great caution in this area.

▶ Student Web Sites

The democratizing tendencies of the Web apply to children as well as adults. It is not surprising, therefore, that the Web is beginning to have some impact on student publications. Students who cannot get their material published in school newspapers or other mainstream publications are turning to the Web to express their unorthodox opinions. According to Selino, "Thousands of high school students have flocked to the Internet in recent years to start underground newspapers, where they may publish articles or art censored from school-sponsored newspapers or simply put their thoughts on Web pages."[40] Their goal is to avoid the scrutiny and censorship of school administrators.

At Westlake High School in Ohio, student Sean O'Brien felt that he was being unfairly treated by one of his teachers. His response was to create a home Web page that included a photograph of his music teacher who was described as "an overweight middle-age man who doesn't like to get haircuts." The high school was outraged and promptly took action. It suspended O'Brien for 10 days, ordered him to delete the Web site, and threatened his expulsion if he failed to comply. His parents filed suit against the school district, claiming that this order infringed on their son's right to free speech.

The central question in the case revolves around the school's right to discipline a student for the contents of a personal Web site. According to the ACLU and other legal scholars who supported O'Brien's lawsuit, a school's efforts to exercise control of home Web sites, what students say outside of school, no matter how outrageous it may be, seems inconsistent with the First Amendment right to free expression. According to this view, students have every right to use the Internet in order to criticize their schools or their teachers.

The legal precedent on the issue is somewhat ambiguous and this whole legal area is evolving quite slowly. The United States Supreme Court has recognized three types of control over student speech in public schools. First, schools can control the content of student newspapers or other student publications such as those associated with extracurricular activities. Second, they can control and seek to curtail profane speech that occurs within the school. And third, they can regulate off-campus speech if that speech causes a "material and substantial" disruption of the school's classroom activities. The third criteria is obviously the only one that may be apposite in this case. Does O'Brien's criticism of his teacher constitute a material disruption? A marginal case can perhaps be made that because the site was read by many of O'Brien's classmates, the music teacher's class was "disrupted." But embarrassing remarks aimed at teachers is probably not what the Supreme Court had in mind. The disruptive activity would have to be much more serious to warrant censorship of what a student says outside of the classroom. For example, in Pennsylvania, the state court sanctioned the expulsion of a student for creating a Web site with violent threats aimed at a teacher and the principal. That case has been appealed to the Pennsylvania Supreme Court and its outcome will undoubtedly set an important precedent.

In the O'Brien case, an out-of-court settlement was reached in April, 1998, in which the O'Brien family was awarded $30,000 in damages. Sean O'Brien also received an apology from the school district, which promptly reinstated him at Westlake High in good standing. The problem of controversial home Web sites will only get worse and may be a moderate but necessary price to pay for the information egalitarianism afforded to all computer users by the Internet. Schools must find a way to discourage and discredit student Web sites that mock teachers or indulge in profane insults by means other than censorship. Web sites advocating violence against students and teachers is much more serious, and in these cases the courts must intervene to protect potential victims.

▶ Spam as Commercial Free Speech

Spam refers to unsolicited, promotional electronic mail usually sent in bulk to thousands or millions of Internet users. Quite simply, it is junk e-mail that is usually a costly annoyance to its recipients. Further, the volume of spam continues to increase exponentially, despite costly efforts to contain it by Internet Service Providers. One provider, HiWaay Internet Services in Alabama, "puts the number of spam messages it blocks per minute at about 150, which equates to 78.8 million per year."[41] Ferris Research estimates that by 2006, 40 percent of incoming mail will be spam as opposed to only 10 percent right now.[42]

The major difference between electronic junk mail and paper junk mail is that the per copy cost of sending the former is so much lower. There are paper, printing, and postage charges for each piece of regular junk mail, but the marginal cost of sending an additional piece of junk e-mail through the digital commons is zero. For instance, some direct marketers who specialize in spam advertising campaigns charge their clients a fee as low as $400 to send out several million messages.

But spam is not cost-free. The problem is that the lion's share of these costs are externalities, that is, they are costs borne involuntarily by others. As Raisch has observed, spam is "postage-due marketing."[43] The biggest cost associated with spam is the consumption of computer resources. For example, when someone sends out spam, the messages must sit on a disk somewhere, and this means that valuable disk space is being filled with unwanted mail. Also, many users must pay for each message received or for each disk block used. Others pay for the time they are connected to the Internet, time that can be wasted downloading and deleting spam. As the volume of spam grows and commercial use of the Internet expands, these costs will continue their steady increase. Further, when spam is sent through Internet Service Providers (ISPs), they must bear the costs of delivery. This amounts to wasted network bandwidth and the utilization of system resources such as disk storage space, along with the servers and transfer networks involved in the transmission process.

In addition to these technical costs imposed by spam, there are also administrative costs. Users who receive these unwanted messages are forced to waste time reading and deleting them. If a vendor sends out 6 million messages and it takes 6 seconds to delete each one, the total cost of this one mailing is 10,000 person hours of lost time.

Purveyors of spam contend that this is simply another form of commercial free speech that deserves the same level of First Amendment protection as traditional advertising. They point out, perhaps correctly, that a ban on spam would not only be impractical but also unconstitutional, since it would violate their constitutional right to communicate. The right to commercial forms of speech has stood on tenuous ground and has never been seen as legally or morally equivalent to political speech. In recent years, however, the Court has tended to offer more substantial protection for commercial speech than it did several decades ago. According to Michael Carroll, "With the development of our information economy, the Court has come to read the First Amendment to provide broader protection over the nexus between the marketplace of ideas and the marketplace for goods and services."[44]

The potential violation of free speech rights by those who want to suppress spam is further complicated by the difficulty of deciding which communications should be classified as spam, that is, as *junk* electronic mail. Should the category of spam include only commercial speech, that is, advertising and marketing pitches, or do certain forms of noncommercial unsolicited e-mail qualify as spam as well?

Consider the controversial case of *Intel Corporation v. Hamidi*. Mr. Hamidi, a former Intel employee, was issued an injunction barring him from sending e-mail to Intel employees connected to the company's network. Hamidi's mail consisted of protests and complaints about Intel's poor treatment of its employees. Intel maintained, and a court agreed, that Hamidi's mass mailings were equivalent to junk commercial e-mail that disrupted its operations and distracted its employees. What makes this case difficult is the fact that Hamidi's speech was noncommercial. He was not advertising a product but rendering an opinion, however alien that opinion might have been in the Intel work environment. His speech seemed to be in the public interest, and yet it was barred by Intel as a nuisance and judged not to deserve First Amendment protection.

A similar incident arose at a Pratt & Whitney factory in Florida, where a union organizing drive used e-mail to contact the company's 2,000 engineers in order to solicit their interest in joining the union. According to Cohen, unions have found e-mail to be "an unusually effective organizing tool, one that combines the intimacy of a conversation, the efficiency of mass-produced leaflets and the precision of delivery by mail to work forces that are often widely dispersed."[45] But companies like Pratt & Whitney argue that these intrusive mass mailings are the same as spam and must be suppressed to avoid the negative effects of spam, such as congestion of their networks.

These and other cases suggest some provocative free speech questions. Should the legal system regard *all* bulk electronic mail, even noncommercial communications, as a form of spam? If the Internet is to realize its full potential as a "democratizing force," shouldn't some forms of bulk e-mail be permitted? What should be the decisive factors in determining when bulk e-mail is intrusive spam and when it is a legitimate form of communication?

What can be done about spam? Should it be subject to government regulations because of its deleterious side effects? If so, should those regulations be imposed at the federal level? Some regulatory possibilities include an outright ban on spam or a labeling requirement. It has been suggested that the federal government could amend the Telephone Consumer Protection Act of 1991 (TCPA), which already makes it illegal to transmit unsolicited commercial advertisements over a telephone facsimile machine. The TCPA could be expanded to include unsolicited commercial e-mail as well as junk faxes.[46] But there would most likely be a constitutional challenge to a complete ban on spam, since it appears to violate the First Amendment. Also, for those who want to preserve the Internet's libertarian ethic, it is unsettling to proscribe communications such as electronic mail based purely on its content.

The second type of legislation might be a labeling requirement of some sort. All unsolicited commercial e-mail and Internet advertising would have a common identifier or a label, allowing users to filter it out if they so desired. With accurate labels, ISPs could more easily control incoming spam either by preventing any unsolicited advertising from their networks or by allowing those ads to reach only the destinations that have agreed to accept such e-mail.

Critics of the latter approach argue that if a labeling requirement were enacted, it would implicitly legitimize spam, and this could have the perverse effect of actually increasing its volume. Spam might become a more acceptable way of advertising, and this could increase the burden on consumers and ISPs to filter out even more unwanted junk e-mail.

Some states, including Washington and Virginia, have adopted laws to deal with spam. The Washington state law, for example, prohibits the transmission of two types of e-mail messages from an email account within the state or to "an electronic mail address that the sender knows, or has reason to know, is held by a Washington resident."[47] The first category is e-mail that conceals the sender's identity and the second is a message that "contains false or misleading information in the subject line."[48]

The new law was used against Jason Heckel, an Oregon resident who mailed a junk message called "How to Profit from the Internet" and falsified his address. In *Washington v. Heckel*, Heckel's lawyers argued that the "Washington anti-spamming law violates the dormant commerce clause," which holds that "certain kinds of state regulation violate the Constitution because they impinge on the congressional prerogative to regulate interstate commerce."[49] Superior Court Judge Palmer ruled that the Washington statute did violate the Federal Interstate Commerce Clause, but he was later overruled by the Washington Supreme Court. The Supreme Court concluded that the law "protected legitimate local interests" and that it did not impose an undue burden on interstate commerce.

Washington's Supreme Court may not have the final word about this matter. If this case (or a related case) is appealed to the Supreme Court, the justices may find that the dormant commerce clause is applicable. State regulations can become a burden on interstate commerce if they create an inconsistent pattern of regulations. This might be a realistic possibility if each state develops its own version of antispam legislation. Consider the opinion of one court in the case of *American Library Association v. Pataki*:

> The courts have long recognized that certain types of commerce demand consistent treatment and are therefore susceptible to regulation only on a national level. The Internet represents one of those areas; effective regulation will require national, and more likely global, cooperation. Regulation by any single state can only result in chaos, because at least some states will likely enact laws subjecting Internet users to conflicting obligations.[50]

Given the problems endemic to a legal approach to spam, perhaps regulating from the bottom up would be a better alternative. This sort of decentralized rule-making would entail a greater reliance on code than on the law. Filters are now available that will weed out spam while allowing legitimate mail to come through, even if spam is not appropriately labeled. Brightmail and other companies provide antispam products that are employed by most corporations. The problem is that e-mail filters rely on *keyword matching*, looking for certain words or phrases that signal spam, such as "Get Rich Quick." But what's needed "is something with more natural language interpretation intelligence."[51] There are fairly sophisticated filters that distinguish junk mail from real mail also being developed by companies like Microsoft. Microsoft Outlook enables users to create rules for screening incoming e-mail with its "rules wizard" functionality that scans and sorts e-mail into different folders, including the trash can.[52] Those who support the bottoms-up philosophy claim that it gives users more flexibility and more control over what they want to allow into their mail boxes.

Once again, we are confronted with a choice between top-down regulations based on deliberative democratic decision making or a bottoms-up approach with fallible yet reasonably effective antispam technology. Of course, the same dangers that accompany the filtering of pornography could be applicable when one filters spam. Filtering protocols, even those that are well intentioned, come with a cost. As Shapiro observes, excessive filtering "may cause our preferences to become ever more narrow and specialized, depriving us of a broad perspective when we likely need it most."[53]

Finally, it is worth noting that the problem of spam could easily be solved through self-restraint and ethical awareness. Those who send spam should recognize that a potent case can be advanced to support the ethical impropriety of this activity. Let us consider spam through the prism of ethical theory, and, for the sake of brevity, confine our remarks to an analysis from a deontological perspective. Spamming clearly violates the spirit of Kant's categorical imperative ("Act according to a maxim which is at the same time valid as a universal law"), which requires us to perform only those actions that can be universalized. Recall that according to Kant, the test of moral correctness is the rational acceptability of a hypothetical, but universal, conformity to a policy or practice. In other words, the universalization process usually demands that we imagine a counterfactual situation. In this case, we must imagine what would happen if all organizations and vendors that had an interest in online advertising adopted a policy of spamming, transmitting large volumes of bulk e-mail through cyberspace on a regular basis. Beyond any doubt, the Internet would become hopelessly congested and the entire system would rapidly become dysfunctional. Spamming therefore is not a coherently universalizable practice, since it entails a pragmatic contradiction to the categorical imperative.[54] The action of spammer X is efficacious only because others refrain from this activity and the network is available for spammer X's bulk e-mail.

▶ Postscript

Spam, pornography, libel, hate speech, threats—all are problematic forms of free expression that pose formidable challenges to cyberspace jurisprudence, which seeks to balance individual rights with the public good. Ideally, of course, individuals and organizations should regulate their own expression by refraining from intimidating and mean-spirited hate speech, refusing to disseminate pornography to children, and repressing the temptation to use spam as a means of advertising goods or services. But in the absence of such self-restraint, Internet stakeholders must make difficult decisions about whether or not to shield themselves from unwanted speech, whether it be crude obscenities or irksome junk e-mail.

Top-down government regulations such as the COPA or laws that ban junk e-mail represent one method for solving this problem. Sophisticated filtering devices, which will arguably continue to improve in their precision and accuracy, offer a different but more chaotic alternative. As we have been at pains to insist here, whatever combination of constraints are utilized—code, law, market, or social norms—full respect must be accorded to key moral values such as personal autonomy. Hence the need for nuanced ethical reflection about how these universal moral standards can best be preserved as we develop effective constraints for aberrant behavior in cyberspace. Otherwise, our worst apprehensions about the tyranny of the code *or* the laws of cyberspace may be realized.

Another option, of course, is to refrain from the temptation to take *any* action against these controversial forms of speech in cyberspace. Some civil libertarians argue convincingly that Internet stakeholders should eschew regulations and filtering and leave the Internet as unfettered and open as possible. We should tolerate all forms of nuisance speech on the Internet just as we tolerate them in the physical world.

If a decision is made to suppress extreme forms of speech, the ethical challenge is to find a way to preserve the liberties of cyberspace while removing speech that is not constitutionally protected, or restricting access to speech that is harmful to minors. The Internet has created a "new marketplace of ideas" with "content [that] is as diverse as human thought."[55] And neither law nor code should disrupt the free flow of ideas and information in this democratic marketplace.

Discussion Questions

1. What is your assessment of the Children's Internet Protection Act (CHIPA)? Do you support the ACLU's views against this legislation?
2. Are automated content controls such as PICS a reasonable means of dealing with pornographic material on the Internet? At what level(s)—parent, school/library, ISP, etc.—should they be imposed?
3. What sort of First Amendment protection do Web sites filled with hate speech or racist speech deserve?
4. Do you agree with the position that anonymity should be preserved in cyberspace? Or should every user's digital identity be mandated when they go online?
5. What should be done about spam? Do we need federal laws? What about relying on state law? Do you agree with the moral arguments presented here about spam?

Cases

The Librarian's Dilemma

Assume that you have just taken over as the head librarian of a library system in a medium-sized city in the United States. You discover that the main library building in the heavily populated downtown area has 16 Macintosh computers, but they are only used sporadically by this library's many patrons. The computers lack any interesting software and do not have Internet connectivity. As one of your first orders of business, you decide to purchase some popular software packages and to provide Internet access through Netscape's Navigator browser. The computer room soon becomes a big success! The computers are in constant use and the most popular activity is Web surfing. You are pleased with this decision, since this is an excellent way for those in the community who cannot afford computer systems to gain access to the Internet. You then authorize expenditures for the same software and Internet access for the library's branches throughout the city.

Soon, however, some problems begin to emerge at the main branch. On one occasion, some young boys (about 12 or 13 years old) are seen downloading graphic sexual material. A shocked staff member tells you that the boys were looking at sadistic obscene images when they were asked to leave the library. About ten days later, an older man was noticed looking at child pornography for several hours. Every few weeks there are similar incidents.

Your associate librarian and several other staff members recommend that you immediately purchase and install some type of filtering software. But other librarians remind you that this violates the ALA's code of responsibility. You reread that code and are struck by the following sentence: "The selection and development of library resources should not be diluted because of minors having the same access to library resources as adult users." Many colleagues urge you to resist the temptation to install these blocking mechanisms, as the use of this technology is a form of censorship. One staff member argues that filtering is equivalent to purchasing an encyclopedia and cutting out articles that do not meet certain standards. But another librarian points out that the library doesn't put pornographic material in its collection so why should it allow access to such material on the Internet?

As word spreads about this problem, there is also incipient public pressure from community leaders to do something about these computers. Even the mayor has weighed in—she too is uncomfortable with unfettered Internet access. What should you do?

In the midst of all this, you learn that Congress has passed the Children's Internet Protection Act (CHIPA). CHIPA requires all public libraries that participate in the federal e-rate program to install filters or other blocking mechanisms in order to prevent access to material that is obscene, child pornographic, or harmful to minors. The e-rate program is simply a discounted rate for Internet access charged to libraries by telecommunications carriers. Your library system received about $80,000 in e-rate discounts last year. If you don't purchase the blocking mechanisms, the budget will have to be cut by $80,000 to make up for the lost e-rate subsidy.

Questions:

1. Is filtering of pornographic Web sites equivalent to an acquisition decision where the library chooses what material to carry or not to carry? Or does it represent an attempt to censor the library's collection?
2. Do libraries have any legal and/or moral duty to protect children from indecent and obscene material?
3. How does CHIPA complicate your decision?
4. Decide on a course of action and defend your position.

Spam or Free Speech at Intel?

Mr. Kenneth Hamidi is a disgruntled former employee of Intel who has problems with the way Intel treats its workers. Hamidi is the founder and spokesperson of an organization known as FACE-Intel (Former and Current Employees of Intel). Many of these ex-Intel employees claim that they have been mistreated in some way by Intel. Hamidi himself was dismissed from Intel for reasons that have not been made public, but he claims to be a victim of discrimination.

Shortly after his dismissal in the fall of 1996, Hamidi began e-mailing Intel employees, informing them of Intel's unfair labor practices. He alleges that the company is guilty of widespread age and disability discrimination, but Intel firmly denies this allegation. According to Intel, Hamidi sent five or six e-mail messages to as many as 29,000 employees over a span of two years between 1996 and 1998. The messages voiced Hamidi's grievances with Intel, especially its employment policies. One message, for example, accused Intel of grossly underestimating the size of an impending layoff. According to court documents, Hamidi offered the recipients of his messages an opt-out option, but only 450 Intel employees chose that option. Hamidi has not explained how he got the e-mail addresses, but despite suspicions raised by his possession of these addresses, Intel presented no evidence that they were misappropriated or taken illegally. After efforts to block the messages were unsuccessful, Intel sent a letter to Hamidi in March, 1998, demanding that he cease sending these e-mail communications. He refused, and Intel went to court to seek an injunction.

Intel's position was that Hamidi's bulk e-mail was the equivalent of spam, congesting its e-mail network and distracting its employees. Intel's lawyers have contended that these unsolicited mailings were intrusive and costly for the corporation. At a minimum, they resulted in "diminished employee productivity," given the time employees spent reading and deleting Hamidi's mail. The company also cited resources consumed to block these messages and the time expended to address employee concerns raised by the content of Hamidi's e-mail. Therefore, the unwanted messages are analogous to trespass on Intel's property: just as a trespasser forces his way on to someone's else's property, so these messages were being forced upon Intel and its employees. The specific legal claim was that Hamidi was guilty of trespass to chattels, which is defined as "the unauthorized interference with possession of personal property which causes injury."[56] In summary, the company's basic argument was that Hamidi did not have a right to express his personal views on Intel's proprietary e-mail system especially after he was put on notice that his messages were unwelcome. They also point out that Hamidi has many other forums to express his opinions such as the FACE-Intel Web site, where many anti-Intel messages often appear.

In June, 1999, a California Superior Court judge agreed with these arguments and issued a permanent injunction prohibiting Hamidi from sending any more bulk e-mail to Intel's employees. The court found that "Hamidi's e-mails are not (under either federal or state constitutions) protected speech."[57]

Defenders of Hamidi's actions argued that the injunction was an unfair overreaction and that his free speech rights were being violated. They claimed that this bulk electronic mail should not be categorized as spam since it took the form of noncommercial speech, which deserves full First Amendment protection. Hamidi's speech involves ideas and opinions that are in the public interest; it is not an attempt to sell goods or services over the Internet. Hamidi, therefore, has a First Amendment right to disseminate his electronic mail messages to Intel's employees even if the company is inconvenienced in the process. Further, they argued that his messages have not caused any injury or impairment to Intel's e-mail system.

Backed by the ACLU and other supporters, Hamidi appealed this judgement to the California Supreme Court, and in April, 2002, that court decided to hear the *Intel v. Hamidi* case.

Questions

1. Does Hamidi's speech deserve First Amendment protection? Should he be allowed to send these messages without court interference?
2. What do you make of Intel's argument that its censoring of Hamidi's bulk e-mail amounts to protecting its private property from trespass?
3. Should there be new laws to clarify this issue? How might those laws be crafted?
4. Assume that you are selected for the panel of judges at the California Supreme Court hearing Intel v. Hamidi. How would you rule in this case? Explain your answer.

L'Affair Yahoo!

Company Background:

Yahoo, founded in 1994 by David Filo and Jerry Yang, was originally developed as a guide to the Web and a way to keep track of Web site addresses. This guide quickly evolved into a commercial web site and a thriving business. In 1995, Yahoo took on Tim Koogle as its CEO. From the outset, Yahoo saw itself as a media company and not just a search engine. During 1996 and 1997, Yahoo added considerable content and communication facilities as it evolved into a full-fledged Internet portal. Yahoo's primary services are called "properties." These properties include navigational services that help users find Web sites and other information more easily. It also includes "community properties," in order to help users communicate with one another. For example, users could access the Yahoo Address Book, which allows them to use an address book from any connected system. There are also e-commerce properties for shopping or making travel arrangements. Millions also use Yahoo for e-mail, instant messaging, scheduling, and personal Web pages.

Yahoo generates most of its revenues through advertising and through deals with e-commerce partners. It recently decided to charge a listing fee for the items sold on its auction sites in order to enhance its revenue stream. Yahoo's vision "declares that advertisers will pay a big premium to be on the Web's biggest and best known site, just as they pay a premium to advertise on a top-rated television program."[58]

Yahoo currently reaches 60 percent of all Net users worldwide and it tracks the visits of 166 million users. Yahoo has expanded mightily into overseas markets. Foreign users now amount to 40 percent of Yahoo's customer base. Yahoo has the biggest global reach of any Internet brand—it offers 23 local versions in 12 different languages. Yahoo has prided itself on good relations with foreign governments. According to *Forbes*, Yahoo devotes much energy to "hitting the international conferences and meeting heads of state to talk Internet policy and plead Yahoo's local interests."[59]

The French Resistance

During the spring of 2000, Yahoo's relations with the French government ran into serious problems. In April of that year, two French antiracist groups (the French Union of Jewish Students and the International League against Racism and Anti-Semitism) filed suit against Yahoo, demanding that they remove swastika flags and other Nazi memorabilia from their American Web site. Some of Yahoo's properties are auction sites that included such items for sale. French law expressly prohibits the display or sale of objects that incite racial hatred, and this includes any World War II Nazi memorabilia. In May, Judge Jean-Jacques Gomez ruled in favor of these two groups. He concluded that Yahoo had violated French law and offended the "collected memory" of France. He ordered Yahoo to make it impossible for French users to access any auction site that contained illegal Nazi items.

Yahoo's lawyers claimed that the company was not able to enforce this ruling. They argued that it would not be technically feasible to accomplish the task of identifying Web users by national origin and blocking access to the contested sites. The judge assembled a panel of three experts to determine whether or not Yahoo's assessment was correct.

The panel consisted of three individuals representing France, Europe, and America. The panel was charged with answering this question: is it technically possible for Yahoo to comply with the judgement against them, and, if not, to what extent can compliance be achieved? The panel concluded that foolproof 100 percent compliance was impossible. But it also concluded that Yahoo could block up to 90 percent of French users by using several levels of detection. Over 60 percent could be blocked by the same technology that Yahoo used to customize the site for French users by providing French banner ads. This entailed tracking their Internet Protocol address, which in most cases reveals the physical location of the user. This would not work, however, for AOL subscribers who do not have fixed IP addresses. It estimated that another 20–30 percent could be identified by requiring users to fill out a "declaration of nationality."

Of course, each method of detection could be easily circumvented. One could employ an anonymizer such as www.anonymizer.com to prevent the IP address from being revealed. And one could also lie about one's nationality on the declaration form.

Based on these results, in November, 2000, the judge put into effect the order he had issued in May. Yahoo was ordered to install a filtering system to block French citizens from these problematic sites. Yahoo was informed that it had 90 days to comply with the court order or face a fine of up to 100,000 francs (about $13,000) per day. In his ruling, the judge referred to Yahoo's ability to detect French Web users since it already pre-selects them for its French-language banner ads. The judge also pointed to Yahoo's other restrictions, citing its policy "of not allowing the sale of drugs, human organs or living animals on its auctions sites."[60]

This unique case triggers many difficult jurisdictional issues. On one hand, France has the right to assert jurisdiction over its citizens and to enforce its own laws. But how can it enforce its laws against a company located in the United States? One of Yahoo's lawyers predicted "that any effort by French authorities to enforce Judge Gomez's judgement in a United States court against Yahoo's United States assets would fail because of the First Amendment, which protects hate speech."[61]

Yahoo's Dilemma

Yahoo officials must now decide whether or not to comply with the French Court's order. They had several options. They could adopt a defensive posture: ignore the court order and continue to allow its auction sites with these controversial items to be made available to French citizens. The company might combine this strategy with an appeal of the French Court's decision. Or it could take blocking measures to shut out French residents from the contested sites to ensure compliance even if they are not fully effective. It also has the option of banning hate material including these Nazi-related items from all of its auction Web sites. This might be accomplished by using software that scans the items before they are made available for sale. This course of action would be the most drastic, since it would be a departure from Yahoo's longstanding policy against the monitoring of its Web properties.

As the November decision began to sink in, Koogle and his colleagues realized that they faced an insuperably difficult decision. How could it balance the interests of its diverse stakeholders without getting embroiled in a protracted legal battle with the French government?

Questions:

1. In your opinion, what should Yahoo do about this situation? Should it make concessions to the French Government?
2. Do you agree with the French Government's efforts to enforce the law against hate speech?
3. What are the broader implications of this case for the future of free speech on the Internet?

References

1. Michael Godwin, *CyberRights* (New York: Random House, 1998), p. 16.
2. *Reno v. ACLU* 521 U.S. 844 [1997].
3. Julie Cohen, "Examined Lives: Informational Privacy and the Subject as Object," 52 *Stanford Law Review* 1373, 2000.
4. "Geography and the Net," *The Economist*, August 11, 2001, p. 18.
5. Lessig, *Code and Other Laws of Cyberspace*, p. 167.
6. *Ginsberg v. New York*, 390 U.S. 15 (1973).
7. Philip Elmer-Dewitt, "Cyberporn," *Time*, July 3, 1995, p. 40.
8. Godwin, p. 223.
9. See *Communications Decency Act*, 47 U.S.C. # 223 (d) (1) (B).
10. Zittrain et al., Amicus Curiae Brief for Appelants, *Reno v. ACLU*, 521 U.S., 1997.
11. Lessig, *Code and other Laws of Cyberspace*, p. 175.
12. *ACLU v. Reno* 929 F. Supp 824 (E.D. Pa [1996]).
13. *Reno v. ACLU.*
14. Max Hailperin, "The COPA Battle and the Future of Free Speech," *Communications of the ACM*, V. 42, No. 1, January, 1999, p. 25.
15. Pamela Mendels, "Setback for a Law Shielding Minors from Smut Web Sites," *The New York Times*, February 2, 1999, p. A10.
16. Carl Kaplan "Free-Speech Advocates Fight Filtering Software in Public Schools," www.nytimes.com, January 19, 2001.
17. Plaintiff's Complaint, *Multnomah Public Library et al. v. U.S.* (402 E.D. PA [2001]).
18. Ibid.
19. Jonathan Katz, *Virtuous Reality* (New York: Random House, 1997), p. 184.
20. See "About Websense Enterprise" available at: http://www.websense.com/products.
21. Jennifer Lee, "Cracking the Code of Online Filtering, " *The New York Times*, July 19, 2001, p. E9.
22. Lessig, "Tyranny in the Infrastructure," *Wired*, March, 1997, p. 96.
23. Cass Sunstein, "The First Amendment in Cyberspace," 104 *Yale Law Journal* 1757, 1995.
24. Plaintiff's complaint, *Multnomah Public Library et al. v. U.S.*
25. Quoted in Amy Harmon, "To Screen or Not to Screen: Libraries Confront Internet Access," *The New York Times*, June 23, 1997, p. D8.
26. *Mainstream Loudon v. Loudon County Library* 2 F. Supp. 2d 783 (E.D. Va, [1998]).
27. Ibid.
28. Ibid.
29. Ibid.
30. See the American Library Association Web site, www.ala.org.
31. Richard Rosenberg, "Free Speech, Pornography, Sexual Harassment, and Electronic Networks," *The Information Society*, Vol. 9 (1993), p. 289.
32. I am indebted to John Finnis' insightful discussion of these issues in *Natural Law and Natural Rights* (Oxford: Oxford University Press, 1980), pp. 216–218.
33. Keith Perine, "The Trouble with Regulating Hate," *The Industry Standard*, July 31, 2000, p. 4.
34. *Yahoo, Inc. v. La Ligne Contre Le Racisme et L'Antisemitisme, et al.* C-00-21275 N.D. Cal [2001].
35. Carl Kaplan, "New Economy," *The New York Times*, February 11, 2002, p. C3.
36. Elaine Lafferty, "Ruling Against Anti-Abortion Website Raises Storm in US over Rights," *The Irish Times*, February 4, 1999, p. 14.
37. *Planned Parenthood v. American Coalition of Life Activist* 41 F. Supp 1130 (9th Cir. [2001]).

38. Michael Froomkin, "Flood Control on the Information Ocean: Living with Anonymity, Digital Cash, and Distributed Data Bases," *University of Pittsburgh Journal of Law and Commerce*, 395 (1996), p. 278.

39. David Brin, *The Transparent Society* (Reading, MA: Addison-Wesley, 1998), p. 27.

40. Jeffrey Selino, "Student Writers Try to Duck the Censors by Going Online," *The New York Times*, June 7, 2001, p. E6.

41. Jennifer Disabatino, "Spam Taking a Toll on Business Systems," *Computerworld*, February 18, 2002, p. 7.

42. Larry Armstrong, "Making Mincemeat Out of Unwanted E-mail," *Business Week*, December 18, 2000, p. 234.

43. Robert Raisch, "Postage Due Marketing: An Internet Company White Paper," available at http://www.internet.com:2010/marketing/postage.html.

44. Michael Carroll, "Garbage In: Emerging Media and Regulation of Unsolicited Commercial Solicitations," 11 *Berkeley Technology Law Journal*, 1996.

45. Noam Cohen, "Corporations Battling to Bar Use of E-Mail for Unions," *The New York Times*, August 23, 1999, p. C1.

46. In April, 2002, however, Judge Limbaugh of the Federal District Court in Missouri has ruled that the ban on unsolicited commercial faxes is unconstitutional. Although his ruling will be appealed, the TCPA is now effectively in a state of limbo.

47. Wash. Rev. Code, 19.190.020(1).

48. Ibid.

49. "Recent Cases," 115 *Harvard Law Review* 931, January, 2002; see also *Washington v. Heckel*, 24 P. 3d 404 [Wash., 2001].

50. *American Library Association v. Pataki*, 969 F. Supp. 160 (S.D.N.Y. [1997]).

51. Disabitino.

52. Armstrong.

53. Shapiro, p. 114.

54. For a more detailed version of this argument, see Richard Spinello, "Ethical Reflections on the Problem of SPAM," *Ethics and Information Technology*, vol. 1, no. 3 (1999): pp. 185–191.

55. *Reno v. ACLU*.

56. *Thrifty-Tel Inc. v. Bezenek* 46 Cal. App. 4th 1559, [1996].

57. *Intel Corp. v. Hamidi*, No. 98A505067, (Cal Super Ct. [1999]).

58. Suein Hwang, "Yahoo's Grand Vision for Web Advertisng Takes Some Hard Hits," *The Wall Street Journal*, September 1, 2000, p. A1.

59. Quentin Hardy, "Yahoo: The Killer Ad Machine," *Forbes*, December 11, 2000, p. 174.

60. John Tagliabue, "French Uphold Ruling Against Yahoo on Nazi Sites," *The New York Times*, November 21, 2000, p. C8.

61. Carl Kaplan, "Ruling on Nazi Memorabilia Sparks Legal Debate," *CyberLaw Journal*, November 24, 2000.

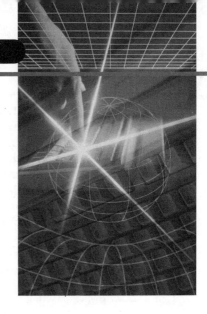

CHAPTER FOUR

Intellectual Property in Cyberspace

Part I: Background on Intellectual Property

▶ Introduction

The struggle to adapt copyright and patent laws to the complex realities of the networked digital age has already been a long and contentious one. In December 1996, a major conference was convened in Geneva to devise a comprehensive international copyright treaty. But to the dismay of Bruce Lehman, the Assistant Secretary of Commerce, and the American delegation, no consensus could be reached on the major issues.

Given the precariousness of maintaining some semblance of control over one's intellectual property in cyberspace, Lehman sought stricter rules and stronger ownership rights for content creators, that is, record companies, book and magazine publishers, movie studios, and software vendors. His efforts were inspired by a Clinton Administration white paper called "Intellectual Property and the National Information Infrastructure" (NII) published in 1995. The white paper concluded that copyright owners should have control over temporary as well as permanent copies of their digital works and that "fair use and other copyright exceptions . . . will no longer be necessary because it will be possible to license uses needed via the NII."[1] The white paper also proposed that much of the cost for policing intellectual property protection be shifted to online service providers who would be liable for the copyright violations of their users.

Pamela Samuelson describes those who advocated this extreme view as *copyright maximalists.*[2] Clearly the maximalist agenda flies in the face of the libertarian approach to intellectual property, which tends to de-emphasize property rights. "Information wants to be free" is a familiar refrain of some libertarians who oppose intellectual property laws that constrain the free flow of information in cyberspace. Those who advocate this point of view are often called *copyright minimalists.*

The minimalist approach has strong support among those who feel that trying to preserve strong intellectual property protection in this digital era is a futile and misguided effort. Esther Dyson, among others, has argued that copyright in cyberspace is an anachronism and that authors will soon be forced to give away their books on the Internet and make money through other activities (such as lectures). According to Dyson, "Chief among the new rules is that 'content is free.'"[3] Similarly, Negroponte writes that copyright law is a "Gutenberg artifact."[4]

Others like John Perry Barlow have deeper philosophical reasons for opposing Internet copyright protection. He argues that ownership of information in this open environment is antidemocratic since it will interfere with the free circulation of ideas. But Barlow understands the paradox of living up to the demand to protect digital information:

> The riddle is this: if our property can be infinitely reproduced and instantaneously distributed all over the planet without cost, without our knowledge, how can we protect it? How are we going to get paid for the work we do with our minds? And, if we can't get paid, what will assure the continued creation and distribution of such work? Since we don't have a solution to what is a profoundly new kind of challenge, and are apparently unable to delay the galloping digitization of everything not obstinately physical, we are sailing into the future on a sinking ship. This vessel, the accumulated canon of copyright and patent law, was developed to convey forms and methods of expression entirely different from the vaporous cargo it is now being asked to carry. It is leaking as much from within as from without.

Barlow's observations suggest one side of the "digital dilemma," which succinctly expresses the key issues at the core of the intellectual property problematic. The ability to reduce all forms of information into a digital format, 1s and 0s, means that it is possible to make limitless, perfect copies of books, videos, and music, and to distribute those products easily and quickly. The ease with which these digital media can be shared is of great concern to many copyright holders who fear that they will have to sacrifice revenues as they lose control over their works. However, the other side of this dilemma is that digital technologies, such as rights-management systems and encryption software, can enclose this information more tightly than ever before. As a result, "The information infrastructure has as well the potential to demolish a careful balancing of public good and private interest that has emerged from the evolution of U.S. intellectual property law over the past 200 years."[5]

Maximalists seek to tighten copyright restrictions through law and technology, but those at the other end of the spectrum are content with the liberation of information from the physical encumbrances that preceded its digitization. Can we stake out a reasonable middle ground between the maximalists and the minimalists? Or are the disagreements and divisions so deep-seated that a tenable compromise is almost impossible? The theme of the digital dilemma will pervade this chapter as we seek to assess the proper scope of intellectual property protection for the digital age. A central axis of discussion will be how the content industry, particularly music and movie producers, have been impacted by digital technology. Is it possible to securely distribute music and movies in cyberspace without compromising intellectual property "safety valves" such as fair use and first sale? How can we capitalize on the promise of digital technology without overreacting to the perils of distributing content over the Net?

We will also consider here a number of other related intellectual property issues triggered by expanded utilization of the Web coupled with the unique features of digital technology. For example, do organizations have property rights in domain names (e.g., www.cocacola.com) once they are properly registered, and what are the limits of those rights? When does the use of another's trademark in a metatag become deceptive or infringe on the trademark holder's property rights? What is the fairest approach to framing and linking to other Web sites, and does linking to another Web site ever infringe on intellectual property rights? Are business method patents necessary to sustain innovation on the Web? And, lastly, what are the social implications of the open source code movement in the software industry?

We will provide some perspective on all of these matters from both a moral and legal vantage point. It seems fitting that we begin by providing an overview of the framework of relevant laws that protect intellectual property along with an account of the most plausible moral grounding of those laws. In addition, keeping in mind Lessig's paradigm introduced in the first chapter, we must consider what combinations of law, code, and moral norms are most appropriate to effectively regulate property in cyberspace without undermining the public good.

▶ What is Intellectual Property and Why Does it Matter?

It is logical to begin this analysis by setting forth a workable definition of property and an overview of its central role in a well-ordered society.

Property is at the cornerstone of most legal systems, yet it is a murky and complex concept that defies a simple definition.

Most contemporary philosophical analyses equate the notions of "ownership" and "property." Hence, the statements "I own that house" and "That house is my property" are equivalent, since they convey the same information. Further, those analyses define ownership as "the greatest possible interest in a thing which a mature system of law recognizes."[6] More simply, ownership of property implies that the owner has certain rights and liabilities with respect to this property, including the rights to use, manage, possess, exclude, and derive income. This is consistent with our legal tradition, which has long recognized that ownership encompasses a number of rights known as the "Blackstonian Bundle," named after William Blackstone who summarized these rights in his famous eighteenth century *Commentaries*. According to Blackstone, the owner has the right to exclude anyone from the property, to use it as he or she sees fit, to receive income derived from that property, or to transfer the property to someone else.

Why do property rights matter so much? The principles of justice, economic efficiency, and political freedom have been invoked to defend the basic structure of property rights. DeLong observes that unless we have unambiguous ownership rights and unless we pay for the goods (i.e., property) that we need, the end result will be greed and chaos: "If you must pay, then it forces thought about what is really valuable and what is not. If the property is free the outcome is obvious: take everything you can get your hands on."[7] The abuse of free goods such as land, air, and water has already led to serious environmental degradation and a "tragedy of the commons." This tragedy of the commons where individual incentives are at variance from the public good is now widely recognized. It is somewhat different with intangible intellectual property but there are some important analogies: personal data sold and exchanged by data brokers can also be abused and overexposed because it has become such a cheap commodity.

Intellectual property consists of *intellectual objects*, such as original musical compositions, poems, novels, inventions, product formulas, and so forth. While the use of physical objects is a zero-sum game in the sense that my use of an object prohibits others from using it, the same cannot be said of intellectual objects. They are nonrival goods, since they can be used by many people simultaneously and their use by some does not preclude their use by others. My appropriation of a special recipe for pasta primavera does not preclude others from enjoying that same recipe. Furthermore, although the development and creation of intellectual property objects may be time-consuming and costly, the marginal cost of making copies is usually negligible.

Some of these characteristics make intellectual property rights more difficult to define and justify especially in open, democratic societies that prize free expression and the free flow of ideas. Assigning property rights to nonrivalrous intellectual objects seems antithetical to many of the goals and traditions of a free society. Those who oppose strong copyright protections often appeal to the First Amendment along with the need for maximum vitality in the marketplace of ideas as a rationale for their opposition. They point to the maximalist agenda, which threatens to suffocate the growth of the public domain.

Nonetheless, for reasons that will become more lucid as this chapter proceeds, limited property rights should extend to the intellectual realm. On its face, an intellectual property right provokes a sense of unease because it implies that someone has the right to certain concepts, knowledge, or ideas. But there are obvious difficulties with the notion that one has property rights in an idea or in similar abstract entities, since this would mean the legal prerogative to exclude others from using and building upon those ideas. This problem is overcome by making a distinction between the idea and its expression, and, in most cases, granting copyright protection to the expression of an idea but not the idea itself. If we can make these important distinctions and develop property rights with reasonable limits and proper "safety valves," it might be possible to protect individual authors without damaging the public interest.

▶ Legal Protection for Intellectual Property

In the United States, the roots of intellectual protection law can be traced back to the Constitution. The founding fathers recognized that such protection was necessary for commercial and artistic advancement. Consequently, the Constitution confers upon Congress the power "to promote the Progress of Science and the useful Arts, by securing for limited Times to Authors and Inventors the exclusive Right to their respective Writings and Discoveries."[8] Specifically, Congress has traditionally chosen to follow this mandate by granting limited copyright and patent protection. We will review here how copyright and patent protection applies in cyberspace, and we include in this summary a third category of trademark protection, since it is pertinent for many of the property conflicts that have surfaced on the Net.

Copyright Laws

Copyright laws give authors exclusive rights in their works, especially the right to make copies. Copyrights now last for an author's lifetime plus 70 years. *Copyright* protects a literary, musical, dramatic, artistic, architectural, audio, or audiovisual work from being reproduced without the permission of the copyright holder. Copyright law also gives the copyright holder the right "to prepare derivative works based upon the copyright works," and "in the case of literary musical, dramatic, choreographic works, pantomimes, and motion pictures and other audiovisual works, to perform the copyrighted work publicly."[9]

In order to be eligible for copyright protection, the work in question must be original, that is, it must be independently created by its author. The work must also be fixed in some tangible medium of expression. Thus, a dance such as the tango cannot be copyrighted but a visual recording of that dance would be eligible for copyright protection. Also, it is important to underscore that copyright protection extends to the actual concrete expression of an idea but not the idea itself. Copyright laws do not protect ideas, concepts, principles, algorithms, and so forth.

Copyright protection has certain limitations considered to be in the public interest. One such limitation or "safety valve" is the "fair use" provision.[10] For example, copyrighted literary works can be quoted and a small segment of a video work can be displayed for limited purposes, including criticism, research, classroom instruction, or news reporting. There are limits, albeit ambiguous ones, on how much of a work can be reproduced. Fair use would enable a teacher to reproduce and distribute a few paragraphs from a book or magazine article, but it would probably not allow reproduction of the whole article or several chapters of the book. Also, making private copies of certain material is considered fair use. In *Sony v. Universal*, the U.S. Supreme Court affirmed that consumers can make a video copy of a television program for their own private use.

Another restriction is the *first sale* doctrine. The first sale provision allows the purchaser of a copyrighted work to sell or lend that copy to someone else without the copyright holder's permission. These limits on copyright law are designed to balance the rights of the copyright holder with the public's interest in the broad availability of books and other artistic works.

Patents

Whereas copyright protection pertains to literary works, patents protect physical objects like machines and inventions along with inventive processes for producing some physical product. A patent can be defined as "a government grant which confers on the inventor the right to exclude others from making, using, offering for sale, or selling the invention for what is now a period of 20 years, measured from the filing date of the patent application."[11]

In order to be eligible for a patent, the invention must be novel, that is, unknown to others or unused by others before the patent is awarded; also, it cannot be described by others in a printed publication. It must also satisfy the criterion of "nonobviousness," that is, it cannot be obvious to anyone "skilled in the art," or it is not patentable. The invention must also be useful in some way. The proper subject matter for a patent is a process, machine, or composition of matter. Laws of nature, scientific principles, algorithms, and so forth belong in the public domain and are not eligible for patent protection.

The scope of patent protection has been expanded significantly over the last several decades. For example, patents are now awarded for new plant varieties developed through experimentation. Patents are also awarded for surgical procedures under certain circumstances. Although software was considered ineligible for patent protection, thanks to the case of *Diamond vs. Diehr*, that has all changed. In that landmark case, the Court ruled that a patent claim for a process should not be rejected merely because it includes a mathematical algorithm or computer software program. In this case "the majority opinion of the Court concluded Diehr's process to be nothing more than a process for molding rubber products and not an attempt to patent a mathematical formula."[12] In other words, the process itself (in this case one for curing rubber) must be original and hence patentable, and if computer calculations are part of the process, then they are included in the patent protection. Subsequent cases have affirmed that any software program is patent-eligible.

Patents have been the subject of some scorn and criticism in certain circles. Since a patent gives the patent holder virtual monopoly power for a long period of time, it enables the producer to charge high prices and reap monopoly rents. This has been a serious source of contention for breakthrough pharmaceutical products, which are sometimes unavailable to indigent patients due to monopoly pricing practices. On the surface, patent protection may seem anticompetitive, but without it, would companies have the incentive to invest hundreds of millions of dollars in order to invent breakthrough drugs or other innovations? The assumption in the Anglo-American capitalist system is that by creating powerful incentives for companies and individuals that take the form of strongly protected monopolies for their innovations, there will be a greater number of breakthrough inventions that will benefit society in the long run.

Trademarks

The final form of legal protection for intellectual property objects is the trademark, which is a word, phrase, or symbol that pithily identifies a product or service. Examples abound: the Nike "swoosh" symbol, names like *Pepsi* and *Dr. Pepper*, and logos such as the famous bitten apple image crafted by Apple Computer. To qualify as a trademark, the mark or name must be truly distinctive. In legal terms, distinctiveness is determined by two major factors: the trademark should be "arbitrary or fanciful," that is, it should not be logically connected to the product (e.g., the Apple Computer logo has no connection to a computer), and the trademark should be powerfully descriptive or suggestive in some way.

A trademark is acquired when someone is either the first to use the mark publicly or the first to register it with the U.S. Patent Office. Trademarks do not necessarily last in perpetuity. They can be lost if one squanders a trademark through excessive or improper licensing. They can also become lost if they eventually become generic and thereby enter the public domain.

According to the terms of the Federal Trademark Act of 1946 (the Lanham Act), trademarks are generally violated in one of two ways: infringement or dilution. *Infringement* occurs when the trademark is used by someone else in connection with the sale of its goods or services. If an upstart athletic shoe company tried to sell athletic shoes and clothing with the aid of the "swoosh" symbol, it would be blatantly violating Nike's trademark. The general standard for infringement is the likelihood of consumer confusion. Trademark owners can also bring forth legal claims if their trademarks are diluted. *Dilution* is applicable only to famous trademarks that are distinctive, of long duration, and usually known to the public through extensive advertising and publicity. Dilution can take one of two forms: blurring or tarnishment. *Blurring* occurs when the trademark is linked with a dissimilar product—for example, using the Disney trademark name to sell suits for men. *Tarnishment* occurs when the mark is portrayed in a negative or compromising way or associated with products or services of questionable value or reputation.

Trademark law does allow for fair use of trademarks and also use for purposes of parody. In fair use situations, the trademark name normally assumes its primary (versus commercial) meaning; for example, describing a cereal as comprised of all bran is different from infringing on the Kellogg's brand name *All Bran*. Parody of trademarks is permitted as long as that parody is not primarily for commercial purposes. Making fun of a well-known brand in a Hollywood skit is probably acceptable, but ridiculing that brand in order to help sell a competing product would most likely not be allowed.[13]

▶ Moral Justification for Intellectual Property

We have considered the various forms of legal protection for intellectual property, and we now turn to the underlying philosophical and moral justification for these laws. It is important to understand the foundation for the legal infrastructure supporting intellectual property rights. Certainly many theories of property have been put forth, but those with the greatest intellectual resonance can be found in the philosophical writings of Locke and Hegel and in the philosophy of utilitarianism. Locke is credited with providing the philosophical underpinnings of the labor-desert theory, while aspects of Hegel's thought form the basis for the so-called "personality theory." Utilitarianism provides the most pragmatic philosophical approach and has been most appealing to economists and legal theorists. Let us briefly review the main tenets of each of these theoretical frameworks.

Labor-Desert Theory

Locke's theory of property has undoubtedly been one of the most influential in the entire philosophical tradition. Stripped of its subtleties, his thesis is simple enough: people have a natural right or entitlement to the fruits of their labor. Thus, if someone takes common, unusable land and through the sweat of the brow transforms it into valuable farm land, that person deserves to own this land. According to Locke, "As much land as a man tills, plants, improves, cultivates, and can use the product of, so much is his property. He, by his labor does, as it were, enclose it from the common."[14] Locke's basic argument is that labor is an unpleasant and onerous activity, and people do it only to reap its benefits; as a result, it would be unjust not to let people possess these benefits. In short, property rights are required as a return for the laborers' painful and strenuous work. However, people should take only property sufficient for their needs.

To be sure, there are numerous problems with Locke's theory, such as the assumption of plenitude. Also, it seems outdated and irrelevant. We do not mix labor with nature but with a complex economic system; a person's labor is only a small input contributing to the production of goods. Nonetheless, the theory does contain a kernel of truth: people ought to receive just rewards for their labor, and when nothing but a property right will be adequate compensation, they should be entitled to that right.

Although Locke had in mind physical property such as land, it would seem that this theory is naturally applicable to intellectual property as well. Should not those who expend intellectual labor be rewarded by ownership in the fruits of their labor and be allowed to "enclose it from the common?" In this case, the relevant resource is common knowledge (i.e., unowned facts, ideas, algorithms, etc.) and one's intellectual labor, which contributes an original creation to this common pool of knowledge, should entitle one to have a natural property right in the finished product such as a novel, a computer program, or a musical composition. Even if this sort of labor is not so unpleasant and difficult, Hughes argues that a property right is still deserved since that labor creates something of social value.[15] It seems only fair that whoever produces something from raw materials, whoever adds value even with minimal effort, should have a title to what they produce. Further, the granting of most intellectual property rights will satisfy the Lockean sufficiency proviso. Nozick contends that the proper interpretation of this proviso is that ownership of property through labor is acceptable if others do not suffer any net harm. He argues that patents, for example, satisfy this proviso since without this incentive, that is, without the prospect of a long, heavily protected monopoly around one's invention, there would probably be no invention and everyone would be worse off.[16]

The Lockean theory may seem archaic, a source of hoary debates about the moral worth of work, but it echoes through many U.S. court decisions about intellectual property. Listen to the eloquent words of Justice Reed, who served on the Supreme Court in the 1950s: "Sacrificial days devoted to . . . creative activities deserve rewards commensurate with the services rendered."[17]

Personality Theory

The basis of the second approach is that property rights are essential for proper personal expression. This theory has its roots in Hegel's philosophy, which describe how "a person must translate his freedom into an external sphere."[18] Hegel argued that property was necessary for the realization of freedom, as individuals put their personality into the world by producing things and engaging in craftsmanship. According to Reeve, "Property enables an individual to put his will into a 'thing.'" Property rights enable the will to continue objectifying itself in the world by insulating its "self-actualization from the predation of others."[19]

Property then is an expression of one's personality, a means of self-actualization. This theory seems particularly apt for intellectual property. As human beings freely externalize their will in various things such as novels, works of art, poetry, music, and even software source code, they create property to which they are entitled because those intellectual products are a manifestation of their personality or selfhood. One recognizes oneself in these productions. They are an extension of a person's being and as such they belong to that person. While not all types of intellectual property entail a great deal of personality, the more creative and individualistic are one's intellectual works, the greater one's "personality stake" in that particular object and the more important the need for some type of ownership rights.[20]

Utilitarianism

The final approach assumes that the *utility principle,* sometimes expressed as 'the greatest good of the greatest number,' should be the basis for determining property entitlements. It has several variations but the main argument is based on the premise that people need to acquire, possess, and use things in order to achieve some degree of happiness and fulfillment. Since insecurity in one's possessions does not provide such happiness, security in the possession, use, and control of things is necessary. Furthermore, security of possession can only be accomplished by a system of property rights. Also, utilitarian philosophers such as Bentham justified the institution of private property by the related argument that knowledge of future ownership is an incentive that encourages people to behave in certain ways that will increase socially valuable goods. It would certainly appear that the basic utilitarian argument can be easily extended to intellectual property.

According to the Landes/Posner version of the utilitarian model, since intellectual products can often be easily replicated due to low "costs of production," there is a danger that creators will not be able to cover their "costs of expression" (e.g., the time and effort involved in writing a novel, producing a music album, or developing a piece of software). Creators cognizant of this danger are reluctant to produce and distribute socially valuable works unless they have ownership or the exclusive prerogative to make copies of their productions. Thus, through financial incentives, intellectual property rights induce creators to develop works they would not otherwise produce without this protection, and this contributes to the general good of society.[21]

The Landes/Posner model takes into account a common feature of most products whose value lies in intellectual property, that is, the magnitude of the upfront costs to create those products. Once the product is created, the marginal cost of producing and distributing each unit is minimal. But if competition drives the *price* down to the marginal cost of production, there will be little incentive to distribute the product. For example, the development costs for Microsoft's Windows operating system (OS) were about $500 million, but the cost of producing and distributing a disk with this OS is next to nothing. If there is no intellectual property protection and competitors are allowed to copy the source code and resell it at a nominal price, Microsoft could not charge a premium price, and therefore it would not be able to recoup its original $500 million investment.

Others have stated the utilitarian theory more simply: we should provide enough intellectual property protection to serve as an inducement for future innovation. It is unlikely that Microsoft will invest $500 million in an operating system, that Disney will make expensive movies, or that pharmaceutical companies will invest in new drug development, unless they can be guaranteed the right to get a return on their investment by controlling their creations, at least for a limited time. Hence the need for some type of protection to spur creativity, especially when creative innovations require a large initial investment.

While all of these theories have been invoked to provide a rationale for intellectual property, James Boyle claims that a more subtle and nuanced justification is rooted in our overly romanticized notion of "authorship." Society has always tended to see its authors as original creators who craft something new. By granting a new work some protection, we can justly reward its author and set that work apart from the public domain. Since the work is original, this protection will not diminish the common stock of knowledge and ideas. According to Boyle, "it is the *originality* of the author, the novelty which he or she adds to the raw materials provided by culture and the common pool which justifies the property right. . . ."[22]

In Boyle's view, this romantic figure of the author and the theme of originality serve as an underlying justification for the strong intellectual property rights that are codified in U.S. law. But these strong rights are socially acceptable because they are qualified by the important idea/expression distinction, which should resolve the tensions between the need for protection and the need to preserve our common reservoir of knowledge. While we might confer a copyright on a specific work, the ideas upon which that work is based remain in the public domain, available for use by other authors. Thus, these three themes—the romantic author figure, originality, and preservation of the idea-expression dichotomy—shape our legal infrastructure on copyright protection.

According to Boyle's analysis, this influential "author vision" has prompted us to be overzealous in our efforts at intellectual property protection and to privatize intellectual goods that ought to remain in the public domain. The Clinton Administration's 1995 White Paper on intellectual property rights on the Internet and later legal developments tend to confirm this tendency. That controversial White Paper articulated concerns about how ease of access on the Internet would facilitate illegitimate copying. It proposed the curtailment of fair use and even planned to put restrictions on the ability to read documents with a browser. The presumption was that cyberspace warranted even tighter protections than real space. But if countries like the United States are too overprotective of their information resources, they run the risk of eventually contracting the public domain because certain intellectual raw materials are owned for a long period of time by their authors.[23]

▶ Recent Legislation

The Digital Millennium Copyright Act (DMCA)

The Digital Millennium Copyright Act (DMCA) is undoubtedly one of the most significant pieces of intellectual property law to be passed in the last decade. This law was enacted by the U.S. Congress in September, 1998.

The heart of this bill is its anticircumvention provision, which criminal-izes the use of technologies that circumvent technical protection systems such as an encryption program.

There are two types of anticircumvention rules in the DMCA. First, it outlaws the act of circumventing "a technical measure that effectively controls access to a [copyrighted] work." For example, if someone pur-chases a CD-ROM video game, there might be a requirement to register with the manufacturer (via modem) so that the CD-ROM will only recog-nize the password forwarded by the manufacturer and will only work in this one machine owned by this particular customer. If this same indi-vidual were to use this CD-ROM in a friend's computer, he or she would be violating the DMCA by circumventing technical measures that control access to the work.

The DMCA also makes it illegal to manufacture or distribute technolo-gies that enable circumvention. According to Ginsburg, "If users may not directly defeat access controls, it follows that third parties should not enable users to gain unauthorized access to copyrighted works by pro-viding devices or services (etc.) that are designed to circumvent access controls."[24] There are exceptions to this statute, including a general exception for interoperability: companies can circumvent technical mea-sures if it is necessary to develop an interoperable computer program (see §1201 f).

Another issue addressed in the DMCA is *intermediary liability*, that is, the liability of third parties for the copyright infringements of others. There have been some adjustments made in the law of contributory in-fringement for Online Service Providers (OSPs). According to the DMCA, these OSPs qualify for immunity from liability, that is, they enjoy safe harbor status, if they are willing to terminate service to repeat copyright infringers and remove material from their sites once they are put on notice that the material infringes copyright.

Criticism of the DMCA has been vociferous since the bill became law. Experts claim that the regulations are ambiguous, complicated, and im-precise. One apparent problem with this law is that it makes access to copyrighted works for fair use purposes difficult. While it appears that the DMCA allows circumvention of a technical protection system for the sake of fair use, "it is less clear whether fair use circumventors have an implied right to make software necessary to accomplish fair use circum-ventions."[25]

The Sonny Bono Copyright Term Extension Act (CTEA)

Another controversial piece of legislation signed into law in 1998 is the Copyright Term Extension Act (CTEA). Some cynics say that this law was a response to Disney's anxiety about the famous cartoon character Mickey

Mouse. Mickey Mouse was scheduled to become part of the public domain in 2004. In order to prevent this, Disney, along with other media companies like Time Warner, heavily lobbied for this legislation. The CTEA extends the term for copyright protection for 20 years so Mickey is safe once again, at least until 2024.

Initially, copyright protection as provided by the U.S. Copyright Act of 1790 was for a 14 year term, renewable for an additional 14 year term. In 1909 the term for copyright became 28 years with a one term extension for a possible total of 56 years. The 1976 Copyright Act established the term of life of the author plus 50 years for individual authors and 75 years for corporate authors (i.e., for companies such as Disney). The CTEA extends these terms by 20 years so protection for individual authors is now life of the author plus 70 years and for corporate authors 95 years. When the copyright expires, the work enters the public domain. Once in the public domain, works can be reproduced and distributed without permission and derivative works can be created without the need for the copyright holder's authorization.

Proponents of the CTEA argued that passage of this legislation was noncontroversial and would have a positive impact on the industry. But critics claim that it hurts the public domain, where almost no new works will be transferred thanks to this extension. That criticism and dismay culminated in a lawsuit filed by Eric Eldred who owns Eldritch Press, which makes works in the public domain freely available over the Internet. The case now known as *Eldred v. Ashcroft* has become a *cause celebre* of lawyers at the Harvard Law School, who have pursued this case all the way to the U.S. Supreme Court, where it will be heard sometime in 2003. The main argument is that the CTEA hurts individuals like Mr. Eldred who are dependent on the public domain. Popular culture itself also depends heavily on a public domain that is being renewed with creative works for others to draw upon as inspiration. Leonard Bernstein, for example, was clearly inspired by Shakespeare's *Romeo and Juliet* when he composed the musical *West Side Story*. Disney itself has benefited immensely from works in the public domain such as Hans Christian Andersen's *Little Mermaid*. Great art and literature also depend on the commons, and on the ability of the artist to dynamically recreate past traditions. As T.S. Eliot wrote, no artist or poet "has his complete meaning alone."[26]

When the CTEA is examined through the lens of intellectual property theory, its justification is dubious. The current term seems like an ample reward for one's work and utilitarian reasoning is unlikely to yield positive arguments on behalf of the CTEA. It is difficult to argue that this retrospective increase in copyright protection will provide a further inducement to creativity. Does an individual or author have a bigger incentive if the copyright on her creative work extends for 70 years after her death instead of 50 years? According to one Court decision, "[a] grant of copyright protection after the author's death to an entity not itself responsible for creating the work provides scant incentive for future creative endeavors."[27] Further, the damage done to the public domain seems to far outweigh any "scant" incentives created by this law. One could certainly argue that this law overprotects property and that it is not in the best public interest. Given the importance of the public domain's vitality for the common good, there is a moral imperative to ensure that this supply of cultural resources is not disrupted by laws that go too far in protecting individual rights.

Part II: Issues for the Internet

▶ Copyright and the Digital Dilemma

Now that we understand the legal framework for intellectual property protection along with its philosophical underpinnings, we can turn to a description and assessment of the most salient issues in cyberspace. We begin with the challenge to copyright protection and the problem of the digital dilemma mentioned earlier. Music and movies are particularly vulnerable since they can be represented in digital format and are in great demand by young audiences.

Digital Music

The rise of digital music has been made possible by a standard known as MP3 (Motion Picture Experts Group, Audio Layer 3). MP3 is an audio compression format that creates near CD-quality files that are 10 to 20 times smaller than the files on a standard music CD. While standard music files require 10 megabytes for each minute of music, MP3 formatted files require only one megabyte. MP3 files are created through a process called "ripping" whereby a computer user copies the contents of a CD into MP3 format. Thanks to MP3, digital music can now be accessed and transmitted over the Web without the need of a physical container such as a compact disk.

This revolutionary distribution method has propelled the music industry into chaos, but it does have certain key advantages. Authors, composers, and performers can publish and distribute their music online without the assistance of recording companies. This low cost distribution method has the potential to create benefits for both the creators of music and their customers. For example, downloadable music might finally alter the balance of power between major record companies and their artists. Moreover, as Fisher points out, this mode of music distribution tends to promote "semiotic democracy." The "power to make meaning, to shape culture" will no longer be so concentrated.[28] Rather it will be more dispersed among a broader range of musicians and artists who do not need to sign a big contract in order to produce and distribute their music.

The downside of this system, of course, is the potential for unchecked piracy. Since MP3 files are unsecured, they can be effortlessly distributed and redistributed in cyberspace. The music industry's response to this threat has been predictable. They have defended their property rights and legally pursued the operators of Web sites that promote digital music file sharing, like MP3.com, along with intermediaries like Napster.

Napster is the creation of Shawn Fanning, a Northeastern University student who left after his freshman year to write this celebrated piece of software. This software operates by allowing Napster users to share MP3 music files with each other, as long as they have installed Napster's free file-sharing software. Once a piece of music is located by using Napster's central directory, a user who wants that music can connect to the computer where it resides and transfer the file. Napster does not store, "cache," or serve any MP3 music files on its own servers, and it is not involved in any copying of music files. The transfer is directly from one Napster user's computer to another's.

In December, 1999, the Recording Industry Association of America (RIAA) sued the company for vicarious and contributory copyright infringement, demanding $100,000 each time a song was copied by a Napster user. Several months later, the rock band Metallica also sued Napster for copyright infringement. The RIAA was particularly anxious about the precedence of allowing copyrighted music to be exchanged so freely and openly. In its main brief, the RIAA summed up the problem quite clearly: "If the perception of music as a free good becomes pervasive, it may be difficult to reverse."[29]

Despite a superb legal team led by David Boies, Napster did not fare well in these legal proceedings. In the summer of 2000, Judge Marilyn Patel granted the RIAA's request for a preliminary injunction ordering the company to shut down its file-sharing service. But two days later the U.S. Court of Appeals for the Ninth Circuit stayed the injunction so that Napster could have its day in court.

In the trial, the plaintiffs argued that a majority of Napster users were downloading and uploading copyrighted music. They estimated that almost 90 percent of the music downloaded by Napster users was copyrighted by one of the recording labels that were a party to this lawsuit. These actions constituted direct infringement of the musical recordings owned by the plaintiffs. Since Napster users were culpable of direct copyright infringement, Napster itself was liable for contributory copyright infringement. Also, since Napster had the ability to supervise the infringing activity and had a financial interest in that activity, it was liable for vicarious copyright infringement.

In its defense, Napster presented several key arguments. It invoked the protection of the 1998 Digital Millenium Copyright Act (DMCA), which provides a "safe harbor" against liability for copyright infringement committed by customers of intermediaries or "information location tools" (i.e., search engines). Napster contended that it was merely a search engine and therefore deserved to be protected by the DMCA. Napster also argued that a significant percentage of the system's use involved legally acceptable copying of music files. According to Napster, many songs were not copyrighted and others were being shared between users in a way that constituted fair use. According to trial documents, "Napster identifies three specific alleged fair uses: sampling, where users make temporary copies of a work before purchasing; space-shifting, where users access a sound recording through the Napster system that they already own in audio CD format; and permissive distribution of recordings by new and established artist."[30] There are four factors that help the court determine fair use: (1) the purpose and character of the use (for example, commercial use weighs against the claim of fair use); (2) the nature of the copyrighted work (for example, creative works receive more protection than factual ones); (3) the "amount and substantiality of the portion used" in relation to the work as a whole; (4) the effects of the use on the market for the work ("fair use, when properly applied, is limited to copying by others which does not materially impair the marketability of the work which is copied"[31]). All of these factors are weighed together and decisions are made on a case-by-case basis.

Napster argued that its users often downloaded MP3 files to sample their contents before making a decision about whether or not to make a purchase. Hence, according to this line of reasoning, Napster's service could even help promote sales of audio CDs. *Space shifting* occurs when a Napster user downloads MP3 files in order to listen to music she already owns on an audio CD. Napster was analogizing its technology to the videocassette recorder. In the 1984 case of *Sony v. Universal City Studios*, the U.S. Supreme Court had exonerated Sony from liability for the illegal copying that could occur by means of its VCR technology. It also held that in general VCRs did not infringe copyright since viewers were engaged in *time shifting*, that is, recording a television show for viewing at a later time. According to Greene, "Relying on the Sony decision, Napster attempted to establish that its service has substantial noninfringing uses and that Napster users who download copyrighted music, like VCR users who record copyrighted television programming, are entitled to a fair use defense."[32]

Despite the ingenuity of Napster's defense, these arguments did not persuade the U.S. Court of Appeals for the Ninth Circuit, which found that "the district court did not err; Napster, by its conduct, knowingly encourages and assists the infringement of plaintiffs' copyrights."[33] It rejected the fair use claim, concluding that Napster had an adverse effect on the market for audio CDs, especially among college students. However, the Appeals Court found that the preliminary injunction was "overbroad," and it placed a burden on the plaintiff to provide Napster with proper notice of copyright works and files being shared on the Napster system "before Napster has the duty to disable access to the offending content."[34] In light of this ruling, Napster is trying to reconstruct its business by converting itself into a subscription music service.

Despite Napster's demise and the legal precedent established by this case, the free circulation of music is unlikely to abate any time soon. At the end of the trial, John Perry Barlow declared, "I think the only way to deal with law on the Internet is to ignore it flagrantly. I want everyone in this room to consider themselves revolutionaries and go out and develop whatever they damn well please."[35]

In addition, new companies are emerging with file-sharing architectures more difficult to contain than Napster. The architectures facilitating this new mode of music distribution are purer versions of peer-to-peer (often referred to as P2P) computing. Unlike the server-based technology, where distribution to clients emanates from a central server, with peer-to-peer, any computer in the network can function as the distribution point. In this way, the server is not inundated with requests from multiple clients. P2P systems enable communications among individual personal computers. For example, personal computer X may ask other PCs in a peer-to-peer network if they have a certain digital file. That request is passed along from computer to computer until the file is located and a copy is sent along to the requester's system.

There is nothing inherently wrong with P2P technology, but if that file has a copyright, this transmission may not be legal. Unlike server-based technology, it is much more difficult to enforce copyright laws with a P2P system since it is difficult to trace the movements of files in this network and there is no central server to shut down. Napster is not a true P2P application since it relies on a central server that stores its directory. Once that server is disabled, the whole network is effectively shut down. But unlike a server-oriented technology, P2P treats all nodes in the network as equals and disabling one node will have minimal impact on the network.

For the music industry, this lethal combination of easily reproducible digital music files, the MP3 format enabling storage, and P2P making illicit distribution impossible to deter, is a recipe for disaster. Now that Napster has been neutralized, the industry is most concerned about true P2P sites such as Gnutella, MusicCity's Morpheus, and Kazaa. Gnutella, for example, is a file-sharing P2P network designed for the purpose of sharing music files and pornographic materials.

It is worth noting that no legal action has been taken against Napster or Gnutella users despite the fact that they are probably guilty of direct copyright infringement. The music industry is not foolish enough to sue its own customers. But what about the moral liability of those who so unabashedly copy copyrighted files? Is there anything morally wrong with such behavior?

Perhaps Kant's moral philosophy can shed some light on this question. If we assume that the theories justifying intellectual property (such as utilitarianism) have some validity, we must conclude that common ownership of intangible property is impractical and inconsistent with the public good. In a dynamic economy, those who produce ideas are motivated by incentives; without property rights, they will create less. Property is a practice, and we contend that this practice makes good economic sense for both physical property and intellectual property. If we want to see blockbuster movies from Disney that cost $150 million to produce, it will be essential to give Disney some copyright protection. While some libertarians resist this way of thinking, most individuals admit that collective ownership of intellectual property, where all creations belong to the intellectual commons immediately, is not feasible. Thus, given the pragmatic necessity of private intellectual property, a universalized maxim that permitted stealing of such property as a standard procedure would be self-defeating. That maxim would say, "It's acceptable for everyone to steal anyone else's private intellectual property." Such a universalized maxim entails a contradiction because it would lead to the destruction of the entire practice of private intellectual property. Since the maxim allowing an individual to freely appropriate another's intellectual property does not pass the test of normative universalization, a moral agent is acting immorally when he or she engages in the unauthorized copying of digital movie or music files. Critics may argue that certain aspects of intellectual property protection make no sense. For example, while they admit that it's logical to protect big budget movies with a copyright and pharmaceutical products with a patent, they disagree with giving copyright protection to music. They may be right about this, but every legal system or practice may appear to have certain incongruities or imperfections. We cannot pick and choose which laws to follow and which to flout or the practice in question would disintegrate as everyone followed his or her own idiosyncratic interpretation of the law. It would be like saying that a house is a valid form of property but things of lesser value like bicycles or clothing are fair game. One can work to modify the copyright laws, but as long as that system has practical significance, one cannot steal another's intellectual property since that act disrespects the whole institution of private intellectual property.

Advocacy of this Kantian argument does not preclude other legitimate moral perspectives on the issue. It *might* be possible for a strict utilitarian to reason that such copying is acceptable when all costs and benefits are calculated. However, if one accepts the set of assumptions we have delineated, the moral argument for respecting all intellectual property rights has considerable persuasive force.

The DeCSS Lawsuit[36]

In January, 2000, eight major Hollywood studios, including Paramount Pictures, Universal Studios, and MGM Studios, filed a lawsuit against three New York men who operated Web sites distributing DeCSS. The DeCSS program allows a user to decrypt a DVD's CSS protection system, so that the user can copy the DVD file to his or her hard drive. (Movies in digital form are placed on disks known as DVDs.) The suit contends that DeCSS is little more than a "piracy tool" that will be used to produce pirated copies of DVD movies for distribution over the Internet. The lawsuit also alleges that DeCSS violates Section 1201 of the DMCA, which makes it illegal for anyone to provide technology that is intended to circumvent access controls (such as encryption) that protect literary or creative works.

DeCSS, the plaintiff's lawyers argue, defeats the purpose of an encryption system known as the Content Scramble System (CSS) by enabling the decryption of copyrighted DVDs without permission of the copyright holder. All DVDs contain digital information, and digitization allows copies of a motion picture contained on a DVD to be stored on a hard disk drive in the computer system's memory or to be transmitted over the Internet. Moreover, there is no degradation of quality and clarity when such digital copies are produced. Given that DVDs are so vulnerable to illicit copying, they have been protected with an access control system called that encrypts the contents. All movies in this digital format are distributed on DVDs protected with CSS. These movies can only be viewed on a DVD player or specially configured PC that has a licensed copy of CSS that contains the keys for decryption.

If computer users want to watch DVD movies on their personal computers instead of a dedicated DVD player, those computers must be using a Mac or Windows operating system. CSS does not support any other operating system at the present time.

In the fall of 1999, Jan Johansen of Larvik, Norway decided that he wanted to watch DVD movies on a computer that ran the Linux operating system. With the help of two friends, he set out to create a software program that would play DVDs on a Linux system. This meant, of course, that it would be necessary to crack the CSS encryption code. Johansen had little trouble doing this, and when he finished writing the DeCSS program, he posted the executable object code on his web site.

Later that fall, Eric Corley wrote about DeCSS for his Web site, 2600.com. At the end of his laudatory article, Corley posted copies of the object and source code of DeCSS. Shortly thereafter the movie studios filed their law suit against Corley and several others.

In February, 2000, Judge Lewis Kaplan issued a preliminary injunction prohibiting the defendants from posting DeCSS on their respective Web sites, pending the trial. Following this court order, two of the defendants settled with the movie studios. But the third defendant, Eric Corley, refused to settle, and the case continued. Mr. Corley removed the DeCSS code from his web site, www.2600.com; however, he added links from his site to a number of other target sites that contained the DeCSS software.

In April, lawyers for the movie studios filed a petition with Judge Kaplan urging him to amend his previous order and prohibit Corley from linking to Web sites that posted the DeCSS code. They argued that although the 2600 Web site no longer contained a copy of DeCSS, the site was functioning as a virtual distribution center for the DeCSS code by virtue of these links.

As the case known as *Universal City v. Remeirdes* continued into the early summer months, the actual trial began. The plaintiffs reasserted their contention that by posting DeCSS on their Web site, the defendants violated the DMCA, since CSS is a technological measure controlling access to these works. The defense challenged the absolute right of the movie industry to control how DVD discs are played. It argued that DeCSS simply preserves "fair use" in digital media by allowing DVDs to work on computer systems that are not running Mac or Windows operating systems. Consumers should have the right to use these disks on a Linux-platform DVD player, and this necessitated the creation of a program such as DeCSS. Their contention was that DeCSS existed to facilitate a reverse-engineering process that would allow the playing of DVD movies on these unsupported operating systems. It had not been written to facilitate the copying or transferring of DVD files in cyberspace. In addition, the defense argued that the ban on linking was tantamount to suppressing an important form of First Amendment expression. Links, despite their functionality, are a vital part of the expressiveness of a Web page and therefore their curtailment violates the First Amendment.

Finally the defense team presented the constitutional argument that computer code itself, including DeCSS, is a form of expressive free speech that deserves full First Amendment protection. This includes both the source code and object code. A computer scientist appearing as an expert witness proclaimed that an injunction against the use of code would adversely affect his ability to express himself. The opposition countered that computer software is more functional than expressive, that is, it is more like a machine that just happens to be built with speech.

On August 17, 2000, Judge Kaplan ruled in favor of the movie industry, concluding that DeCSS clearly violated the DMCA. He ordered Eric Corley to remove the DeCSS software from his web site along with any links to sites containing that program. In his ruling, Judge Kaplan rejected the notion that the DMCA curtailed the "fair use" right of consumers. He did agree that source code is a form of expressive speech. But, on the other hand, DeCSS "does more than convey a message ... it has a distinctly functional, non-speech aspect in addition to reflecting the thoughts of programmers."[37] Hence it is not worthy of full First Amendment protection.

The case was appealed to the United States Court of Appeals for the Second Circuit. In November, 2001, that court concluded that there was no basis for overturning the district court's judgement.

Beyond the narrow legal question addressed in this case, there are obviously much larger issues pertaining to the First Amendment and its apparent conflict with property rights. To what extent should the First Amendment protect computer source code? Is that code expressive enough to deserve full First Amendment protection? Does the First Amendment also support a basic "freedom-to-link," an unrestricted right to link to other Web sites, including sites that contain rogue code such as DeCSS?

This case also raises questions about the DMCA law itself. How can "fair use" be preserved if copyrighted material is in encrypted form and programs like DeCSS are outlawed? Is this ban on the publication of DeCSS ordered by the courts equivalent to a ban on fair use? According to Harmon, critics of the anticircumvention provision "worry that it goes far beyond the specific copyright challenges of the digital age to give copyright holders broad new powers over how the public uses their material."[38] Is there a better way to balance the rights of copyright holders, who rely on protective devices, with free speech rights and the fair use concept?

Software Ownership and the Open Source Code Movement

Software is a special form of intellectual property that can be protected by a patent or copyright. It can also be classified as a trade secret, but reliance on this weaker form of protection would be too risky. Software is different from other forms of intellectual property and it doesn't neatly fit under either legal framework. Its source code resembles a literary work that deserves copyright protection, but unlike other literary works, it has a functional nature. It does resemble a "machine," which seems to mean patent protection is more suitable. But there are certain asymmetries between software and machines, such as the user interface. Is that interface also eligible for patent protection? Further, what accommodations would be made for distributing software in cyberspace? Software has been especially vulnerable to piracy and the Internet clearly increases its vulnerability.

Some argue that given its origins and unusual nature, software should not be eligible for strong copyright or patent protection. Richard Stallman, president of the Free Software Foundation, has argued with great insistence that all software should be free. Stallman claims that ownership of software programs is obstructive and counterproductive. Hence, software should be in the public domain, freely available to anyone who wants to use it, modify it, or customize it. He regards software licensing fees as an enormous disincentive to use programs since they obviously exclude worthy users from enjoying the use of many popular programs. Ownership also interferes with the evolution and incremental improvement of software products. According to Stallman,

> Software development used to be an evolutionary process, where a person would take a program and rewrite parts of it for one new feature, and then another person would rewrite parts to add another feature; this could continue over a period of twenty years. . . .The existence of owners prevents this kind of evolution, making it necessary to start from scratch when developing a program.[39]

Stallman concludes that since the ownership of programs is so obstructive and yields such negative consequences, this practice should be abolished.

This way of thinking has apparently led some to engage in piracy in order to promote the goal of widespread software availability. For example, in March, 1994, MIT student David LaMacchia was charged with computer fraud for operating a computer bulletin board on the Internet called CYNOSURE, which distributed copies of various copyrighted software programs. LaMacchia was not accused of actually uploading or downloading any of the programs, and he did not collect any money or materially profit from this activity in any way. While many were quick to condemn LaMacchia's efforts to act like Robin Hood in cyberspace, some legal scholars urged caution, since an indictment might chill the transmission of information in cyberspace.

Thanks in part to Stallman's efforts and the ascendancy of the Internet, many Internet stakeholders have begun to reassess the propriety and utility of software ownership. As a result, the *open source* movement, once on the fringe of the industry, has picked up momentum. The open source software model generally means that software is distributed free and the "source code" is openly published and accessible for modifications. Idealists like Stallman believed that proprietary software was virtually immoral, but leading proponents of this movement do not look at the issue in moral terms. In their view, open source code is not morally superior to conventional software. Rather, the open source approach leads to the development of better software code, that is, code with fewer bugs and more features contributed by the talented programmers who have access to the program.

During the past few years, there has been a noticeable trend among major software vendors to make their code more openly accessible on the Internet. In 1998, Netscape surprised the software industry when it initiated project mozilla.org, releasing the source code for its Navigator browser. In addition, the open source code movement has been energized by the limited success of programs such as PERL and the LINUX operating system, a variation of UNIX that runs on personal computers. Any user can download LINUX free of charge. LINUX was written by Linus Torvalds when he was an undergraduate at the University of Helsinki. It is quickly becoming a feasible alternative for UNIX and other proprietary operating systems.

Open source code software gives computer users direct access to the software's source code, enabling them to fix bugs or develop incremental enhancements. The premise is that the collective programming wisdom available on the Internet will help create software that is of better quality than any single individual or group of individuals in a company could construct. The Internet is also a factor in the movement's momentum, since it makes collaborative work much easier.

In a highly influential essay entitled "The Cathedral and the Bazaar," Eric Raymond illustrated why a dispersed group of hackers and programmers working on their own ("the bazaar") can develop higher quality software than a more cohesive group of professional, high-paid programmers employed by companies such as Microsoft or Oracle ("the cathedral"). He explained that the former approach is far superior because it can tap into the decentralized intelligence of many talented individuals loosely connected to a program by means of the Internet. The core difference underlying the cathedral versus bazaar approaches is the latter's capacity for finding and fixing bugs more rapidly. According to Raymond,

> In the cathedral-builder view of programming, bugs and development problems are tricky, insidious, deep phenomena. It takes months of scrutiny by a dedicated few to develop confidence that you've wrinkled them all out. Thus the long release intervals, and the inevitable disappointment when long-awaited releases are not perfect. In the bazaar view, on the other hand, you assume that bugs are generally shallow phenomena—or, at least, that they turn shallow pretty quick when exposed to a thousand eager co-developers pounding on every single new release. Accordingly you release more often in order to get more corrections, and as a beneficial side effect you have less to lose if an occasional botch gets out the door.[40]

The open source code trend is likely to intensify only if software companies can make their money from software services and support rather than through the sale of the software. One benefit to vendors should be decreasing labor costs. According to Andrew Leonard, "There's never been a more cost-effective way to contract out services than to use this type of free labor."[41] Open source software represents a new business model that may be risky and yet highly effective for both vendors and users. It promises to be less expensive, more versatile, and more customizable, and all of these features will greatly please many frustrated software users.

The benefits of the open code approach are beyond dispute, but one problem is that it could create a dangerous free-for-all in the exchange of software programs. The current system of ownership and licensing agreements allows the creators of software to maintain control and integrity over their systems. The lines of accountability and responsibility are unambiguous. But that would change if proprietary software systems became the equivalent of common property. Products that are modified by unqualified programmers and redistributed could contain serious flaws and problems and it would be exceedingly difficult to assign blame and liability. Another drawback is security. It's possible that a hacker might insert dangerous code into an open source product that gets redistributed to unsuspecting users.

Further, this open framework for the Internet supported by the open code movement could have major implications for how the Internet will be regulated in the future. When software code is proprietary, that is, the legal property of a particular vendor such as IBM or Apple, it can be regulated more easily by the state. But open code defies such regulation and control since users can substitute their own routines or lines of code in a particular program. Without a fixed code controlled at a single source, it becomes impossible to set a standard of protocols or routines that a software program should or should not contain. If, for example, the state insisted that the code for all Internet browsers include a routine that would automatically calculate and collect a federal tax for certain Internet purchases, this regulation would be difficult to enforce if the browser code is customizable by programmers all over cyberspace. Thus, depending upon one's views on government regulation, open code is either a liberating or subversive force in the struggle for sovereignty between the individual and the state.

Despite the growing enthusiasm for open and free source code, many companies, like Microsoft, still choose to protect their software products and to tightly control distribution. It should be apparent, however, that none of the forms of intellectual property protection described above (copyrights and patents) are especially well suited for software. The source code of software written in languages such as C++ or JAVA is a literary creation, but software is also functional, and because of its functional nature it is inconsistent with copyright law. But does this utilitarian feature imply that patent protection is more appropriate? It doesn't quite fit under patent protection either, because in addition to behaving as a machine, it is also an expressive literary work. Also, although software may be innovative, it is not really *inventive*. The problem, of course, is that software is both useful and literary; it is a machine and yet it is also expressive like a work of art.

Furthermore, as Pamela Samuelson and her co-authors have observed, software programs "bear much of their know-how on and near their face," and this know-how is "vulnerable to copying."[42] It is well known that Steve Jobs, cofounder of Apple, first saw a graphical user interface in a Xerox research laboratory. For someone with imagination and technical acumen, creating that interface in original source code is not a problem. Samuelson goes on to explain that if the primary value of software is useful behavior, copyright law is not the proper protective mechanism because it doesn't protect useful behavior. And if most software is really more innovative than inventive, it shouldn't be eligible for a patent.

It follows therefore that software may need a unique form of legal protection, probably some hybrid of patent and copyright law that takes into account the special characteristics of software. Samuelson suggests a new framework that protects the "sources of value" in software: the literal source code, the useful behavior produced by that code, the know-how embodied in the program, and the program's overall design. Yet any new framework should also encourage future innovative software programs. Accordingly, Samuelson proposes the following framework:

- Traditional copyright protection for the literal code

- Protection against behavior clones for a market preserving period

- Registration of innovative capabilities to encourage knowledge sharing

- Menu of off-the-shelf liability principles and standard licenses

The market preserving period will allow innovators to recoup their investment, and it will vary depending upon the specific segment of the software industry in which the product competes. In general, this period will be much shorter than the 20 years currently granted for most patents. This new framework needs more elaboration but it does represent a reasonable direction for regulating this unusual form of intellectual property. It appears to strike the right equilibrium between the need to promote innovation and competition and the need to reward those innovators for their substantial investments.

Digital Rights Architectures

Throughout this chapter we have expressed how difficult it is for intellectual property laws to keep pace with the transforming power and capabilities of the Internet. As more and more people gain access to electronic distribution, intellectual property is being devalued through illicit copying in cyberspace. It is no surprise, therefore, that code and technology may soon supplant the law as the driving force of regulation in the future. The law has sought to balance the public interest of knowledge-sharing with the private interest of content providers who want to protect their work. But code may work more to the advantage of private interests and therefore shift that balance in a dramatic fashion.

This brings us once again to the digital dilemma. Digital technology makes it much easier to reproduce, distribute, and publish information. But thanks to code in the form of trusted systems and digital rights architectures, it is also possible to control or enclose digital information to a degree never before possible. When buttressed by laws such as the DMCA that forbid circumvention of these protection systems, the digital content becomes hermetically sealed.

One prominent technology that is giving content providers enhanced control over their material is known as *trusted systems*. A trusted system consists of hardware and software programmed to follow certain rules or usage rights that express how and when a digital work can be used. According to Mark Stefik, "Trusted systems can take different forms, such as trusted readers for viewing digital books, trusted players for playing audio and video recordings, trusted printers for making copies that contain labels (watermarks) that denote copyright status, and trusted servers that sell digital works on the Internet."[43] Content providers would distribute their work in cyberspace in encrypted form in such a manner that they would be accessible only by users with trusted machines.

Rights management systems can also be utilized to determine what rights a user has with regard to content. According to Ku, "Used in conjunction with a trusted system, rights management is the ability of a publisher of a work to define what rights subsequent users of her work will have to use, copy, or edit the work."[44]

While the trusted system approach may seem like an ideal solution to the problem of intellectual property protection on the Internet, it also poses some unique challenges. How would fair use coexist with trusted systems? Would critics, scholars, and teachers need to go through elaborate mechanisms to access their material? Further, these systems enable content providers to choose who will access their material, and its possible that certain groups might be excluded from viewing or listening to certain material. If trusted systems are not constructed properly, they could eviscerate the fair use provisions of copyright laws and make creative works less accessible to the general public.

Another problem with trusted systems is the potential for invasions of privacy. These systems will allow content creators to keep precise tabs on who is accessing and purchasing their material. This raises the Orwellian specter of demands for this information from lawyers, government officials, or other curious third parties. Do we really want anyone to keep tabs on which books we read or what kind of record albums we purchase?

It seems evident that trusted systems have the potential to change the ground rules for intellectual property protection. Code can be far more efficacious than law in guarding against infringement, and code working in tandem with law can be even more formidable. But what will be the cost to other valuable social goods such as fair use and personal privacy?

Trusted systems illustrate Lessig's argument that code can be more powerful and comprehensive than law in regulating the Internet. Code allows for almost perfect and foolproof control that is beyond the capability of a more fallible legal system. In effect, the code threatens to privatize copyright law without the appropriate checks and balances (such as fair use and limited term) that we find in public copyright law.

This problem can be mitigated, however, if these systems are designed and coded with the proper ethical awareness. Digital rights management systems should be given a chance, but they should be constructed with sensitivity to traditional values such as fair use and privacy. If this code can be developed responsibly and avoid the excesses of overprotection, it could ease the burden on the legal system's efforts to enforce property protection in cyberspace and minimize future state regulations. Rights management systems *could* be tools that facilitate self-regulation, but only if they are developed in a morally competent fashion.

▶ Business Method Patents in Cyberspace

As we observed, the scope of patent protection has broadened considerably during the last several decades. Software, surgical procedures, plant variations, and so forth are now eligible for patents. But until a few years ago, business methods were off limits for this proprietary right. Examples of business methodologies might include Federal Express's famous hub and spoke delivery system or a bank's money market account. The notion of patenting such novel ways of doing business seemed to be folly, an abuse of the patent system.

In the 1990s, however, the Patent and Trademark Office (PTO) began granting patents for some business methods, treating them as process patents. In 1998, the U.S. Court of Appeals for the Federal Circuit ratified the general business method patent in the *State Street Bank and Trust Co. v.*

Signature Financial Group, Inc. case. The *State Street* case upheld a controversial patent granted to Signature Financial Group for a data processing system that was designed to churn out mutual fund asset allocation calculations. The Appeals Court overturned a lower court ruling and held that the transformation of data by a machine into a final share price was a practical application of an algorithm (and not an abstract idea), since it produced "useful, concrete, and tangible results."[45] The Court stated that business methods were not different from other methods or processes that were traditionally eligible for patent protection. It concluded that "patentability does not turn on whether the claimed method does 'business' instead of something else, but on whether the method, viewed as a whole, meets the requirements of patentability as set forth in Sections 102, 103 and 112 of the Patent Act."[46] The upshot of this case was quite clear: software-enabled business methods (or processes) can be patented as long as they meet the criteria for a patent such as novelty and nonobviousness.

This ruling opened the floodgate for business method patents, and since many of these patents were for online business methods, they became known as "cyberpatents." By 1999, the number of e-business patent applications to the PTO doubled to 2,600.[47] Two of the most prominent examples of such patents included Priceline.com's "name your price" model, where buyers posted the prices they would pay, and Amazon.com's single click method, which allows qualified customers to make their purchase with one click of a mouse. Priceline's patent has been the subject of intense scrutiny because it is so broad and general. Despite the criticism, Priceline has zealously defended its patent, which it regards as one of the most strategically important assets of the company.

In the fall of 1999, Expedia, Inc., owned by Microsoft, offered its Hotel Price Matcher Service. This service bore a strong similarity to Priceline's. The Expedia consumer could name his or her price for a room in a certain locale and Expedia would look for a match among the hotels that participated in this service. Pricleine promptly sued Microsoft, claiming that Microsoft's Expedia travel service infringed on the Priceline patent, allegedly copying the methods and processes set forth in that patent. During a conference, Jay Walker, the founder of Priceline, confronted Microsoft's CEO Bill Gates, but was rebuffed: "On being informed that Priceline.com considered its patent rights to be a competitive asset, Mr. Gates became agitated and told Mr. Walker that he would not allow patent rights to stand in the way of business objectives."[48]

According to Priceline, the patent protection for the "name your price" model was essential in order to attract "venture capital investment."[49] Lewis suggests a similar argument: "For new businesses attempting to engage in e-commerce, a solid patent can be the determining factor as to whether a venture capitalist invests or does not invest in the entrepreneur's business."[50] In the information age, intellectual assets take on far greater import than physical ones and they become the basis for a corporation's differentiation strategy. It stands to reason that corporations will want to protect those valuable assets from being replicated by free riders through patents or other legal mechanisms.

In its complaint for *Priceline.com v. Microsoft*, the company argued that its invention was the result of an "extended effort" to solve a recurrent management problem: "the inability of buyers and sellers properly to connect supply and demand." The Priceline invention helps resolve the intractable problem of "unfilled demand and unused supply" through a system of buyer-driven electronic commerce.[51] Further, according to Priceline, no one had been able to practically solve this problem until its "name your price" methodology was introduced.

While there may be some merit to these arguments, critics of business method patents argue that these methods do not deserve a patent because they do not require major capital investments. There is a big difference between investing in the process to develop a new pharmaceutical product, which can sometimes cost up to $1 billion, and investing in a method for an online business. Patents also limit competition on the Web. Expedia's situation is a case in point—its foray in to the online C2B travel business was delayed by the Priceline lawsuit, and if Priceline wins, Priceline could monopolize this segment of Internet commerce. In addition, companies developing new business models must be constantly on the alert so that they do not inadvertently infringe on registered business patents. These administrative transaction costs amount to a waste of resources and an impediment to innovation. Finally, from a purely economic perspective, business method patents are costly since they allow companies to reap monopoly rents, which leads to a deadweight loss of consumer surplus for society. Hence, unless the benefits of these patents clearly outweighs these costs, it is difficult to make the case that a policy supporting cyberpatents is really welfare-enhancing.

The future of cyberpatents is unclear due to their controversial nature. Some Internet companies argue that they do foster innovation and growth, but others observe that the Internet and the Web took shape without the need for these patents. It is always possible, but by no means likely, that Congress will intervene and prohibit these patents or raise the standard for innovation. Regardless of what the future holds for cyberpatents, they certainly raise many questions. The critical question is whether these patents are really necessary to stimulate innovation in cyberspace. Will future Internet companies be constrained by the lack of patent protection for their innovations? Will investors and venture capitalists be less forthcoming unless they can be assured that the companies in which they invest have exploited patent protection and safeguarded their intellectual assets?

▶ Domain Names and Interconnectivity Issues

The emergence of the World Wide Web has created a number of new ethical disputes. Some of these disputes involve domain names for Web sites while others arise from the interconnected nature of the Web. Everyone recognizes that the Web is greatly enhanced by the ability to link to other sites, but when do unauthorized hyperlinks become a problem from a moral or legal stand point?

Ownership of Domain Names

Every Internet Web site is identified by a unique domain name such as www.disney.com. A domain name is equivalent to a telephone number or an electronic address. The names were originally distributed by a company called Network Solutions on a first-come, first-served basis for a fee. In the year 2000, the oversight of domain name distribution was handed over to a nonprofit organization known as ICANN (see Chapter 2).

As one would expect, there have already been numerous domain name disputes. One of the problems that has frequently arisen is known as the twins phenomenon, where two parties have a legitimate claim to the same name. Several years ago, Hasbro Inc. prevailed in a legal dispute against Internet Entertainment Group (IEG) in its efforts to lay claim to www.candyland.com. This domain name was first secured by IEG when Web sites were relatively novel and not widely used by private industries. Hasbro holds a trademark on this famous children's board game and maintained that IEGs Web site of the same name, which featured pornographic material, was a clear case of trademark dilution.

The second major problem is caused by *parasites*. Parasites operate by registering a name quite similar to a famous name in order to piggyback on its allure and recognition. For example, someone might try to register a domain name such as www.disneysgreat.com in order to take commercial advantage of Disney's valuable brand name by luring unsuspecting users who believe that it has an official affiliation with Disney to this Web site.

The third problem is *cybersquatting*. Cybersquatters are individuals who unscrupulously register certain domain names in order to resell them to organizations that have a claim to the same name for which they own the legal trademark. One resourceful cybersquatter registered the domain names based on the names of major investment banks, such as jpmorganonline.com. Some of these banks paid thousands of dollars to reclaim these names.

The issues generated by these domain name controversies tend to be mired in legal niceties, but there are certainly moral considerations at stake. At the core of most disputes is a conflict between legitimate claims of trademark owners and the free speech rights of aspiring domain name owners. Should the property right in a trademark hold sway in cyberspace as it does in real space? And, if so, at what point does the proprietary right of a trademark begin to encroach upon free speech rights?

The issues are complicated but we can begin to sort them out by the examination of two case studies. Consider, for instance, the Web site called www.scientology-kills.net., which carries some trenchant criticism of the scientology movement and peddles t-shirts with the same epithet. Scientology has sued this Colorado Web site owner for trademark violation, claiming that this domain name "dilutes the distinctiveness of the mark," which could "tarnish the reputation of the owner."[52] The free speech issue at stake is whether or not the domain name *itself* expresses a viewpoint or opinion. In this case does "scientology-kills.net" constitute an editorial comment about scientology that should not be suppressed?

The normative and legal issues in this case are difficult to disentangle. The legal issue is dilution, but whether this sort of criticism amounts to dilution is a matter of debate. Should domain names be allowed to express a negative opinion as long as they do not deceive or mislead visitors to their site? Is this a reasonable place to draw the line in these disputes?

A strong case can be made that suppressing the "scientology kills" domain name would set a dangerous precedent. The domain name is becoming a medium for expressing one's opinions and this should be acceptable as long as one does so within certain parameters, that is, without being deceptive, defamatory, and without seeking commercial gains by the unfair leveraging of another's trademark. The domain name in question is making an observation that Scientology is a dangerous movement; it is an inflammatory remark expressing a debatable and controversial opinion, but it seems to be within the bounds of one's right to free expression.

To be sure, a trademark is an important property right, a valuable social good that is one side of this moral equation. But on the other side is the normative starting point of the First Amendment right to free speech. Arguably, a Web site that is a.) not deceiving visitors or seeking commercial gain through its parody of a trademark, and b.) responsibly expressing an opinion without defamation, should be allowed to use trademarked names like "scientology" as part of a domain name that expresses an idea or particular viewpoint. There may be cases where dilution is so material that it does become morally relevant and those cases must be judged accordingly, but overall the common interest would seem to be served by giving the benefit of the doubt in some of these disputes to the weightier claim of free speech.

In a different case, Steve Brodsky, an orthodox Jew from New Jersey, established a Web site called www.jewsforjesus.org. The site had no affiliation with the Jews for Jesus movement, which embraces Jesus as the Messiah and seeks to convert Jews to Christianity. This site, however, proclaimed the following message: The answers you seek are already within your faith. It also provided a link to a site called Jewish Outreach, which reinforced the theological principles of the Jewish faith. The Jews for Jesus organization, whose actual Web site has the domain name, www.jews-for-jesus.org, sued for trademark infringement and won the case. Brodsky was enjoined from using his domain name.

Although similar to the scientology domain name case, this case has some new wrinkles and is fraught with a lesser degree of moral ambiguity. In the scientology case, there was no allegation that the domain name itself was deceptive. But according to the Jews for Jesus organization, Brodsky's domain name was blatantly deceptive and had undoubtedly been chosen for the sole purpose of intercepting those looking for the legitimate Web site of Jews for Jesus. They maintained that this was akin to false advertising, since Brodsky was representing his Web site as something that it wasn't. But defenders of Brodsky argue that his use of this domain name should be protected by the First Amendment. Brodsky is not selling a product or a service, but expressing an idea. They contend that in this case, trademark law is being invoked to quash free expression. It is difficult to see, however, how Brodsky's domain name, which differs only in punctuation from the Jews for Jesus domain name, expresses an opinion, and hence the free speech defense appears to be on shaky ground.

These two cases are representative of the many disputes that will continue to arise as users stake out property rights in their domain names. One of ICANN's first major initiatives was to develop a procedure for handling trademark disputes, called the Uniform Dispute Resolution Procedure or UDRP. The UDRP has established certain criteria to determine whether an organization has the right to a domain name. The complainant must prove that "the domain name is identical to or confusingly similar to a trademark or service mark to which it has rights." The complainant must also demonstrate that the registered domain name is being used in bad faith. Paragraph 4(b) of the UDRP lists four circumstances as evidence of bad faith:

(i) the domain name was registered primarily for the purpose of selling it to the complainant or a competitor for more than the documented out-of-pocket expenses related to the name; or

(ii) the domain name was registered in order to prevent the mark owner from using it, provided that the registrant has engaged in a pattern of such registration; or

(iii) the domain was registered primarily to disrupt the business of a competitor; or

(iv) by using the domain, the registrant has intentionally attempted to attract users for commercial gain by creating a likelihood of confusion as to source or affiliation.[53]

UDRP seems like a reasonable response to the cybersquatting problem as long as the definition of "bad faith" is not interpreted too broadly so that legitimate free speech rights are impaired. Many credit the UDRP with eliminating the most flagrant forms of cybersquatting, and the procedures are generally regarded as equitable. Nonetheless, according to a recent 2001 study, 81 percent of the cases have been decided in favor of the complainant, that is, the party that holds the trademark.[54] It is difficult to draw any real conclusions from this study without looking at each individual case, but it suggests one requires a pretty convincing case to prevail against the trademark holder.

Linking and Framing

At the heart of the Web's interconnectivity is the simple but ubiquitous hyperlink. By clicking on pieces of text or images known as hypertext links, a user could easily move from one HTML document to another. This is one of the most beneficial features of the Internet because it greatly facilitates online research, along with the ability of users to navigate the diffuse offerings on the Web. But should Web page authors have an unrestricted right to link to HTML documents on other Web sites? When does linking violate copyright laws and thereby infringe on property rights?

Some of the problems associated with freewheeling Internet linking surfaced in the *Ticketmaster v. Microsoft* case of 1997. Ticketmaster sued Microsoft, claiming that the "Seattle Sidewalk" guide on Microsoft's Web site provided links that infringed its trademark because it "circumvented the beginning pages of Ticketmaster's Web site, which displays advertisements, products, and services of entities with which Ticketmaster contracts, and ... linked directly to the subsidiary pages of the Web site." In other words, Ticketmaster did not necessarily object to the link itself; rather, it protested the way the link was done because it bypassed the home page and went directly to a subsidiary page within the Ticketmaster Web site. This practice has become known as *deep linking*. According to one analysis, "This case raises the question of whether site proprietors may dictate to others how and where to link their pages."[55]

From a legal standpoint, it can be argued with some plausibility that the trademark infringement allegation has some merit. Linking to a position within a Web site and bypassing the home page may convey to the casual user that there is one site instead of two because it may give the impression of being a seamless whole. There could therefore be some blurring of the property lines in the consumer's mind.

Aside from the legal questions, there are more transcendent normative questions—should there be an absolute right to link on the Internet? Those who support this position maintain that a link is merely a convenient pointer to another site, to information that is publicly available on the Internet. They also contend that putting a Web site online constitutes implicit permission to allow links from other Web sites.

However, the position that Web site authors have an inherent right to link to any other Web site in any manner possible may go too far. To begin with, a hyperlink is more than a pointer since activating the link actually delivers the linked Web page to one's browser. This is clearly different from just listing an address or a phone number and may increase the Web publisher's liability. For instance, what if the target Web site contains defamatory material? Are the Web sites linking to that site and delivering pages to their users also responsible for disseminating that defamatory content? Is there a moral or legal duty to review a site before establishing a link?

None of these issues have been properly sorted out and there are few legal precedents to offer guidance. Clearer legal guidelines will probably emerge from future lawsuits that resolve some of these matters. But how might we assess linking from a strictly moral point of view? This is a complex and multifaceted question so we will confine our analysis to two issues: (1) is there an unequivocal right to link to other Web sites in cyberspace in any manner whatsoever; and (2) is the Web site publisher who links to another site morally accountable in any way for the content of that second site?

Beyond any doubt, linking is a valuable social good that is consistent with the chief purpose of the Internet: open communication and the seamless availability of information. In most cases, linking should be encouraged, and it should not be necessary to seek permission every time a link is made to another Web site. Rather, it seems reasonable to assume that participation in the World Wide Web implies permission to link. But it does not imply an unrestricted right to link to any site in any manner. The relevant moral principle here seems to be *autonomy*. If autonomy is duly respected, Web site publishers will refrain from imposing their activities on unwilling parties. Organizations that want to share in the benefits of the Internet should not be required to completely relinquish their autonomy when they are setting up a Web page. There must be some limits on the activity of linking in order to fully respect the autonomy of Web site publishers. It seems reasonable to assume that most Web sites do not mind incoming links but if a Web site makes it quite explicit that it does not want any incoming links or desires to license those links, this preference should be honored. In addition, a Web site should also be able to dictate the specific terms of how those links will be constructed—a site may have good reasons for forbidding deep linking, such as the loss of eyeballs for advertising on the home page, which translates into a loss of revenues. Thus, in the Microsoft–Ticketmaster dispute, Microsoft should have respected Ticketmaster's preference to have the link made to the home page instead of a subsidiary page. These simple constraints on linking will balance the public good with the autonomy of Web site producers.

This brings us to the more difficult question of liability—should we hold Web site publishers accountable for any defamatory or illegal material at the linked Web site? On the one hand, the Web site publisher is delivering the content of the second page to the user's browser and so is contributing in a direct way to the dissemination of the defamatory material. Yet it does seem burdensome to expect a Web site publisher to be intimately familiar with the material on the target Web sites to which it links. There must be some level of responsibility here, but it is quite difficult to fix precisely what that level should be. For example, if a teacher sets up a civics class Web site for a high school and inadvertently links to a Web site with pornography (for instance, www.whitehouse.com instead of www.whitehouse.gov), and that pornography is not concealed in some obscure location on that Web site, it is reasonable to conclude that he shares some blame for misdirecting these students. In general, then, a Web site publisher should have at a minimum a general familiarity with the contents of the sites to which he is linking. It is not too burdensome to expect a cursory overview of the site, but it does seem extreme to require intimate knowledge of all the subsidiary pages. The moral principle "ought implies can" is apposite here.

Thus, in summary, responsible and prudent linking policies would encompass the following: avoid linking to sites that explicitly prohibit such linking; link in the manner requested by the site to which one is linking; have a general familiarity with the content of the linked site in order to avoid misdirecting one's users; and, finally, avoid any impression or indication that the linkage implies an endorsement in any way of one's own products or services.

Ticketmaster and Microsoft settled their lawsuit out of court in early 1999, and both parties agreed not to disclose the terms of the settlement. But Microsoft did agree to point visitors to the Ticketmaster home page instead of a page deep within the Ticketmaster site. The legal community hoped that this case would establish a precedent on linking, but that has not happened. As a consequence, there is still some ambiguity about the legal propriety of deep linking.

Another practice related to linking is known as *framing*. This occurs when a Web page creator designs a Web page that always displays a frame containing the name of the Web site and other identifying marks, such as a logo. This frame stays on the screen when the user views content at the framed site so that whenever the user links to another site, he always sees the name and logo at the originating Web site. A lawsuit filed by the *Journal Gazette* in Fort Wayne, Indiana against the Ft-Wayne.com

Web site alleges that the site's framing technique is equivalent to theft of its material. The Web site linked to articles in the paper and by using framing, "altered the display of the newspaper's article by placing its own ads and site address in the browser window."[56]

According to Dyson, this sort of framing "harms the content provider trying to sell advertising or simply wanting to maintain its own identity."[57] Those who are the "victims" of framing such as the *Journal Gazette* often allege unfair competition and claim that framing can confuse users regarding the connection between the framed site and the framing site. Those who practice framing contend that they are merely providing a convenient one-stop-shopping service to their users and that there is no damage to the framed site There have been no court rulings on whether framing is a lawful activity.

Metatags

Metatags are invisible codes that are incorporated into HTML code, that is, the hypertext markup language that is used to construct Web sites. The name is derived from the practice of "tagging" all of the objects on a Web page—for example, the title of the page is included within title tags. Metatags represent a brief description or summary of a Web page's contents, usually no longer than one or two words. The Web page for the Museum of Fine Arts (MFA) in Boston might include the following metatags to describe its Web page: MFA, art museum, Boston, Museum of Fine Arts, etc. Although these codes cannot be seen by the user, they will be recognized by most search engines looking for specific sites. If someone enters the search term "MFA" into Yahoo or some other search engine, one of the Web sites retrieved will be the site for the Museum of Fine Arts in Boston. For some search engines, the more times a term appears in a metatag the more prominence that site is given when the list is returned to the user.

Since metatags are virtually nontransparent, their use is difficult to monitor. How can we be sure that a Web site has "tagged" its contents accurately and honestly? According to Meek Jun, "Meta tags often contain popular search terms that have little or nothing to do with the content of the relevant HTML page but are nevertheless inserted for purposes of luring Internet users to a particular Web site."[58]

The legal battle waged between Terri Welles and Playboy Enterprises Inc. epitomized the high stakes involved in the use of metatags. Ms. Welles was a Playboy centerfold model in 1981 and she now operates a Web site that features photos of herself and other models, biographical material, and a personal appearance calendar. The site's metatags include the words "Playmate" and "Playboy." Playboy Enterprises objected to this, contending that the Playmate or Playboy metatag implied an ongoing affiliation with the "Playboy empire." Welles's use of this tag, they argued, would confuse users who would be misdirected to her site instead of those directly connected to Playboy Enterprises.

When Welles refused to desist from using the tag, the company filed a $5 million trademark infringement suit. It also sought an injunction preventing Welles from using the Playboy trademark. But Judge Judith Keep refused to grant Playboy its injunction, concluding that use of terms like "Playmate" on Welles's Web site was fair use (*Playboy v. Terri Welles* Civ. No. C-97-3204 N. D. Cal [1997]). The ruling stipulated that Welles "could use the trademarked terms in her meta tag because they accurately reflected the contents of her site."[59] Playboy appealed, but the Ninth Circuit Court of Appeals refused to hear the case and so the original ruling stands.

The Welles case may well establish a firm legal precedent, but some argue that a more nuanced legal solution will be essential if metatags are not to be abused. Just because a trademarked name reflects the contents of a Web page, does that mean that it can then be used as a tag? If I write extensively about the Boston Celtics on my amateur sports news Web page, does that mean that I should be allowed to embed the phrase "Boston Celtics" in the site's metatags? This is a legitimate interpretation of Judge Keep's ruling, but users might be ill-served by granting such wide latitude in the use of terms as metatags. On the other hand, in this test case, Welles has done more than merely write about Playmates. She has had a direct and prolonged affiliation with this organization, which does give her Web site a certain credibility. Therefore, one could argue that this makes her right to the use of these terms as metatags more compelling.

As we have intimated, a serious moral problem that often emerges in the employment of metatags is deception. For example, some Web site developers use the trademarks of more established competitors, seeking to exploit the equity of a brand name. If company A is selling a new brand of women's clothing online, it might embed the term "Talbot's" among its metatag keywords to steer users looking for the Talbot's Web site to its own Web site. This practice has been labeled as "search engine baiting." When metatags are clearly being utilized only to deceive and mislead users, the case against them is morally unambiguous. Tags should not be casually used to fool search engines and lure unsuspecting users from the sites they were seeking. This amounts to false advertising that can cause confusion among consumers.

Consider also other related, controversial practices such as *spamdexing*. Spamdexers list metatag keywords multiple times so that search engines relying on the frequency of terms in a metatag as part of their search algorithm will be more inclined to place their Web site closer to the top of its retrieved list of hits.

To make matters worse, some search engines have become complicit in metatag abuse by selling "keyed banner ads." Some search engines sell keywords to advertisers so that when that particular keyword is entered as a search term, a banner ad for the company that has purchased the keyword appears above the search results. Advertisers can purchase generic keywords such as "toys," which is typically not a problem. But they can also purchase a competitor's trademark. Assume that an online toy company (let's call it "KidsStuff") purchases the Disney trademark from a particular search engine so that when a user enters the search term "Disney," they will see the KidsStuff banner ad above the list of retrieved sites.[60]

In all likelihood, this questionable practice of keying a banner ad to a competitor's trademark constitutes a violation of the Lanham Act. But are consumers deceived by this practice? Let's assume that I am looking for the online Disney store to buy some toys; I enter "Disney" as a search term and what is returned is a list of sites matching the term. Although Disney is on the list, closer to the top is KidsStuff.com (thanks to spamdexing) and above the list is a bold banner ad for KidsStuff. Will people take the bait and check out KidsStuff on the way to the Disney store? Galbraith argues that many will take this detour due to the force of *inertia marketing*. According to this theory, "Search engine users will take the first and most convenient route to the solution of their task."[61] Although the law here is unsettled, one could argue that KidsStuff's actions violate the Lanham Act because it uses a trademark without permission; moreover, it uses that trademark to free ride on the substantial brand equity of Disney. This fictitious company's actions are also questionable from a moral perspective. The company appears to be guilty of deception by diverting people looking for the Disney site. It has arguably violated the common moral principle "do not deceive," and there is little moral justification for such deception aside from purely self-serving interests. Although a sale may never even occur at KidsStuff, it has created "initial interest confusion," and benefited improperly from the brand equity of another company.[62]

Thus, just as there is bad faith use of trademarks in domain names, there can be bad faith use of trademarks in metatags. There are, however, many tough cases like the one involving Ms. Welles and Playboy Enterprises. This is surely not a straightforward case of deception. The keywords like Playboy are not being used to create a false impression of an affiliation with Playboy since there was some affiliation in the past that lends credibility to Welles' descriptive summary of her current activities. Trademarks should be safeguarded, but not at the expense of valid free speech rights.

Creative Integrity

The final issue under consideration is being termed *creative integrity* since it involves the ability of authors to maintain control over their artistic and literary works on the Internet. Digitized artistic works are inherently plastic and easily manipulated. Users can transform and recreate digital images that they encounter on the Internet and to retransmit those images throughout cyberspace. They can digitally edit photographs, videos, or even online art works.

Do such re-creative activities violate trademark and copyright laws? Do they infringe upon a creators well-deserved property rights? Should authors have the prerogative to prevent the digital manipulation and editing of their materials on the Internet? Or is such activity a valid way for someone to interact with a digital work?

An infamous case that has brought some of these issues to the forefront is the "Distorted Barbie." This represents a Web art reproduction of Barbie that has been digitally modified as a commentary on the Barbie doll icon of American culture. The artist who created this is Mark Napier, and on a Web site sponsored by his supporters, one can find the following description of his creation:

> Artist Mark Napier is the author and creator of The Distorted Barbie, a Web-based exploration in words and images of the impact Barbie and all her baggage have had on our bodies and culture. The site is a poetic and potent piece of Internet art.

Barbie's "owner," the Mattel toy company, was not convinced by any of this "poetry." It strongly protested and demanded that this distorted Barbie be immediately removed form Napier's Web site, called Interport. Mattel and its lawyers have invoked the moral rights defense. *Moral rights,* a translation of the French term *droit moral*, bestows on an author control over the fate of his or her works. In the United States, moral rights are protected by the law embodied in the Visual Artists Rights Act of 1990 (VARA), which applies only to the visual arts. According to VARA, a creator has the right to prevent revision, modification, or distortion of his or her work. The visual arts protected by VARA include: paintings, drawings, prints, sculptures, and photographs taken to be shown at an exhibition. VARA protects works only of "recognized stature."

VARA gives an author two basic rights: the right of attribution and the right of integrity. The right of attribution protects an author's work from being attributed to someone else. The right of integrity bars distortion or alteration that might impair the author's reputation or stature as an artist. But should VARA apply to the distorted Barbie or to other digital works?

Here again we encounter the familiar conflict between property rights and free speech, which has been a common theme in the last two chapters. Napier's site is not seeking commercial gains from Barbie and it would appear that his creation is a form of art. Hence at the present time, it seems to be a legitimate form of fair use, similar in some ways to Andy Warhol's reproductions of Brillo boxes and Campbell's soup cans. Like Warhol, Napier is simply using popular commercial products as the raw material and inspiration for his artistic endeavors. It seems perfectly logical in this age "where girls bond with Barbie and dream of broadcast exploits of Sabrina the teenage witch" that this would become the stuff of creative activity.[63] In certain key respects the distorted Barbie, however offensive some may find it, offers a valuable commentary on this era not for commercial gains but for its own sake. A strong case can be made that such artistic impulses should not be stifled by excessively broad copyright and trademark restrictions.

We admit that the Distorted Barbie is one of many tough cases that make it so difficult to sustain that precarious but necessary balance between fair use and intellectual property protection. But suppression of artistic reproductions based on commercial icons seems to err on the side of overprotecting the Internet.

▶ Postscript

The astute reader will recognize something paradoxical about the trends in intellectual property protection. On the one hand, digital information is facilely duplicated and transmitted in cyberspace. The Internet's original architecture, predicated upon content-blind packet switching, is largely responsible for this. This open architecture has posed a great threat to the movie and music industries, which are becoming increasingly anxious about their ability to protect their intellectual investments. On the other hand, new technologies and restrictive laws are conspiring to enclose information, to contain it more thoroughly than ever before. Laws like the DMCA and the Sony Bono Copyright Term Extension Act overprotect intellectual property and advance the copyright maximalist agenda to the chagrin of those who want openness and free-flowing information on the Net. Cyberpatents broaden the scope of patent protection in a way that threatens to stifle innovation. And digital rights architectures can control the distribution of digital information so tightly that they virtually preclude fair use and first sale.

As we have implied, these laws are misconceived and need some revision, and digital rights architectures must be sensitive to well-established values such as fair use. At the same time, a strong case can be put forth that we still need reasonable intellectual property protection. For many reasons, it would be impractical to transform cyberspace into a copyright-free zone, as some have glibly proposed. We need laws that have a sense of measure and proportionality. In Aristotle's terminology, the goal of regulators should be to "hit the mark" and not to fail through excess (*hyperbole*) or defect (*elleipsis*), that is, to avoid overly strong or feeble protections. In a world where intellectual property has such exceptional value, the challenge to get it right could not be more important.

Discussion Questions

1. What limits, if any, should there be on a user's right to link to other Web sites? Should there be laws clarifying and protecting the right to link?
2. What is the significance of the open code movement? Comment on the pros and cons of open code software.
3. Explain how trademark ownership can conflict with free speech rights. How should these competing claims be resolved?
4. Comment on this observation from Esther Dyson's essay entitled "Intellectual Property on the Net": "The issue isn't that intellectual property laws should (or will) disappear; rather, they will simply become less important in the scheme of things." [64]

Cases

The www.nga Domain Name Dispute

The National Gun Association [NGA] of America is a powerful lobbying organization established over fifty years ago to protect the public's constitutional right to own firearms. The organization has millions of members concentrated in the western and southern regions of the country. It has a strong presence in Washington D.C., where it advocates against efforts to restrict the right to own a gun. The NGA's vocal support of that right has spawned opposition groups that believe the NGA helps contribute to a climate of violence through its encouragement of gun ownership.

The NGA has a Web site, www.nga.org, where it disseminates information on the right to bear arms and other issues related to gun ownership and gun control. The site also informs members about impending legislation and advises them how to register their opinions with elected officials. The Web site is quite popular with members and averages over 25,000 hits a day.

One of the more radical groups opposing the NGA, called Pacifists for Gun Control (PGC), has set up a nonprofit organization that distributes literature and organizes its own lobbying efforts. It has created a Web site for which it was able to secure the domain name www.nga-assassins.org. The PGC has admitted that one purpose in using this domain name is to intercept users looking for www.nga.org. In its keyword metatag it uses "National Gun Association," and "NGA." Its home page has the following message:

Don't be fooled by the NGA.

Look here to see the damage that guns can really do!

The PGC's Web site is filled with material on the perils of gun ownership and the virtues of gun controls, particularly for automatic weapons and handguns. There are also links to other sites that discuss the excesses and the tendentious views of the NGA. Through the contents of this Web page, the PGC seeks to convert gun owners and others sympathetic to the NGA's objectives to its ideological views regarding violence and fire arms.

The NGA would like to block the use of this domain name on the grounds that it is deceptive and misleading. It also believes that its trademark "NGA" has been violated and diluted. The PGC contends that it is merely exercising its free speech rights and that this domain name is expressing an editorial comment about the NGA. It is using this derivative domain name to help propagate its political ideas about gun ownership. It also points out that NGA members who might be temporarily diverted to this site can easily move on to the real NGA Web site, so no harm is done.

The NGA is considering its options—perhaps it should pursue a lawsuit for trademark infringement or file a claim with ICANN.

Questions

1. Is this a free speech issue? Does the PGC have any right to use this domain name?
2. Assume that the NGA files a claim with ICANN and this dispute is subjected to the UDRP. Which side would prevail based on the UDRP's criteria?

Patent War on the Web: Amazon vs. Barnes & Noble

Rarely do patents awarded by the United States Patent and Trademark Office attract much attention. But patent no. 5,960,411 ("411"), awarded to Amazon.com in September, 1999, has stirred some controversy. The patent in question was granted for Amazon's "one-click" ordering system, which was introduced by Amazon in September, 1997. Thanks to this system, a consumer can complete a transaction over an electronic network by utilizing only a "single action," typically the click of a computer mouse. Amazon.com, a leading purveyor of online books, videos, music, and many other products, developed this model to improve upon its shopping cart model of making online purchases whereby users would add items to the virtual shopping cart, then proceed to a checkout screen. At the checkout screen, the user verifies the shipping address, fills in or checks over billing and credit card information, selects shipping preference, and then clicks to execute the order. The one-click system reduces the sequence of steps at the checkout screen to one step after the user has selected the items for purchase. According to the patent application: "The single-action ordering system of the present invention reduces the number of purchaser interactions needed to place an order and reduces the amount of sensitive information that is transmitted between a client system and a server system."[65] This assumes, of course, that the user has visited the Amazon site before and has provided necessary shipping and billing information that is kept on file by Amazon.

In May, 1998, Barnes & Noble (BN), Amazon's main competitor in the online book business, launched its own expedited ordering system known as "Express Lane." It was widely recognized that Express Lane was a "me-too response as [BN] continues to lag behind Amazon."[66] BN's model relies on a product page that contains a description of the items the user would like to purchase and from that page the user can place the order. Like Amazon's model, "only a single action need be taken to complete the purchase order once the product page is displayed."[67]

Amazon immediately took BN to court and sought a preliminary injunction preventing them from using this Express Lane functionality since it was in violation of patent 411. BN claimed that there were serious questions about the validity of the 411 patent and it argued that the injunction was not warranted since there was not a reasonable likelihood of Amazon's success based on the merits of its case. But Judge Marsha Pechman of the U.S. District Court for the Western District of Washington disagreed with BN, and in December, 1999, she granted the preliminary injunction sought by Amazon. Barnes & Noble was forced to add a second "verification" step in order to maintain Express Lane.

The decision was not well received in the software industry. Richard Stallman, president of the Free Software Foundation, organized a boycott of Amazon. And critics like publisher Tim O'Reilly challenged Amazon CEO Jeff Bezos in the press. In an interview with *The Wall Street Journal*, O'Reilly said "What I find most offensive about business-method patents is that fundamentally they allow somebody to patent an idea. . . . This is at odds with so much that we hold sacred."[68] Bezos responded by arguing that while business method patents were valid and necessary, they should only have a duration of three to five years. This was a compromise position, but in most statements Bezos left little doubt that the one-click technique was a legitimate patent. According to Bezos, "We spent thousands of hours to develop our 1-Click process, and the reason we have a patent system in this country is to encourage people to take these kinds of risks."[69]

Barnes & Noble appealed Judge Pechman's ruling to the U.S. Court of Appeals for the Federal Circuit. The Appeals Court concluded in February, 2001 that "BN has raised substantial questions as to the validity of the '411 patent.'"[70] Consequently it vacated the injunction and it remanded the case for trial to U.S. District Court.

Questions:

1. Does the Amazon one-click method meet the standards for a valid patent?
2. Do you agree with Bezos's suggestion that cyberpatents (or business-method patents) should only last for three to five years?
3. Are online patents such as the ones awarded to Amazon and Priceline necessary for "the progress of science and the useful arts" in the context of cyberspace? Which philosophical theory best supports your position?
4. Some say that Amazon and other Internet companies like Priceline are adapting old ideas to a new forum. Should a company be allowed to get a patent for doing this?

Morpheus: The Next Napster?

Music City is a privately held Tennessee software company that develops and distributes peer-to-peer file-sharing software. The product is called Morpheus. Along with Kazaa, Music City has licensed the peer-to-peer infrastructure program from a Dutch company called Fast Track. Fast Track is a distinctive peer-to-peer technology that relies on supernodes. These supernodes are computers within the P2P network, but they are extremely fast systems with high bandwidth connections. These features make them well suited to route and distribute requests for files. Unlike P2P networks such as Gnutella, where requests are sent to other peers on the network (and those peers are all equal), peers on this Fastrack platform send requests to supernodes in order to search and download content. As a result of this innovative approach, Fast Track's performance is far superior to the performance of Gnutella, which has a difficult time supporting more than 100,000 simultaneous users without performance degradation.[71]

Morpheus and Kazaa are both growing rapidly in popularity, especially after Napster's sudden demise. Morpheus now claims 20 million clients who use the system to transport copyrighted music and to "swap pirated TV shows and films over the Internet."[72] And 64 million people have downloaded Kazaa.

Morpheus has been compared to Napster since it enables users to search and download music files. But the Morpheus architecture has some notable differences. Morpheus users do not connect to a central MusicCity server. Rather Music City gives its users on the Morpheus network the addresses of supernodes. The *supernode* is just another Morpheus user who has a high bandwidth connection; that computer serves as the file directory server. According to Truelove, these supernodes are "conceptually equivalent to Napster indexing servers," since they keep track of music files and their locations on the network.[73]

Music City provides the supernode addresses to members of the Morpheus network. In later versions of Morpheus (1.2 and 1.3), the supernode addresses are included with the client software, so there is no longer a need to connect to Music City's server to receive those addresses. That list is revised and updated automatically each time a user connects to a supernode.[74]

The Morpheus P2P network based on the Fast Track platform has multiple uses. Software producers can use it to distribute their software products while amateur movie producers, photographers, and other artists can deploy this technology to distribute their digital works. Like other P2P networks, the Fast Track software "cannot differentiate between copyrighted and non-copyrighted material transferred over a network created with the software."[75] Hence it is similar to the Web's underlying protocol, http, which allows users to download Web pages regardless of their copyright status.

The music and movie industries have claimed that Music City and Kazaa BV are culpable of contributory and vicarious copyright infringement. Worried about the impending Napsterization of films, the Motion Picture Association of America (MPAA) has file a lawsuit against the principal suppliers of Fast Track products including Grokster, Kazaa BV, and Music City. The plaintiff claims that the software is a tool used for the wholesale piracy of videos and music. In the case of *Metro-Golwyn-Mayer Studios Inc., et al. v. Grokster, Ltd., et al.,* the main issue will be whether or not Music City has the same moral and legal liability of Napster. Music City contends that it is simply a software company without any direct involvement in the file-swapping of its users. While the Morpheus network of users employs the company's software, that network functions independently of Music City servers. Music City's only role is to provide supernode addresses to those who download the software. On its Web site, the company seeks to immunize itself from liability by pointing out that its users are searching a "public network" over which it has no control. Users do not connect to the Music City servers in order to share files with one another. In their response to the allegations of copyright infringement, Kazaa and Music City present the following argument: "Like the makers of a Web browser who do not control the sites being browsed, or the e-mail software providers who do not monitor the attachment to its users' messages, Kazaa [and Music City] simply provide a data-sharing software application and a peer-to-peer software stack without monitoring the specific data being shared or controlling its users' behavior."[76]

Questions

1. Do you agree with Music City's position that they should not be held liable for the copyright infringement of Morpheus users?

2. Jack Valenti, head of the MPAA, was reported to be quite distraught when he heard that Stanford students were downloading pirated movies. His comment was, "There's a great deal of thievery going on on college campuses."[77] Do you agree with Mr. Valenti's characterization of these activities? Are Morpheus users guilty of "thievery" when they download copyrighted video or music files?

References

1. Pamela Samuelson and Hal Varian, "The 'New Economy' and Information Technology Policy," Working Paper, University of California, Berkeley, July 18, 2001.
2. Pamela Samuelson, "Confab Clips Copyright Cartel," *Wired*, 5.03, March 1997, p.62.
3. Esther Dyson, *Release 2.0* (New York: Broadway Books, 1997).
4. Nicholas Negroponte, *Being Digital* (New York: Alfred A. Knopf, 1995), p. 58.
5. National Research Council, *The Digital Dilemma: Intellectual Property in the Information Age* (Washington, D.C.: National Research Council, 2000).
6. A.M. Honore, "Ownership," in A.G. Guest (ed.), *Oxford Essays in Jurisprudence* (Oxford: Oxford University Press, 1961), p. 108.
7. James DeLong, *Property Matters* (New York: The Free Press, 1997), p. 340.
8. *U.S. Constitution*, Article I, § 8, clause 8.
9. 17 U.S.C. § 106.
10. Paul Goldstein, *Copyright's Highway* (New York: Hill & Wang, 1994), p. 20.
11. William Fisher, "Business Method Patents Online," March, 2000; available at: http://eon.law.harvard.edu/property00/patents.
12. Henri Hanneman, *The Patentability of Computer Software* (Deventer, The Netherlands: Kluwer Academic Publishers, 1985), p. 87.
13. Background material in this section was found in Joe Liu, "Overview of Trademark Law"; available at http://cyber.harvard.edu/law.
14. John Locke, *The Second Treatise of Government* (Indianapolis: Bobbs-Merrill, 1952), II: 20.
15. Justin Hughes, "The Philosophy of Intellectual Property" in *Intellectual Property*, ed. A. Moore, (Lanham, MD: Rowman & Littlefield, 1997), pp. 107–177.
16. Robert Nozick, *Anarchy, State and Utopia* (New York: Basic Books, 1974).
17. *Mazer v. Stein*, 347 U.S. 201 [1954].
18. G.W.F. Hegel, *Philosophy of Right*, (trans. T. Knox) (New York: Oxford University Press, 1967), p. 40.
19. Hughes, "The Philosophy of Intellectual Property," p. 144.
20. Ibid.
21. See William Fisher "Property and Contract on the Internet.," 1998; available at http://cyber.law.harvard.edu/ipcoop/98fish.html
22. James Boyle, *Shamans, Software and Spleens: Law and the Construction of the Information Society* (Cambridge, MA: Harvard University Press, 1996). p. 23.
23. For more about Boyle's important book, see my review of *Shamans, Software and Spleens* which appears in *Ethics and Information Technology*, vol. 1, no. 2 1999, pp. 161–163. Some of the material here is drawn from that review.
24. Jane Ginsburg, "Copyright Legislation for the 'Digital Millennium,'" 23 *Columbia-VLA Journal of Law and the Arts*, 137, 1999.
25. Pamela Samuelson, "Intellectual Property and the Digital Economy: Why the Anti-Circumvention Regulations Need to be Revised," 14 *Berkeley Tech. Law Journal* 519, 1999.
26. T.S. Eliot, "Tradition and the Individual Talent," *Selected Essays* (New York: Harcourt Brace, 1950), p. 4.

27. *United Christian Scientists v. Christian Science Board of Directors*, 829 F.2d 1152 (D.C. Cir. [1987]).

28. William Fisher, "Digital Music: Problems and Possibilities," 2000; available at http://www.law.harvard.edu/Academic_Affairs/coursepages/tfisher/Music.

29. Plaintiffs Brief, *A&M Records v. Napster, Inc.* 2000 WL 573136 (N.D. Cal. [2000]).

30. United States Court of Appeals for the Ninth Circuit, *A&M Records et al. v. Napster*, 239 F.3d 1004 [2001].

31. *Harper & Row Publishers, Inc. v. Nation Enters*, 471 U.S., 539, 85 L. Ed. 2d 588 (1985).

32. Stephanie Greene, "Reconciling Napster with the Sony Decision and Recent Amendments to Copyright Law," 39 *American Business Law* 57, 2001.

33. *A&M Records, Inc. v. Napster*, 239 F. 3d 1004 (9th Cir. [2001]).

34. Ibid.

35. Quoted in John Alderman, *Sonic Boom: Napster, MP3 and the New Pioneers of Music* (Cambridge, MA: Perseus Books, 2001) p. 180.

36. For a more thorough treatment of this case, see "Note on the DeCSS Trial" in R. Spinello and H. Tavani (eds.) *Readings in Cyberethics* (Sudbury, MA: Jones & Bartlett, 2001), pp. 226–230.

37. *Universal City Studios, Inc. v. Reimerdes* 111 F. Suppl. 2d 294 (S.D.N.Y. [2000]).

38. Amy Harmon, "Free Speech Rights for Computer Code," *The New York Times*, July 31, 2000, p. C1.

39. Richard Stallman, "GNU Manifesto," 1985, www.gnu.org/manifesto.html.

40. Eric Raymond, "The Cathedral and the Bazaar." The latest version of this essay can be found at http://www.tuxedo.org/~esr/writings/cathedral-bazaar.

41. Andrew Leonard, "Open Season," *Wired*, May, 1999, p. 142.

42. Pamela Samuelson, et al., "A New View of Intellectual Property and Software," *Communications of the ACM*, vol. 39, no.3, 1996, p. 24.

43. Mark Stefik, "Trusted Systems," *Scientific American*, March 1997, p 79.

44. Raymond Ku, "The Creative Destruction of Copyright: Napster and the New Economies of Digital Technology," 69 *University of Chicago Law Review*, 2002.

45. *State Street Bank and Trust Co. v. Signature Financial Group, Inc.* 149 F. 3d 1368 [1998].

46. Ibid.

47. Kelly Higgins, "IT Exploits Patents to Protect E-Assets," *InternetWeek*, July 17, 2000, pp. 78–80.

48. Priceline.com Press Release, August 11, 1999; available at: http://www.corporate-ir.net.

49. Ibid.

50. Christopher Lewis, "What is a Cyberpatent's Value to Emerging e-Business," December, 1999; available at http://www.lclark.edu/~loren/cyberlaw99f.

51. Complaint, *Priceline.Com, Inc. v. Microsoft Corporation and Expedia, Inc.* (U.S. Dis Ct. Cn, [1999]).

52. Courtney Macavinta, "Scientologists in Trademark Dispute," *CNET News.com*, January 29, 1998.

53. Uniform Domain Name Dispute Resolution Policy [UDRP] (1999) available online at ICANN's Web site, http://www.icann.org.

54. Julia Angwin, "Are Domain Panels the Hanging Judges of Cyberspace Court?" *The Wall Street Journal*, August 20, 2001, p. B1.

55. Emily Madoff, "Freedom to Work Under Attack," *New York Law Journal*, June 23, 1997.

56. Carl Kaplan, "Lawsuit May Determine Whether Framing is Thieving," *Cyber Law Journal*, http://www.nytimes.com/library/tech/98/05/cyberlaw.

57. Esther Dyson, *Release 2.1* (New York: Random House, 1998), p. 199.

58. Meeka Jun, "Meta Tags: The Case of the Invisible Infringer," *The New York Law Journal*, October 24, 1997.

59. Carl Kaplan, "Former Playmate Wins Round in Fight over Web Site Labels," *Cyber Law Journal*, November 13, 1998; http://www.nytimes.com/library/tech/98/11/cyberlaw.

60. For a more detailed account, see Richard Spinello, "The Use and Abuse of Metatags," *Ethics and Information Technology*, vol. 4, no. 1, 2002, pp. 23–30.
61. Christine Galbraith, "Electronic Billboards along the Information Superhighway," 41 *Boston College Law Review* 847, 2000.
62. See the ruling in *Brookfield Communications Inc. v. West Coast Entertainment Corp.* 174 F. 3d 1036 (9th Cir. [1999]).
63. Charles Mann, "Who Will Own Your Next Great Idea," *Atlantic Monthly*, September, 1998, p. 183.
64. Esther Dyson, "Intellectual Property on the Net," *Release 1.0* (New York: Random House, 1994).
65. *Amazon.com, Inc. v. BarnesandNoble.com* 239 F. 3d 57 (U.S.P.Q 2d [2001]).
66. Thomas Weber, "Battle over Patents Threaten to Damp Web's Innovative Spirit," *The Wall Street Journal*, February 10, 2000, p. B1.
67. *Amazon.com, Inc. v. BarnesandNoble.com.*
68. Julia Angwin, "'Business-Method Patents, Key to Priceline, Draw Growing Protest," *The Wall Street Journal*, October 3, 2000, p. B4.
69. Quoted in Weber, "Battle over Patents."
70. *Amazon.com, Inc. v. BarnesandNoble.com.*
71. "P2P and the Gnutella Myth," Webnoize Study, April, 2001; available at http://news.Webnoize.com.
72. Scott Woolley, "Steal this Movie," *Forbes*, February 18, 2002, p. 66.
73. See Mark Lewis, "Does Morpheus' Architecture Save MusicCity from Legal Liability," *Webnoize News*, August 23, 2001.
74. Ibid.
75. Ibid.
76. *Metro-Goldwyn-Mayer Studios Inc., et al. v. Grokster, Ltd., et al.* CV 01-08451 (Dis Ct. C.D. Cal. [2001]).
77. Scott Woolley, "Steal this Movie."

CHAPTER FIVE

Regulating Internet Privacy

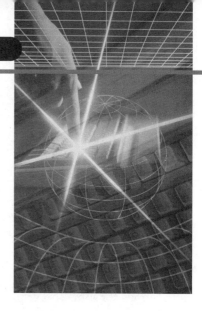

▶ Introduction

The information age has created a more open society where privacy seems to grow scarcer with each technological innovation. Personal information on the Internet has become even more of a commodity that can be collected, exchanged, or recombined with relative ease. The Internet and its supporting architectures have made it much easier to track and monitor individual behavior. Identifying serial numbers embedded within computer chips or software programs that allow traces to an end user's identity threaten to end the electronic anonymity that has so far characterized many interactions in cyberspace. And Web bugs and cookies allow for an unprecedented level of surreptitious Internet surveillance.

The public seems to be ambivalent and even nonchalant about privacy issues until their collective consciousness is jarred by some startling new revelation. On occasion some organization discovers that it has transgressed a certain threshold, and it is forced to withdraw a plan that simply goes too far. For example, DoubleClick, the online ad agency, was portrayed as villainous after it announced plans to link offline customer data with people's Web-browsing behavior. In February, 2000, the Federal Trade Commission (FTC) began investigating the company for unfair and deceptive trade practices, as the press pilloried the high-profile DoubleClick for its questionable conduct.

In addition, as a result of sophisticated surveillance and monitoring technologies, the networked workplace has become a virtual panopticon where workers' movements and interactions are more visible than ever before to their managers. Hence, the employee's right to privacy, which was once regarded with some respect, now appears to be in greater peril than ever.

Privacy is threatened in many other environments as well, and its co-existence with the Internet and electronic commerce seems to be particularly tenuous. The debate over privacy continues to intensify and there is little doubt that this issue will be a dominant ethical concern for many years to come. As Marc Rotenberg has observed, "Privacy will be to the information economy of the next century what consumer protection and environmental concerns have been to the industrial society of the 20th century."[1]

What are the ramifications of this steady erosion of personal and workplace privacy? Once lost, can it ever be retrieved? What are reasonable expectations for some sort of privacy protection as one retrieves information from the Internet or shops at Web sites hungry for consumer data? Are children at an even greater risk for invasions of privacy by benign-looking Web sites? What is the appropriate scope of privacy protection in the workplace? Finally, do some privacy protections go too far and undermine free speech rights in cyberspace?

We will attempt to consider these and other related questions in this chapter, but first we must review why the right to privacy is of such fundamental importance from a legal as well as moral perspective. This will help us to appreciate why its gradual but persistent erosion cannot be taken so lightly.

▶Definition and Theory of Privacy

Privacy is not a simple concept that can be easily defined. Perhaps the most basic and inclusive definition dates back to a seminal *Harvard Law Review* article written by Samuel Warren and Louis Brandeis in 1890. They differentiated the right to privacy from other legal rights and conceived it as the right to some measure of solitude in one's life. According to these jurists, "Recent inventions and business methods call attention to the next step which must be taken for the protection of the person and for securing the individual . . . the right 'to be let alone.'"[2]

This general definition is a good starting point, but it is obviously inadequate, since the "right to be let alone" is rather broad and imprecise. A more suitable definition has been formulated by Ruth Gavison. She defines privacy as the limitation of others' access to an individual with three key elements: secrecy, anonymity, and solitude. Secrecy (or confidentiality) involves limiting the dissemination of knowledge about oneself; anonymity refers to the protection from undesired attention; solitude is the lack of physical proximity to others.[3] Although the right to secrecy, anonymity, and solitude must be subject to certain limits for anyone who participates in civil society, Gavison has laid the groundwork for a more nuanced understanding of what the right to privacy should entail.

It is also possible to distinguish several types of privacy such as psychological privacy or communication privacy. The focus of our attention, however, is primarily *information privacy*. It concerns the collection, use, and dissemination of information about individuals. The right to informational privacy is the right to control the disclosure of and access to one's personal information. In Gavison's terms, it is the right to some level of secrecy or confidentiality.

If one culls the vast terrain of privacy literature, two generic privacy theories stand out: the *control theory* and the *restricted access theory*. Gavison's approach is an example of the restricted access theory, in which privacy amounts to restricting access to information about oneself in certain contexts. According to the control theory, advocated by philosophers like Fried, "One has privacy if and only if one has control over information about oneself."[4]

There have been many attempts by philosophers to ground or justify this right to privacy, but the most convincing approaches regard the right to privacy as an instrumental value that supports other basic rights such as property, security, and freedom. A primary moral foundation for the value of privacy has been its role as a condition of freedom (or autonomy): a shield of privacy is essential in most societies if one is to freely pursue his or her projects or cultivate intimate social relationships.

According to James Reiman, without privacy there are two ways in which our freedom can be appreciably attenuated.[5] First, there is the risk of an *extrinsic loss of freedom*, since the lack of privacy often makes individuals vulnerable to having their behavior controlled by others. Sensitive information collected without one's permission and knowledge can be a potent weapon in the hands of those in positions of authority. Such information might be used to deprive individuals of certain rewards and opportunities such as job promotions or transfers or may preclude eligibility for insurance and other important necessities. This thwarts our autonomy, our basic capacity for making choices and directing our lives without outside interference. As Carol Gould has observed, "Privacy is a protection against unwanted imposition or coercion by others and thus a protection of one's freedom of action."[6]

There is also the risk of an *intrinsic loss of freedom*. It is common knowledge that most people will behave differently when they are being watched or monitored by others. In these circumstances, it is normal to feel more inhibited and tentative about one's plans and activities. According to Zuboff, it is not uncommon to find "anticipatory conformity" among those who are constantly observed.[7] As Richard Wassestrom puts it, without privacy, life is often "less spontaneous and more measured."[8]

Who can forget a movie like *The Truman Show*, which vividly illustrated humankind's primal need for some type of private space?

In summary, then, without the benefit of privacy we are more subject to the manipulation and control by others and we are more inhibited and timid about the pursuit of our goals and activities. According to Foucault, this is precisely the "panoptic effect" that most prison systems seek to achieve. The inmate feels that he is in a "state of conscious and permanent visibility that assures the automatic functioning of power."[9] But do we really want to establish or perpetuate such demoralizing conditions in our homes and offices?

James Moor has developed a related and equally convincing justification of privacy. Recall his contention (see Chapter 1) that there are shared "core values" that are basic for human existence. These values include life, happiness, freedom, knowledge, ability, resources, and security. Although privacy is not a core value, according to Moor, it is the expression of a core value, that is, the value of security. Without privacy, it is difficult to be and feel secure. Moreover, privacy takes on special significance in a computerized networked culture, which poses strong risks for privacy and hence for our personal security. According to Moor, "People have a basic right to be protected, which from the point of view of our computerized culture, includes privacy protection."[10] Privacy, therefore, is in effect elevated to the same level as the other core values, since in our information intensive culture, some degree of privacy is essential for security and by extension for human flourishing.

Almost everyone intuitively recognizes the validity of these arguments and the significance of the right to privacy. We all want some measure of privacy and solitude in our lives. Problems come about because the right to privacy often conflicts with other basic rights and the task of determining which right should take priority is a formidable challenge for ethicists and public policy makers. As we observed in Chapter 3, there is a conflict between strong privacy rights and free speech. Some free speech advocates, for instance, regard privacy regulations as a form of censorship since they conflict with an organization's right to communicate or to transmit information. If we protect privacy through more comprehensive laws, they argue, we risk losing the right to freely exchange valuable consumer data.

As we shall see, the threats to one's autonomy and personal security are heightened by using the Internet since one's zone of privacy is appreciably diminished in this open and fluid environment. We will first consider the precise nature of those threats and then discuss some appropriate policy responses.

▶Personal Information on the Internet

Novice Internet users are frequently astonished to learn about the plethora of personal data that is now available online. Consider the following scenario. Suppose that you live in a prosperous, leafy suburb of Milwaukee and that you are quite curious about your new eccentric neighbor. Something about her demeanor is rather unsettling and unusual. So you decide to do some investigating even though you don't even know her name. You know only her address, but that is sufficient to get started: the Infospace search engine's "Find neighbors" option quickly allows you to find out other information such as her name and phone number using the reverse lookup option, which requires only an address to initiate the search. You then access another popular search engine called "Alta Vista" and this search turns up the name of the company she works for. You then go to the Milwaukee City Tax Assessment Online database, key in the address, and within seconds you find out the assessed value of her property, her current property tax, and the fact that she has a partial personal exemption because she is a surviving spouse.

You have spent about 15 minutes on the Internet and you have just begun scratching the surface of this woman's background. You could continue on and probably build a pretty thorough profile of this woman by using other search engines and Web sites. But where does one draw the line in the search for another individual's personal data? Has anything immoral happened here in this incident of "cybersnooping"? Does it make any difference if we make no revelations to others or take no actions based on our findings? Is there anything wrong with the search engines that facilitate this process? Should this type of data be subject to some sort of regulation in order to limit online stalking and similar abuses? Should online privacy be a greater priority for public policy makers?

The question we must first consider is whether information residing on the Internet should be so "public" and hence easily accessible. Most of the data that has become fodder for search engines has always existed in a public or pseudo-public format (such as a phone book and court records) and it has now become digitized. The trend of posting court documents on the Internet is especially unsettling since those documents sometimes contain highly sensitive data. For example, individuals filing for personal bankruptcy "must disclose Social Security, bank, and credit card numbers, account balances, and even the names and ages of their children."[11]

On one hand, it is easy to see the benefits in having this information more accessible, especially for media investigations that may further the public interest. Converting information into an electronic format and providing a better mechanism to search that data seems to be perfectly acceptable. Civil libertarians have long argued for the freedom of information in a democratic society since the alternative leads to secrecy and governmental control of information.

On the other hand, personal data is being made available in these online databases, which are accessible to search engines without our knowledge and consent. Further, there is more going on here than a mere conversion of data from hard copy to digital format. The Internet makes this data globally and instantaneously accessible. Our nosy neighbor probably would not pore through documents stored in city hall for hours to find out about his neighbor, but if it just takes 15 minutes on the Internet, there is more of a temptation to snoop around. Court documents were always public but few individuals would take the time to physically check through these documents. Also, what makes this data more of a threat is the possibility for recombination of disparate and hitherto unconnected data elements. Businesses could build or augment customer databases using this publicly available data, such as court records, which could easily be searched with software agents. Our hypothetical example illustrated that with little effort, a fairly thorough profile of someone could be constructed by even a casual user. This could create some potential for mischief, and as a result many people will soon prefer to keep their backgrounds as concealed as possible.

Thus, there is a *qualitative* difference between the requirements of physically tracking down data and the ease of finding it on the Internet with the aid of search engines. But is the answer stricter government regulation of online databases? The problem is that such regulations could have an unwanted chilling effect on the distribution and accessibility of valid information.

A feasible alternative might be to work out a responsible middle ground between an outright ban (or detailed restrictions) and a completely *laissez-faire* approach. One could argue that for security purposes there are certain data elements that should *never* be in a public, online database, and this includes social security numbers, which are links to a wealth of other sensitive information. These databases should also exclude mothers' maiden name information, which is used for identification verification at banks and other financial institutions. The ethical justification is that the potential for harm increases exponentially when such items are made so readily available.

So far this is a line that online databases haven't yet crossed, but they have tested the waters. Several years ago Lexis-Nexis, a company that collects personal data on millions of people and resells it to subscribers, provoked the ire of regulators and privacy advocates when it began including social security numbers, birth dates, and mothers' maiden names on its "P-Trak" database. Thanks to the negative publicity, the company reversed itself and has vowed to exclude these items from its reference lists in the future.

If we try to harmonize the need for freedom of information and the imperative of privacy, it is reasonable to conclude that online data systems have many positive benefits. However, we propose that there should be some limits and conditions such as the following:

- Exclusion of sensitive unique identifiers such as social security numbers, birth dates, and mothers' maiden names.

- Exclusion of all unlisted phone numbers.

- Clear provision of an opt-out option so that people can have their names promptly removed from a database.

- Prohibition of reverse social security number look-ups.

▶ Consumer Privacy on the Internet

Privacy-Invasive Technologies

Prior to the information age, the transactions that occurred between vendors and consumers were private affairs, nobody's business but the two parties involved. They were also quickly forgotten. The local baker knew you by name but probably couldn't remember what sort of breads and pastries you purchased last month. This has changed rather dramatically in the information economy since computers can remember everything for an indefinite period of time. If we use a shopping card at our local supermarket, a data warehouse is storing the details of our purchases, and sometimes this data is shared with food producers and others for targeted marketing campaigns.

There are two distinct phases to this systematic loss of our privacy as consumers. The first might aptly be labeled as the *database phase*. The emergence of database technology in the early 1980s made it possible to collect, store, and retrieve copious amounts of information efficiently and economically. During this period our personal data was transferred to computerized records, which became the foundation of consumer profiles. These profiles were often based on public records sold by government agencies at the state and local levels. For instance, car registration and license information has been digitized and relied upon in the past as a major source of marketing data to reach certain groups of consumers.

Another source of data for these systems is the information generated by various consumer transactions such as telephone or mail orders, memberships, warranty cards, or even rebate coupons. This data too can serve as the building blocks for richly detailed customer records. Pharmaceutical companies, for example, build their databases from consumers who call 800 numbers, subscribe to magazines, or fill out pharmacy questionnaires.

The popular retailer Consumer Value Stores (CVS) sent a mailing to diabetes patients advertising a new breakthrough drug called Rezulin. CVS contracted with a direct mail marketing firm to mine its prescription databases for insulin users. Everyone on this customer list was then sent the literature from CVS, although the mailing was funded by Warner-Lambert, which makes Rezulin. Some consumers were incensed by this violation of their right to patient confidentiality and resented that CVS singled them out as diabetes patients. Despite this backlash, the company has defended the mailings because they provided valuable information for their customers.[12]

Some corporations, such as Metromail, function exclusively as data brokers. They specialize in aggregating and maintaining myriad data about consumers. Metromail's National Consumer Data Base includes detailed information on 103 million people in the United States. Metromail is especially proficient in tracking important transitions in people's lives. For example, if someone has moved to a new house, their name will be provided to junk mailers or other vendors for 25 cents a name. These individuals are obviously prospects for new home furnishings and appliances, long distance telephone service, and so forth.

The use of data warehouse software and more sophisticated storage devices such as optical disk technology has greatly aided the preservation of voluminous consumer data. It has also made data mining activities possible. American Airlines' Sabre Group was recently criticized in the press when it announced plans to build a data warehouse of its travel reservation information that would then be made available for sale to outside agencies. Thanks to the Internet, if Sabre were to sell that data it could be transferred effortlessly over this global network. This easy transmission of stored data and the heavy reliance on the Internet and on private digital networks to help conduct business has ushered in the *network phase*. Consumers routinely communicate with vendors by e-mail, post messages to electronic bulletin boards on the Internet, and visit Web sites where they can browse an online catalog and purchase products. In this phase, information has become more mobile than ever before, and connectivity facilitates an unprecedented level of monitoring by prying eyes located all over the network.

The steady ascendance of electronic commerce has meant that the new battleground for consumer privacy protection is now shifting to Web site vendors. A survey by the Federal Trade Commission (FTC) found that 92 percent of commercial Web sites collect personal information, while only 14 percent disclose their information-gathering practices to consumers.[13] Some of these sites are selling or exchanging this information, often without the user's knowledge or consent.

Electronic commerce transactions often leave a revealing trail of *personally identifiable information*, including one's name, address, e-mail address, and phone number. Personally identifiable information can also include demographic data such as age or gender, and this data can be especially helpful for market research. Many Web sites collect this information as users sign up at the site or identify themselves by requesting a catalog or making a purchase.

This sudden surge of Web-based activity has led to some particularly egregious violations of privacy. Consider the problematic case of Geocities, an online community of 2 million personal Web sites. In late summer of 1998 it was forced to revise its information collection policies in order to avoid a Federal Trade Commission lawsuit. New members of Geocities seeking to establish their own personal Web sites were required to fill out a registration form and had to supply information such as their exact income along with their level of education. Members were assured that Geocities "would not share this information without their permission, but will use it to gain a better understanding of who is visiting Geocities."[14] According to the FTC, however, such "permission" was granted as long as the user did not check a box that would allow one to opt out of future marketing offers. Most users in fact did not check this box and as a result their information was widely distributed to other Internet companies such as CMG Information Services or Infobeat. At a minimum, Geocities is culpable of deceiving its customers. It should have abided by its promise not to give out personal information as sensitive as salary data, and it should have provided a lucid and straightforward mechanism so that users could grant their permission to have that data disclosed.

Information about consumers can also be collected without the consumer's knowledge or consent. Many Web sites monitor clickstream data, the information generated as a user surfs the Web and communicates with different Web sites. One way in which Web site vendors can track the movement of their customers is the use of cookies. These cookies are small data files that are written and stored on the user's hard drive by a Web site when the user visits that site with a browser. They contain information such as passwords, lists of pages within the Web site that have been visited, and the dates when those pages were last examined. When the user revisits the Web site that stored the cookie, the user's computer system quietly sends the cookie back with all of its relevant information. Cookie functionality does not require the consumer's identity since the cookie relies primarily on a unique identifier. But a Web site can correlate anonymous cookie data with identifiable personal information, if, for example, the user has registered or made a purchase at that Web site.

Cookies represent a modest means of monitoring a user's movements when they visit a particular Web site. If a customer visits an online bookstore, a cookie can reveal whether she browses through sports books or is more apt to look at books on wine and gourmet foods. If a user comes to this store merely to window shop in cyberspace, cookies can provide the retailer with valuable information that could be the basis of a targeted promotion for that user's next visit.

The most controversial manifestation of this technology is the third party cookie. These are cookies placed across a network of related sites so that users' movements can be tracked not just within a certain site but within any site that is part of this network. Online ad agencies like DoubleClick rely on a common cookie that allows it to deliver custom ads any time a customer enters a DoubleClick affiliated site. It also allows DoubleClick to monitor clickstream data across this network.

Another covert surveillance device is the *Web bug*. A Web bug (or "Web beacon") is embedded as a miniscule and invisible graphic on a Web page and it can track everything one does on a particular Web site. They are sometimes placed on Web pages by third parties such as online advertising agencies. These versatile bugs have many uses. They can be deployed to count the number of visitors to a Web page, track the Web pages a visitor looks at within the site, count the number of times a banner ad has been opened, and so forth.

These "bugs" can also be used in certain forms of e-mail. For example, Web bugs have become an interesting feature of HTML mail, which allows users to create and transmit colorful e-mail messages. Some users embed tiny images invisible to the recipient in the e-mail message, which is triggered through the instruction to open the image file. This Web bug allows the sender to ascertain whether or not the e-mail message has been read by the recipient. Privacy advocates claim that such practices are improper because they "open a new window of surveillance on a traditionally private sphere of communications."[15]

Clickstream data can yield a wealth of information about the user's IP address, browser type and version, all URLs (Uniform Resource Locators) entered at a Web site, all products viewed, and so on. Every move one makes in cyberspace then becomes an indelible part of the clickstream record. This record could be anonymous or it could be linked to an actual identity. Thus, through the voluntary disclosure of information and through the automatic collection of data by devices such as cookies and Web bugs, Web site operators can build a fairly thorough profile of their visitors and customers. What we have is an unprecedented level of *data profiling,* "the term used to denote the gathering, assembling, and collating of data about individuals in databases which can be used to identify, segregate, categorize and generally make decisions about individuals known to the decision maker only through their computerized profile."[16]

This clickstream data is collected not just by commercial Web sites but also by online advertisers like DoubleClick and by Internet Service Providers (ISPs). ISPs are in an excellent position to monitor a user's entire clickstream since every mouse click or command is sent through the ISP. According to Pollock, "Virtually all netizens (Internet users, for the uninitiate) access the Net through an ISP. As you are searching your way merrily along the strands of the WWW, however, your friendly ISP is collecting information regarding where you have been. The information recorded is called a 'click stream' and records every Web site you've visited."[17]

Why do companies engage in all of this data profiling? The objective is targeted marketing and advertising. It's far more effective to send a user a targeted banner ad as opposed to a generic ad—such marketing techniques eliminate some of the risk and uncertainty in this process. Targeted campaigns mean that the response is more predictable.

For example, let's say that Mary Merlot likes to purchase wine online from http://www.wineandspritis.com. On her first visit to the Web site, she purchased several bottles of cabernet sauvignon and spent some time looking at some French wines such as Pouilly Fuisse. Thanks to the purchase she has made, the Web site has collected her name, address, phone numbers, e-mail address, and American Express Card number. It has also monitored the wines she looked at but did not purchase and has acquired information about her browser, IP address, and so forth. This information is stored on the cookie that is deposited on her hard drive when she exits the Web site. The next time she enters the Web site, that cookie is retrieved and she receives customized promotions based on her profile—a banner ad for a new French restaurant in her city, a recommendation to check out the latest imports from France, and a discount if she buys two or more cases of this wine.

While Mary Merlot may appreciate these offers and this level of personalization, she may have some valid concerns about what might happen to all of this data. Will it be sold to third parties for additional marketing campaigns? The temptation to do so is powerful. According to Reidenberg, "The ease of collecting and storing personal information coupled with enhanced capability to use it create tremendous commercial pressures in favor of unanticipated or secondary uses . . . [that] generate additional value."[18] Mary might also be at some risk if this data is recombined with other data and provides someone with more clues about her lifestyle. The line between online and offline data is blurry at best and there is a chance that once these two forms of information coalesce,

Mary's life will be an open book. Unless commercial Web sites like winesandspirits.com have a policy enabling her to opt out of such transactions and she takes the initiative to do so, her fears are probably well founded.

Policy Considerations

How can Mary's information be protected? How can she retrieve some semblance of control over all of this personal information? Should there be laws to guard against data profiling and mining without the consumer's permission? Law, of course, is not the only solution. Recall Lessig's framework: there are other constraints besides law such as code (or technology), norms, and the marketplace. These constraints are not mutually exclusive so the answer might well be arriving at the right mix of constraints.

If we choose the legal solution, a comprehensive law protecting consumer privacy would most likely embody two simple values, *notice* and *choice*. Companies and organizations should be required to inform consumers about how their data will be used and not use that data for any other purpose without the consumer's consent. There are two variations of this model. The first is the "opt-in" approach whereby individuals must explicitly approve secondary (or even tertiary) uses of their personal information. For example, if one provides credit data to a bank to apply for a loan, the bank cannot sell that data to a marketing company without permission. The second is the "opt-out" approach whereby individuals are notified that their personal data will be used for secondary purposes unless they disapprove and notify the vendor accordingly. If informed consent is to work properly, regulations would need to ensure that consumers have knowledge and opportunity, that is, they must be made aware of any projected reuse in a timely fashion and be given a reasonable opportunity to restrict it.

Some argue that tighter legal restrictions are necessary. Kang, for example, has proposed a statute that would prohibit a Web site from retaining transaction information once the transaction is completed unless the user gives his or her consent.[19]

As part of a legal solution, the government could also change the rules about information ownership. After all, who really owns credit, medical, or other data about individuals that is collected? The current laws are ambiguous, and consequently most organizations that gather this data have assumed such ownership. However, it is by no means evident that the activity of data collection automatically engenders any property rights. But who deserves the most legitimate ownership claim on this data?

A controversial paradigm suggested by several scholars regards an individual's personal information as his or her private property. According to this paradigm, individuals should have property rights in all personal information about themselves, especially since they have the greatest stake in how that information will be used. If our information really has economic value, we should receive something in return when a corporation makes some profit from its reuse. By giving individuals such property rights, society recognizes both the economic value and the proprietary nature of personal information.

Once information is regarded as personal property, as an asset with legal attributes, the legal system can begin to develop a set of laws and appropriate regulations that will define when information should be protected from misappropriation, how individuals should be compensated when their information is used by a third party, and when information must be relinquished for the sake of social or public policy or even technological priorities. Property rights are not absolute and just as one's physical property may be subject in extreme cases to eminent domain, one's personal information must at times be sacrificed for the common good.

Although this legal approach may be theoretically sound, it may be difficult to implement due to many practical problems. Users would be forced to negotiate with every vendor or Web-based business seeking their information. This could have a debilitating effect on the free flow of commercial data, and it could also be a time-consuming process for both parties.

Those who advocate the need for the constraint of law, that is, for privacy legislation to protect consumers in online transactions, point to the poor track record of industries that have adopted some type of self-regulation. They are skeptical that business will have the moral discipline needed to police itself. In their view, only federal legislation establishing uniform national privacy standards will be sufficient to protect consumer privacy. Further they point out that the regulatory model has been effective in many European countries.

In purely economic terms, the loss of privacy is a market failure. It is a negative externality analogous to various forms of environmental degradation. The sale or exchange of data between two parties imposes a cost on the data subject: his or her information is being sold, and this results in a loss of privacy. The cost is not borne by the two parties who engage in the transaction but instead is borne involuntarily by the data subject. But can the market fix this failure? Will companies realize that consumers care about privacy and begin to enact privacy-protection policies and architectures that will attract consumers?

The "invisible hand" of the market sometimes nudges companies to abide by certain social and moral norms for purely pragmatic reasons, but is this likely to happen with privacy rights? Some industry experts argue that commercial Web sites must take privacy more seriously or "they will have to risk the wrath of consumers."[20] If privacy is important to consumers, some vendors may eventually come to recognize this by making and keeping promises of confidentiality. This will enhance the confidence and trust of their customers. The demands of consumers and competitive pressures, therefore, might force businesses to establish stronger privacy and security standards. A commitment to confidentiality and tight security may mean higher prices, but consumers who care about their privacy will not balk at paying a premium for this privilege. This may be especially true in cyberspace where electronic commerce has not reached its full potential due to lingering concerns over privacy protection. Some consumers may be willing to pay a bit extra for ironclad guarantees of security and confidentiality in their online transactions.

It seems highly unlikely, however, that free market mechanisms alone can reverse the trend of privacy erosion on any significant scale. The biggest problem is that the vast majority of consumers are not really energized about this issue. Also, some businesses will attempt to take advantage of privacy concerns through opportunistic marketing. The payoffs and marketing benefits of trading in the commodity of information may be too great to rely on market forces alone to bring under control predatory information collection practices.

The third broad approach involves reliance on industry norms and self-regulation. Those norms are often expressed in industry codes of conduct, which member firms are expected to follow. The assumption is that organizations that collect and disseminate personal data will impose constraints on themselves in order to avoid infringing upon their customers' privacy rights. Companies could decide to regulate themselves for several reasons. They may seek to preempt government regulations, which they fear could be more onerous than their own self-imposed constraints. Or they may have purer motives and be convinced that they must act with ethical probity since privacy standards deserve their respect.

Some U.S. trade organizations, such as the powerful Direct Marketing Association (DMA), have long advocated this approach and have developed privacy principles for its members. These principles require that online companies post and follow privacy policies telling consumers how information about them will be used. The DMA has a seal of approval for Web sites that have a track record of fidelity to these principles. Similar standards have been developed by the Online Privacy Alliance and a consortium of companies that make up the Network Advertising Initiative. For these groups, self-regulation means a clear privacy policy along with providing consumers an opportunity to opt out of the secondary or tertiary uses of their personal data.

Finally, we must not overlook the role consumers can play in the safeguarding of their own privacy rights with the help of technology. In the absence of government regulation, consumers may take privacy matters into their own hands by adopting Internet architectures such as P3P and insisting that online businesses cooperate. We will discuss this approach in more detail in a later section. Suffice it to say at this point that used properly and conscientiously, a code-based solution *could* have the potential to achieve the right balance between privacy rights and economic efficiency.

Moral Considerations

How might we assess Mary Merlot's plight from a moral standpoint? Is there anything truly immoral in collecting this data and selling it without her permission to generate extra revenues? Given the importance of privacy as a condition for security in an information intensive society, a potent case can be constructed that those corporations infringing on privacy rights are acting immorally. They are committed to policies that create the risk of harm for people. As we have noted, when information is sold and recombined a more thorough profile of the data subject is created, and this creates the risk of manipulation by other private parties or organizations. One of the big problems that can occur through electronic profiling is that people can be judged out of context. The fact that Mary Merlot buys a sizable amount of wine online may lead some who examine her profile to jump to the conclusion that she has a drinking problem, when, in reality, she entertains with some frequency. Monitoring technologies, profiling, and far-reaching searches often threaten the presumption of innocence. According to Lessig, in these situations, "the burden is on you, the monitored first to establish your innocence and second, to assure all who might see these ambiguous facts that you are innocent."[21]

Of course, some argue that this threat to privacy is overstated. Singleton, for example, maintains that consumer databases do not present a new or unique threat and are no worse than more traditional ways of gathering and disseminating information such as gossip, which was the basis for information exchange prior to technology. Gossip exchanged freely through informal networks within small communities could cause much more harm than private sector databases, which are at least more accurate and impersonal than gossip. Consumer databases are simply the formalization of more direct information flows that took place between consumers and merchants in those small towns. They represent a more efficient way of keeping track of a customer's special needs, their preferences, their credit record, and so forth. Thus, if we do not regulate this more harmful exchange of personal information in private conversation, "we cannot justify regulation of consumer data bases."[22]

Singleton further argues that the collection of information in commercial contexts is no different from the gathering of information that takes place in more informal and casual ways. And information about a person's buying habits "belongs to the person providing the product as well as the person consuming the product."[23] We may be annoyed when vendors use that information to solicit more business but such annoyance does not justify stringent regulation.

But Singleton underestimates the dangers attendant upon the misuse of personal information. Sophisticated IT systems have the power to capture, recombine, and classify personal information efficiently and inexpensively. A credit card company, for example, may build a record of identifying information (name, address, phone number, etc.), include a purchase history, and recombine this with financial data purchased from other sources. These profiles may then be packaged and resold to other interested parties—perhaps insurance companies would like to know more about us before renewing someone or assessing a premium. As Oscar Gandy has pointed out, this collection and reuse of personal information is part of a broad *panoptic sort*, a "complex discriminatory technology" that is utilized to sort people into different categories. The danger of the panoptic sort is that "personal information is not only used to *include* individuals with the marketing scan, but may also be used to *exclude* them from other life chances linked to employment, insurance, housing, education, and credit."[24]

Privacy-invasive architectures are much more powerful and intrusive than local gossip and essentially enable a systematic infringement of privacy rights that can have significant and long lasting consequences. People like local vendors and the town gossips forget most of the minute details they learn about their fellow citizens in day to day interactions. But IT systems such as comprehensive data warehouses *never* forget. Also, as people are categorized and profiled, they can become easy targets of discrimination that can eventually exclude them from essential services. They can suffer economic losses and even public embarrassment. These profiles create an asymmetry of information between the consumer and those corporations that provide essential services. This whole process thereby enhances corporate power and diminishes the freedom of consumers.

The stakes in preserving privacy are much higher than Singleton seems to realize. If it were simply a matter of passing information along electronically instead of through the medium of gossip, there would not be such a problem. However, there is much more to the panoptic sort than the mere diffusion of information. Personal data is captured, recombined, and classified so that profiles can be built that categorize people in certain ways. For example, one data broker sells lists of gay men by culling periodical subscriptions and even calls to AIDS hotlines. This is only one of many examples of how technology classifies us, initially for the sake of marketing efforts. But as these lists become disseminated throughout cyberspace and combined with other lists, who can predict for what discriminatory purposes they will ultimately be used? Thus, from a natural rights perspective we can reason that privacy rights must be respected, given the significant risk of harm that occurs when those rights are cavalierly ignored. Human beings have a natural right to security, a basic human good intrinsic to our humanity because it is essential for our flourishing as human beings. In an information-based, networked economy, the goal of achieving such security is elusive without some type of privacy protection. Hence there is a moral imperative, a fundamental duty, to safeguard privacy rights in order to ensure a person's security and overall well-being. This flows from the general moral obligation that is at the heart of a natural rights ethic: respect every basic human good in each one of your acts and polices. It is also consistent with Kant's second formulation of the categorical imperative: "Act so that you treat humanity, whether in your own person or in that of another, as an end and never as a means." For Kant, this principle is "the supreme limiting condition in the pursuit of all means."[25] We cannot set aside our responsibility to respect these basic human goods or aspects of human personality in every person whose well-being we influence.[26]

Of course, what constitutes respect for privacy rights is not all together clear and a matter of some debate. But at the core of a privacy policy manifesting respect of this basic right are the principles of notice and choice. Privacy policies should be prominently displayed and in those policies companies should explain what data they are collecting and for what purpose the data is to be used. Also, companies should get permission before they resell identifiable personal data that has been collected to another Web site or organization. Finally, consumers should have the prerogative to examine and correct if necessary any sensitive data, especially health care and financial data, since inaccuracies could be quite costly. If every company conscientiously followed the broad lines of such a policy, it could be concluded that they were manifesting respect for privacy rights. One might surely argue for more robust protection. We are merely presenting a reasonable, minimal standard.

What about the use of cookies and other surreptitious technologies? Most Web merchants see cookies in benign terms, maintaining that they really do no harm. For the most part these merchants are correct. Also, it is difficult for Web sites to work without cookies; otherwise there is too much discontinuity between user visits or within a single visit—a customer cannot abandon a virtual shopping cart and return to that cart to complete an order without the help of cookie technology.

At worst, cookies seem to be an annoyance, easily handled by users who can set their Web browsers to selectively block cookies. But there is some reason to be concerned about these technologies since they can function as a form of covert surveillance that conjures up an unsettling "Big

Brother" image. After all, cookie technology is analogous to having some-one follow you through the mall with a video camera.

While we recognize the value of this simple technology, we must not underestimate the potential for harm in the way cookie technology cur-rently functions. What if off-beat or pornographic Web sites visited on a whim send their respective visitors cookies without their knowledge? Those cookies are then residing on one's hard drive and could be opened by a nosy employer or someone else with access to that computer. That person might draw unsettling inferences from the presence of these cookie files. Also, Web sites could begin to package and resell this data that they have acquired by watching their customers. The increased use of third party cookies is also worrisome, since they would enable the con-struction of a fine-grained profile of a user's Web browsing habits. But the biggest problem, as DoubleClick discovered, is forging a link between anonymous online data and offline data that identifies an individual user. Assume, for example, that an individual visited an array of AIDS sites, and that information becomes part of a profile that includes personally identifiable offline data. An insurance company might mine this profile and discover this information, leading to an adverse decision about coverage.

From a moral perspective, the primary issue appears to be the con-sumer's loss of autonomy. Should any company be allowed to deposit a cookie file on a user's hard drive without their knowledge and consent? One could argue that this is presumptuous and disrespectful of a user's right to control his or her "private space," which should include the disk space of their personal computers. When things are delivered to our physical space without our consent (e.g., junk mail) we at least know about them. What is troublesome about cookies is that most users have no idea that these files tracking their movements have been accepted by their computer systems.

There is actually a fairly simple solution to this problem. A policy of informed consent might go a long way to making cookie technology morally palatable for those who have a problem with this technology. Browsers already have the capability to prompt users before they accept a cookie, but the default setting is to let Web sites transmit these files with-out asking that question. Instead, the default setting could be altered so that users are informed that a cookie file will be deposited and given an opt-out option if such an option is viable. If a Web site requires a cookie, it should state why that is so. Above all, it should spell out specifically how the information collected by a cookie will be utilized, so that the Web surfer can make an informed decision.

▶ The United States and Europe: Divergent Paths to Privacy Protection

Now that we have considered the general avenues for dealing with privacy, the use of law, industry norms, and reliance on the marketplace, it is instructive to compare the different strategies followed by the U.S. and Europe in their quest to provide privacy rights for their citizens. The United States has relied on a philosophy of self-regulation, while legal rights have been downplayed. The U.S. solution is predicated on the belief that a healthy combination of market pressures and industry self-regulation is the best path to privacy protection. The goal is to cultivate adequate protection that is compatible with economic growth. This is not to suggest that there are no laws protecting privacy in the U.S., but instead of comprehensive laws, there are targeted regulations that protect privacy rights in certain sectors such as health care. These sectoral statutes are enacted when sensitive information is at stake or the data subjects are too vulnerable. In such situations, it is too risky to put faith in the self-correcting mechanisms of the marketplace. By contrast, in Europe, privacy is treated as a basic human right deserving the full protection of the law, so the country has developed broad, cross-sectoral legislation. In this section we first consider privacy legislation in the U.S. There are a few new laws that have been enacted to protect privacy in the context of the Net, but in most cases consumer laws developed before the rise of e-commerce must now be applied to Internet transactions.

Privacy Legislation in the U.S.

In the 1960s the legal right to privacy, recognized decades earlier by Warren and Brandeis, had become more formalized thanks to several landmark Supreme Court cases such as *Griswold v. Connecticut*. In this pivotal case, the Supreme Court ruled that a Connecticut law that barred the dissemination of birth control information violated the right to marital privacy. The majority opinion also stated that each individual was entitled to "zones" of privacy created by First, Third, Fourth, Fifth, and Ninth Amendments to the Constitution. The justices agreed that privacy was a right "so rooted in the traditions and conscience of our people as to be ranked as fundamental" (*Griswold v. Connecticut* [381 U.S. 479, 1965]).

Shortly after the Griswold decision, Congress began to enact selective legislation to protect that privacy. It is difficult to discern a pattern or coherent plan in this legislation since the catalyst for a particular law was sometimes a public event that captured attention. We will not discuss every piece of privacy legislation, but we will cite enough examples to provide a reasonable overview.

In 1970 Congress passed the Fair Credit Reporting Act (FCRA), which regulated and restricted disclosures of credit and financial information by credit bureaus. The Fair Credit Reporting Act sets standards for the legitimate use of credit reports and delineates consumers' rights in disputing those reports. The responsibility of enforcing this act belongs to the Federal Trade Commission (FTC). In general, according to this act, a consumer's credit report should be released or provided to a third party only in response to a court order or in response to a written request from the consumer who is the subject of the report. Credit information can also be given to those third parties who have a "legitimate business need" for the information, and the meaning of that ambiguous phrase has been further clarified in recent years. As credit report information becomes more accessible online, the FCRA should offer consumers some protection by these limits on disclosure.

The FCRA was followed up by the Right to Financial Privacy Act in 1978, which required a search warrant before banks could divulge financial data of their customers to federal agencies. Federal investigators must make formal written requests to examine a subject's banking records and that subject must be given notice of the request so that he or she can challenge it. The FCRA will offer similar protection for online banking records and related data.

In the 1980s Congress continued to pass legislation intended to better protect privacy rights of U.S. citizens. In 1984 it passed the Cable Communications Policy Act, which prohibits cable TV companies from collecting or disseminating data about the viewing habits of their customers. A related piece of legislation was the Video Privacy Protection Act of 1988, which bars rental video stores from disclosing lists of videos watched by their customers. This act was passed as a reaction to public outrage after journalists were able to retrieve Robert Bork's video rental records during his contentious (and unsuccessful) Supreme Court confirmation hearings. Some have argued that Congress may have overreached when it passed the Video Privacy Protection Act, but there are valid reasons behind safeguarding this sort of information. As Rosen argues, "People are reluctant to have their reading and viewing habits exposed because we correctly fear that when isolated bits of personal information are confused with genuine knowledge, they may create an inaccurate picture of the full range of our interests and complicated personalities."[27]

In 1994 Congress was prompted to protect motor vehicle records, and so it passed the Driver's Privacy Protection Act. This piece of legislation prohibits the release or sale of personal information that is part of the state's motor vehicle record (social security number, name, age, address, height, and so forth) unless drivers are provided an opportunity to opt out. Prior to the enactment of this legislation, the sale of this data to third party marketers, a lucrative business for many states, would usually occur without permission or notification. The catalyst for the passage of this act was the murder of actress Rebecca Schaeffer by a crazed fan who obtained her address from the California Department of Motor Vehicles.

More recently, in 1998 Congress passed the Children's Online Privacy Protection Act (COPPA), which forbids Web sites from collecting personal information from children under age 13 without parental consent. This legislation was in response to growing complaints from parents. Enforcement of COPPA, however, has not been so easy. Many child-oriented Web sites just meet the letter of the law by merely posting a disclosure that the site is not for children, or they believe a child who enters an age or clicks the OK button when asked if the user is at least 13 years old. Despite these implementation problems, the law is having some salutary effects. According to Wasserman, "At the very least, the law has compelled some sites to rethink the way they communicate with kids."[28]

And in 1999 Congress passed the Gramm-Leach-Bliley bill, also known as the Financial Services Modernization Act. The main purpose of this deregulatory legislation was to make it easier for banks to merge with companies selling securities and insurance. The act also contained a key provision requiring financial services companies to disclose their information privacy policies in writing to their clients once a year. They must also provide their customers with an opt-out form that enables consumers to forbid the selling or sharing of their financial information. The burden is on the customer to return the form. So far, as one might expect, the opt-out forms are being returned at a surprisingly slow rate. Critics contend that the privacy notices are too confusing (some are several pages long, and enshrouded in legal terminology) and that an opt-in system where privacy is the default would have been a better solution.[29] Some companies have gone beyond the law and adopted the opt-in approach. In response to this legislation, FleetBoston developed a new privacy policy, stating that "the company won't share nonpublic customer data with non-affiliated third parties for marketing purposes unless the customer authorizes it to do so."[30] The company has deliberately adopted this proactive privacy policy to gain the loyalty and respect of its customers.

Finally, in April, 2001, new rules went into effect to protect medical privacy. Those rules were mandated by the Health Insurance Portability and Accountability Act (HIPAA), and they prohibit health care providers from using and disclosing patient information without patients' consent. This would mean, for example, that hospitals can no longer sell the names of pregnant women to manufacturers of products such as baby formula. Patients now have the right to access, examine, and copy the information in their medical records. The restrictions also limit the disclosure of health information to the "minimum necessary" for a specific purpose (such as paying bills). This provision is designed to end the practice of releasing a patient's whole record when only several specific pieces of information are needed. And new criminal and civil sanctions have been established if medical data is improperly used or disclosed.

What becomes evident as one examines this legislation is that the attempt to protect personal privacy in the United States through legal measures has been highly reactive and unfocused. As a result, what we have is an ad hoc, fragmented approach rather than a coherent body of privacy legislation predicated on a set of privacy principles. Also, as Smith observes, there is something disingenuous about some of this legislation: "In each instance when it enacted 'privacy-protection' legislation, Congress played tricks on the American people."[31] For example, the video privacy law does allow video stores to release the names and address of their customers along with the category of movies they have rented. If someone makes a habit of renting "dirty adult movies," this disclosure could be embarrassing.

The reason for this was the Clinton Administration's preference for a philosophy of self-regulation for privacy matters. It also maintained that responsibility for privacy protection belonged primarily with the private sector and not with the government. In Lessig's terms, the aim is to let industry norms, enforced through public pressure and other means, become the primary regulator of privacy on the Net. There are, of course, some exceptions to this, such as the adoption of regulation for the protection of children's privacy and medical privacy. Furthermore, this philosophy of self-regulation is apt to be reinforced in the Bush Administration, which has so far resisted comprehensive, cross-sectoral privacy legislation.

Privacy Protection in Europe

The situation is quite different in Europe, however. For some time European countries like Sweden and Germany have adopted a much more proactive approach to the protection of privacy rights than the United States has. Part of the reason behind this different philosophy is Western Europe's conceptualization of privacy as a matter of "data protection," and its view that privacy is rooted in basic human rights. There has also been a long-standing assumption that the state must have an interest in protecting personal information.[32] Unlike Americans, Europeans have not become preoccupied with interminable debates about the justification of privacy as a normative concept.

Data protection legislation in some European countries was formulated as far back as the early 1970s. The data protection law of the German state of Hesse was the first such law in the world. Several years later, in 1973, Sweden passed its Data Protection Act, which was designed to prevent "undue encroachment on personal privacy." The purpose of these early laws was to control the process of data processing, particularly the processing of the copious information required by the emerging social welfare bureaucracies. According to Mayer-Schonberger, European legislatures in the early 1970s saw the need to enact "functional data protection norms focusing on processing and emphasizing licensing and registration procedures aimed at controlling *ex ante* the use of the computer."[33]

During the 1980s, data processing became much more decentralized. As a consequence, there were no longer just a few massive central databases, but a variety of databases on mainframe and minicomputer systems dispersed throughout Europe. This gave rise to a second generation of "data protection" laws, where "existing individual rights were reinforced, linked to constitutional provisions, broadened, and extended."[34] The focus shifted to the individual, who was given the right to have some say over the process of data collection and transfer. Subsequent legislation has strengthened and reinforced those rights.

In addition, enforcement of privacy legislation has not been taken lightly. European countries such as Germany, the Netherlands, Italy, and Sweden have established government agencies dedicated to the objective of privacy protection. In Sweden, for example, the Data Inspection Board (DIB) issues licenses to keepers of commercial databases containing consumer information and carefully monitors any matching or recombining of data from one database system to another.

In October, 1995, acting on behalf of all of its member countries, the European Union Parliament adopted *Directive 95/46/EC on the protection of individuals with regard to the processing of personal data and the free movement of such data*. The goal was to harmonize the different rules and regulations that had been developed by the member states. It is known simply as the European Union Directive on Privacy. The directive imposes an obligation on each member of the European Union to enact legislation that will implement these privacy norms. According to Andrews, "The goal of the European law is to prohibit companies from using information about their customers in ways the customers never intended—for example, selling it to other companies for use as a marketing tool."[35]

Since the promulgation of this directive, which must be translated into specific laws in the member countries, there have been fears that it would disrupt electronic commerce between Europe and the United States. The directive contains a provision that enjoins countries within the European Union from disseminating personal data to any country that does not guarantee the same level of protection. This might mean that Europe could block the transfer of data by multinational corporations that operate in Europe and the United States. This law would also seem to prevent

U.S. e-commerce companies from gathering any consumer data from European customers unless it complied with certain privacy standards, even if this activity is typically part of the online transaction.

The primary objective of this ambitious European Directive is clearly articulated in Article 1: "to protect the fundamental rights and freedom of natural persons, and in particular the right to privacy with respect to the *processing of personal data* [emphasis added]." The directive concentrates on the processing of data or the flow of information between organizations; less attention is paid to how data is collected and stored.

Article 6 delineates several important principles regarding that processing: "Member states shall provide that personal data must be (a) processed fairly and lawfully; (b) collected for specified, explicit, and legitimate purposes and not processed in a way incompatible with those purposes . . . (c) adequate, relevant, and not excessive in relation to the purposes for which they are collected and/or further processed; (d) accurate and, where necessary, kept up to date. . . ." With Article 6, the directive is mandating a certain level of data quality, ensuring that data is adequate, relevant, precise, and accurate.

Also important for understanding the core principles of this directive is Article 7, which seeks to explicate the "criteria for making data processing legitimate." Data may be processed when the data subject has provided his or her consent; the processing is necessary for the performance of a contract between the organization and the data subject; the processing is necessary "in order to protect the vital interests of the data" or for the "performance of a task carried out in the public interest." There are special restrictions for data of a sensitive nature (such as information concerning one's ethnic background or religious affiliation). The directive also gives the data subject the right to know about the processing of his or her personal data along with the right to access that data and correct mistakes. Finally, the directive stipulates that European Union citizens even have the right to a national privacy agency in order to enforce all of these rules and protections.

The directive obviously imposes a constraint on the reprocessing of data. Data cannot be processed for new purposes that are incompatible with the purpose for which it has been collected. Presumably, if Amazon.com collects certain information (name, shipping address, e-mail address, books ordered) for the purpose of completing an online sales transaction, it cannot reprocess that information, i.e., package and sell it to a market company for direct marketing offers aimed at this data subject, unless it has that data subject's consent. Elgesem points out, however, that "the notion of further processing of data in a way that is not incompatible with the purpose for which it was collected is a difficult one to interpret."[36] For example, is the purpose for which the information was originally processed the purpose of the processor or the "subjective purpose of the data subject?" It's probably not the latter, but to what extent do the expectations of the data subject become relevant in determining the parameters for legitimate reprocessing of that subject's information?

We cannot settle this issue here, and perhaps country-specific laws will resolve some of this ambiguity. But Elgesem argues that the directive seems to embody "the ideal that the data subject shall be able to form reasonable expectations concerning how personal data will be processed."[37] At the same time, not all processing has to be justified to the data subject if it is for a vital national interest (e.g., the collection of tax revenues). There are three different questions that emerge: "1) is the processing predictable?, 2) does the processing constitute a socially justifiable activity?, and 3) is the processing justified to the data subject, i.e., has he actively or passively consented?"[38] Affirmative answers to Questions 1 and 2 are a necessary condition for the legitimate processing of data according to Elgesem's interpretation of the directive. But there may be cases where processing is justifiable (i.e., it is predictable and a socially justified activity) in the absence of an affirmative answer to Question 3 (the data subject still objects to the processing).

There are other ambiguities with the directive that will be difficult for member states to interpret. The directive requires that any "identifiable person" must be guaranteed these privacy rights. According to Reidenberg, "The scope of this definition is not the same across the Member States; what some Member States consider 'identifiable' others do not."[39] As a result, some European countries have developed different criteria for what constitutes anonymous information, which is not subject to the protections guaranteed by the directive.

Despite these ambiguities, the European directive provides a model statement of principles that could be translated into a regulatory system protecting privacy rights. Aside from a comprehensive legal framework spelling out the specific privacy rights of consumers, there would be some need for a bureaucratic infrastructure to monitor compliance and to deal with offenders. As noted in Chapter 2, there has been some movement in the international community to harmonize privacy standards and to adopt this EU directive as a worldwide model.

While there is no denying the benefits of this model, some governments representing both developed and developing countries may be reluctant to invest in that bureaucracy or to assemble an information police force to protect the privacy of their citizens. The "business cost" of these regulations also cannot be ignored. One British company, Netstore PLC, estimates that "it will cost more than $100,000 to develop a process that lets people access their data, which is a directive requirement."[40]

Yet reliance on the heavy hand of government may be the only truly efficacious way of offering citizens durable privacy protection.

▶Privacy and Internet Architectures

So far in this chapter we have illustrated some of the key architectures that have contributed to the erosion of privacy. Databases and their retrieval algorithms have permitted the accumulation of vast amounts of personal data that can easily be culled by curious users and opportunistic corporations. On the World Wide Web, architectures like cookies and Web bugs make it possible to monitor users as they shop at different Web stores. These architecture could become especially pernicious since they allow data to be collected transparently, without the user's knowledge and consent. What will be the implications for privacy if future Internet architectures continue to work so stealthily?

The debate about Internet architectures and privacy intensified in early 1999 with the introduction of Intel Corporation's plan to put identification numbers in its next generation of computer chips, the Pentium IIIs. The primary purpose of the embedded serial number was to authenticate a user's identity in a business transaction and to allow organizations to better track their computer equipment. Unlike digital certificates, which can be falsified, this appeared to be a much less fallible way of ensuring an individual's true digital identity.

Privacy advocates, however, had a much different perspective, and immediately asked the FTC to demand that Intel recall the chips. With protests escalating and an impending boycott threat, Intel conceded to modify the chips so that the serial number was disabled unless a user turned it on. Even this solution did not satisfy Intel's critics, who pointed out that PC makers could easily remove the software patch that disables the serial number and ship their products with the serial numbers turned on. Others worried that intruders could still break into a system and turn on the switch.

There is no question that the Intel serial number would enhance the security of online commercial transactions and help prevent fraud or personal theft of personal information. But the tradeoff is the potential for a significant loss of privacy. Like the identifying mechanism of cookies, this architecture could also enable Web marketers to clandestinely track consumers on the Web by retrieving that serial number. Although Intel has disavowed any intention to build a master database of customer names linked to serial numbers, who knows what the future could bring?

Digital identification hard-wired into machines epitomizes the new authenticating architectures of cyberspace, which will verify identity, but also allow the identified user to be tracked online without consent or knowledge. Once again, we realize how technology makes it possible to raise monitoring and profiling to a new and more disturbing level.

Is it possible, however, to fight fire with fire, to use architectures that protect privacy rather than put it in harm's way? Can code be used to constrain the activities of those who are so anxious to exploit consumer information? We have seen two distinct approaches to data protection: the U.S.'s reliance on market forces and self-regulation and the European Union's heavy reliance on law. We now turn to a fuller discussion of the role of code in solving this problem.

One privacy-protective architecture that has considerable promise is known as the Platform for Privacy Preferences Project, or P3P, developed by the World Wide Web Consortium (W3C). P3P standardizes the comparison between Web site privacy polices and the user's privacy preferences. The P3P protocol will include rules that guide Web browsers as they read and interpret privacy policies (in a machine-readable format) on commercial Web sites. The user's preferences will be embedded into the browser and P3P will only allow users to provide their personal data at sites that are consistent with those preferences. The user will be warned before entering a Web site that collects more information than he or she is willing to provide or that has other data policies with which the user is uncomfortable. Presumably, the participating Web site's policy will include information such as whether it provides e-mail addresses to third parties or makes use of cookies, and that information will be in a format that can be read by the P3P-compliant browser. The goal of P3P is to empower users to make informed choices about whether to accept or reject a Web site's privacy practices. The more enthusiastic proponents of P3P maintain that this approach "will be far more effective than any new laws."[41]

Obviously, P3P will work only if Web sites adopt this standard and express their privacy policies in P3P's special machine readable dialect. Only then can the browser software compare that policy with the user's preferences. Major software vendors such as Microsoft have thrown their full weight behind this standard by incorporating this protocol into Version 6 of its Internet Explorer browser. In addition, some of the Internet's biggest companies such as AOL Time Warner, IBM, and AT&T have made a firm commitment to P3P, and they have vowed to make their Web sites P3P compliant. But others, including Amazon.com and Disney, are more skeptical about the promise of this technology and have adopted a wait and see attitude for the present time.

P3P is certainly not a privacy panacea, but it represents the first generation of technological tools that give the user control over how he or she wants to divulge personal data. There are several benefits associated with the use of P3P. First, widespread adoption of P3P will encourage standardization and simplification of privacy policies; since that policy must be in machine-readable format, it cannot be expressed in undecipherable legal language. P3P also has the potential to make it easier for users to access privacy statements before they enter a Web site; sometimes those statements are obscured, but P3P will ferret out the policy and allow a proper screening by the end user. P3P has its limitations though. It cannot ensure enforcement of privacy policies: if some corporate Web site decides to violate its policy, P3P will have little recourse. Nonetheless, if P3P is embraced by most commercial Web sites and its specification is further enhanced, this technology could play an important role in helping consumers to safeguard their privacy.

▶A Prescription for Privacy

In Europe, privacy is not left to the whims of the marketplace or the precariousness of self-regulation. This solution, which relies on law as the chief mechanism to safeguard privacy, is probably well suited for the culture and political tradition of Europe. The idea of the beneficent state controlling the economy has had considerable appeal in most European countries for quite some time. But in the United States, where the image of the paternalistic state is not as strong, a more nuanced solution may be optimal.

Where confidentiality breaches could lead to serious harm, comprehensive federal legislation is essential. In the United States there are already laws that protect credit and financial data (such as the Fair Credit Reporting Act), and new rules (HIPPA) to safeguard sensitive medical information. In determining which kinds of information deserve regulatory protection, the principle of proportionality should apply, that is, the need for government regulation should be commensurate with the potential for injury if the information is divulged inappropriately.

A tenable case could be advanced that regular consumer data, including clickstream data, does not satisfy the principle of proportionality. A user's shopping profile and purchasing patterns are much less sensitive than medical or financial profiles. Nonetheless, we have been at pains to insist here that even if that sort of data is improperly disclosed, there is a risk of harm. So this data too deserves some measure of protection. One viable option that deserves consideration is reliance on mechanisms like P3P that hold out great promise for privacy regulation without the need for a new legal framework. P3P or related privacy enhancing architectures represent a way for the online industry to regulate itself through the discipline of technology. It recognizes implicitly that users do have a property right in their information, and yet it does not require that the legal regime be overhauled to protect that right.

Of course, as we have argued in this chapter, all companies that operate on the Web have a deep moral duty to respect the privacy rights of consumers. Hence in the absence of regulations, they should voluntarily embrace sound privacy policies based on notice and choice along with technologies like P3P as an ideal means of living up to that duty. They will be required to disclose their privacy policies openly and honestly in a statement (in machine-readable format) like the one formulated by CoolCatalog:

> We collect click stream data in our HTTP logs. We also collect your first name, age and gender to customize our catalog pages for the type of clothing you are likely to be interested in and for our own research and product development. We do not use this information in a personally identifiable way. We do not redistribute this information outside of our organization. We do not provide access capabilities to information we may have from you, but we do have retention and opt-out policies, which you can read at our privacy page http://CoolCatalog.com/Privacy/Practice.html. The third party Privacy-Seal.org provides assurance that we abide by this agreement.[42]

To work most effectively and to further ensure consumer confidence, P3P will also require self-auditing and monitoring by third party "seal organizations," such as Truste, that would give a seal of approval to co-operating Web sites and take punitive action against those who violate their policies. Given the growing concerns that consumers have about privacy, it is likely that the market will reward those online firms that do participate.

Ethical self-regulation facilitated by technology has the potential to be a viable prescription for privacy protection, as long as it is supplemented by sectoral-specific statutes that protect sensitive information such as medical data. The essence of this approach is reliance on privacy enhancing architectures such as P3P as long as those architectures are responsibly deployed. This approach will not work unless participating vendors truly respect the core value of privacy. They must embrace this issue with an attitude of moral sincerity, otherwise there will be temptations to look for loopholes or exploit shortcomings in the system. There is no substitute for organizational integrity, which breeds the conscientiousness and self-discipline that are essential for effective and durable self-regulation.

While there is much to be admired with the European approach, the drawback is the financial burdens that accompany an elaborate regulatory regime. Economists like Coase have long been skeptical of relying too heavily on government regulations due to the magnitude of the costs necessary to regulate so many externalities like privacy erosion. The European Directive, for example, requires an expensive bureaucratic infrastructure for its enforcement. Coase and others believe that government intervention is not always welfare-enhancing, and that sometimes such intervention does more harm than good, especially if self-interested policy makers are captured by industry interests. According to Coase, "There may be some regulation which is beneficial, but this is not true of most of the activities of the regulatory agencies."[43] While we do not share this extreme pessimism about the efficacy of government intervention, there is something to be said for viewing government regulation with a healthy dose of skepticism. A case can be made that such regulation should be used sparingly—if a decentralized approach emphasizing responsible use of code can determine an adequate level of information privacy, it might be better than relying too heavily on a centralized solution.

As Lessig has intimated, the resolution for an intricate problem such as privacy in cyberspace will necessarily involve a complex interaction between code, law, industry norms, and the marketplace. The European paradigm gives precedence to law, and United States is willing to let the marketplace work out a scheme of privacy protection and intervene only when the costs of market failure are excessive. We propose here another alternative for reflection and debate: the primacy of ethical self-regulation facilitated by code as a way of dealing with the shortcomings that accompany reliance on the invisible hand of the market or the all too visible hand of government.

But we should also recognize the validity of the European perspective. The rule of law may be the most appropriate mechanism for assuring privacy protection, especially if most companies persist in ignoring their ethical responsibilities. If that directive is successfully implemented in Europe, it could become a model privacy policy for many other countries around the world.

▶Privacy in the Workplace

Privacy Rights at Risk

During the past two decades, technology has significantly redefined the nature of work as corporations and users rely more heavily on information technology to manage their information resources and help control their far scattered operations. IT has enabled many corporations to redesign the flow of work and to automate more routine processes. The Internet has clearly played a major role in all of this by expediting interorganizational communication and enabling the online business models discussed in Chapter 2.

But there is a more ominous side to this transformation of the workplace. Technology has also facilitated greater control over employees and a heightened intrusiveness into their private lives. Some omniscient employers, for example, check the whereabouts of their employees through electronic monitoring, maintain health surveillance data banks, and regularly check up on an employee's electronic mail, voice mail, and Web surfing habits. There is a real danger that the workplace is becoming a panopticon where workers' activities and interactions are transparent to the corporate hierarchy. An American Management Association Survey in 1999 revealed that 45 percent of all companies interviewed conducted electronic surveillance, and it is quite likely that this number has expanded considerably.[44]

What is also disturbing is that more and more workplace activities fall under the watchful eye of technology. Some monitoring systems, such as Silent Watch, record every keystroke an employee makes, including those that are deleted. If an employee types an angry e-mail but deletes it before issuing the SEND command, every keystroke is still recorded. Employers are particularly keen on monitoring clickstream data and Web site activities since they are anxious to find out who has been wasting company resources at recreational sites. Products from companies like eSniff.com will monitor all network activities and single out transactions or requests that appear out of the ordinary.

Most workers accept this ongoing surveillance as part of the new reality for the twenty-first century work environment. But when the U.S. federal court system's chief administrator devised a plan to monitor the network activities of federal judges and their staffs, there was a powerful backlash. The intent was to install software that would detect access to Web sites providing pornography, gambling, music, or streaming video. The judges took matters into their own hands and disabled the intrusive software, claiming that it amounted to a "large-scale violation of privacy."[45] In the face of this concerted opposition, the monitoring plan was shelved.

Employers from both the public and private sectors claim that monitoring is essential to guard against the loss of trade secrets and to prevent abuses of their computer systems. They also contend that monitoring helps in performance evaluation. Customer service representatives who interact over the phone are monitored for accuracy, thoroughness, and politeness.

Despite the occasional rebellion, there is little sign that this trend is on the wane. Most employers seem to have no problem with this practice. But moralists and social theorists see it as a perilous policy. Sewell and Barker, for example, argue that we cannot be indifferent about this matter, but must adopt a "critical disposition towards workplace surveillance that can be used to engage with its 'dangerous side.'"[46] They argue that at the very least, questions should be posed in each context about the necessity and legitimacy of the surveillance, which should lead us to "confront and challenge the basic reasoning behind its existence."[47]

Comparing U.S. and European Policies

It is probably not surprising that the European legal system differs from the U.S. system on the issue of workplace monitoring. In the United

States, there are virtually no laws that expressly forbid workplace surveillance. The Fourth Amendment to the Constitution stipulates the "right of the people to be secure in their persons, houses, papers, and effects, against unreasonable searches and seizures." But this right applies only to the government and not to private organizations, so it offers little protection in the workplace. In addition, the Electronic Communications Privacy Act of 1986 "amended the federal wiretap law to protect cellular telephones, electronic mail, pagers, and electronic data transmissions" from unauthorized wiretaps.[48] But the ECPA makes an exception for private communications systems and it excludes telephones or devices "furnished to the subscriber or user by a provider of the . . . communication service in the ordinary course of its business."[49] Thus, the ECPA offers little protection for workers' privacy rights.

On the other hand, the laws in many European countries, such as France and Italy, offer much more extensive protection. In Italy, the Italian Workers Statute "prohibits remote surveillance of workers by video camera or other devices" unless agreed to by the union for the sake of a business necessity; even then, a worker has the right to challenge the surveillance.[50] In addition, the Italian courts have interpreted this law broadly, forbidding software installed exclusively for the purpose of monitoring and controlling a worker's performance.

Similarly, French law has been equally sympathetic to employee privacy rights. Consider Article 120-2 of France's Labor Code: "No one may place restrictions on the rights of persons and individual or collective liberties which are not justified by the nature of the task to be accomplished and proportional to the objective sought."[51] The French courts have interpreted this broad statue in favor of employees. According to Rothstein, "Courts have penalized employers for collecting or processing electronic data concerning employees without informing employees in advance, consulting with the works council or submitting a declaration to the CNIL [National Commission on Data Processing and Liberty]."

What accounts for this discrepancy in how employee privacy is regarded in the U.S. and in Europe? Rothstein contends that the basis of this different treatment is continental Europe's emphasis on dignity. While Americans talk about the value of privacy and the need to weigh that value against economic concerns, in most European countries "the value most frequently mentioned in the electronic surveillance context is human dignity."[52] The worker's dignity must not be disregarded just because the worker is at his or her place of work. Dignity connotes intrinsic worth and each person has dignity by virtue of his or her rationality and autonomy. When workplace surveillance is seen as an affront to dignity (rather than a violation of abstract privacy rights), it is easier to appreciate its potential perniciousness and its threat to the workers wellbeing.

The Case for E-Mail Privacy Rights

Before concluding this chapter, it would be instructive to engage in a moral analysis of a single but representative aspect of worker surveillance: the employee's right to e-mail privacy. Do corporations have a right to inspect the electronic mail of their workers or should employees be able to communicate via e-mail without the fear that their messages will be read by managers? Before we discuss this issue, some additional background on workplace privacy is in order.

Thanks in part to technological advancements and other pressures, we seem to be entering a new era where there is a diminished respect for workplace rights such as privacy. There appear to be several factors accounting for this change. Intense global competition and the exodus of American jobs to foreign countries with low labor costs has strengthened the position of many corporations while it has simultaneously weakened the bargaining leverage of once powerful unions. In our litigious society there is also a greater threat of liability hanging over the corporate world. For example, corporations can now be held liable for negligent hiring if they fail to adequately check the background of their employees. And, of course, sophisticated surveillance technologies have created unparalleled opportunities to exercise control. All of this has been especially perilous for privacy rights in the workplace, which are not well protected in American law.

While most organizations do support the notion that their employees are entitled to some level of privacy protection, they have adopted policies that allow for e-mail monitoring. Employees are usually notified that their e-mail is not considered private and can be read at any time by their managers or by other authorized company officials. The core argument justifying this policy is simple: an electronic mail network, including its contents, is owned by the employer, and hence the employer has a right to inspect these messages whenever it is deemed necessary. Employers contend that they have the right to read e-mail to make sure that employees are not using company property for private purposes. There is an apparent conflict between the rights to ownership and privacy, and the employer claims that property rights should take precedence. Certainly in countries such as the United States, there is a tradition of supporting the right of property owners to monitor their property, so the employer is on pretty firm legal ground.

Those who support e-mail monitoring also point out that employers can be held liable for what their employees transmit over a corporate e-mail system, either to those within the company or to external parties. If an employee uses that system to send offensive images to selected female workers, the company might be held legally liable for sexual harassment if it can be demonstrated that it was too tardy in taking corrective actions. The potential for such liability has clearly increased the incentive to filter and monitor e-mails transmitted through the workplace.

Supporters also argue that the law is firmly on their side. In case after case, judges have affirmed that corporations have a right to monitor their employees e-mail even if they do not inform them about their intentions. Consider the case of *Smyth v. Pillsbury Co.*, which has established an important precedent since the ruling originated in a U.S. federal court (as opposed to a state court). In this case Smyth filed a wrongful discharge suit against Pillsbury. He was terminated for inappropriate use of the company's e-mail system. In one e-mail message in which Smyth was expressing his disgust with some of his managers, Smyth said that he would "kill the backstabbing bastards." According to Smyth, Pillsbury had informed its employees that e-mail communications were confidential. Pillsbury officials, however, said that all employees were told that their electronic mail should not be considered "secure" and could be inspected by the company at any time. The United States District Court for the Eastern District of Pennsylvania ruled in Pillsbury's favor. The court stated that company e-mail does not demand privacy protection because e-mail by its very nature is a public medium of communication, and employees should therefore have no expectation of privacy in their e-mail messages.

Despite this ruling, there are several plausible moral arguments supporting reasonable workplace privacy rights, including a *prima facie* e-mail privacy right. One argument centers on each person's fundamental right to autonomy, to make choices freely and direct one's activities. As we observed earlier in this chapter, privacy is often a critical prerequisite for the exercise of one's autonomy, particularly in an information-intensive environment. Moreover, autonomy is a basic aspect of one's humanity according to moral common sense and most philosophical traditions. Thus, respect for the autonomy of others is a moral imperative that cannot be arbitrarily jettisoned or overridden for the sake of economic expediency. As Pat Werhane has argued, disrespecting the right to autonomy in the workplace "is equivalent to disrespecting employees as persons."[53]

Without some degree of privacy, some zone of personal space where a worker's thoughts and actions are not totally visible, it would be difficult to retain one's autonomy. Since workplace autonomy is contingent on privacy, it follows that workers must have some privacy rights where they work.

Of course, this does not imply that employees have complete freedom in the workplace environment, since they are accountable to their employers for fulfilling the normal demands of their jobs. Autonomy and privacy must be circumscribed appropriately to help meet those demands. It does mean, however, that unless there is a legitimate *need to know,* employers should not be conducting surveillance of their employees.

The vast majority of employers would probably agree with all this, at least from a theoretical point of view. They do not deny that their workers are entitled to *some* level of privacy protection. Most employers, for example, do recognize that they should not spy on their workers at home or pry too deeply into the irrelevant details of their personal lives. Their tendency, however, is to acknowledge a narrow right to privacy, while civil libertarians would argue for a more robust right. There is also disagreement over the propriety of methods used to collect information about employees. Some corporations have employed questionable methods such as polygraph tests, psychological testing, and covert surveillance cameras to acquire data about their workers.

Given these disagreements, how do we achieve a responsible equilibrium between worker's privacy rights and the corporation's need for information? There seems to be at least two important guidelines that can help us to delineate the appropriate privacy zone for employees. First, employers should only gather *relevant* information about their employees. For prospective employees this will undoubtedly include job history and other important background information, while for employees already on the job it will include data related to job performance or the furtherance of corporate objectives such as quality customer service. Second, an employer should only utilize *ordinary* and common methods of acquiring information, that is, "the supervisory activities that are normally used to oversee employees' work."[54] Employers should not routinely use extraordinary data collection methods, which include the deployment of hidden surveillance devices, secret cameras, wiretaps, polygraph testing, and so forth. As Des Jardins argues, extraordinary means of data collection such as "blanket surveillance of all employees" are illegitimate under ordinary conditions because they are so intrusive and potentially harmful.[55] Hence they should not be adopted unless the circumstances themselves are extraordinary. For instance, suspicion that trade secrets were being pilfered or that company property was being misused would certainly justify the use of extraordinary measures to ensure their protection. Also, for financial institutions, a record of all contact with customers, including e-mail, may be necessary for verification purposes. In some cases certain extraordinary methods may also be necessary for quality control purposes.

Monitoring and reading electronic mail in a systematic fashion is a form of surveillance and hence falls under the classification of extraordinary data collection methods. Clarke defines *surveillance* as the "systematic investigation or monitoring of the actions or communications of one or more persons."[56] When a company's policy permits its managers to monitor and to routinely read their employee's electronic mail on a regular basis, that policy is promoting activities that are tantamount to surveillance.

Even if one concedes that monitoring or interception of e-mail messages is a form of surveillance and is an extraordinary means of inquiry into employee activities, it may not be immediately apparent that *this* type of surveillance is really dangerously intrusive and harmful. It is important to consider, therefore, precisely how such e-mail surveillance is an invasion of one's privacy.

Clearly, when one's electronic mail messages are randomly inspected, one's privacy is violated since confidentiality (or secrecy) and anonymity are lost. Recall that these are two key elements of Ruth Gavison's definition of privacy. The information in the message is no longer confidential since it is read by a third party (a systems administrator or a manager) and the names of the sender and receiver are exposed so both lose their anonymity.

But in what ways could this be officious and harmful? For example, many interactions in the workplace intersperse business and personal information; this often happens inadvertently when workers allude to certain aspects of their personal lives as they exchange business information with co-workers. It seems unfair and unrealistic to demand that workers refrain from doing this at all times. Also, employees who regularly work from 9 A.M. to 5 P.M. (and in many cases for much longer hours) often have no choice but to conduct some personal business affairs from their offices. As a result, those companies that routinely inspect e-mail will sometimes become privy to an employee's personal business affairs or perhaps to sensitive details about an employee's family life. Further, the loss of anonymity could be consequential in some situations. For example, the correspondence between two workers, Joe and Marie, might be perfectly innocuous and professional, but Marie's manager might draw an unwarranted inference from the frequency of those communications or it may be referenced out of context. This might affect management's perception of her character and ultimately her future position in the company.

Given the harm that can come to individuals through surveillance and this attendant loss of confidentiality and anonymity, it is tenable to reach the conclusion that employees deserve at least a *prima facie,* or conditional e-mail privacy right. Well-founded suspicions of fraudulent behavior, the transmission of defamatory or offensive material over the Internet, or other forms of employee misbehavior would justify a suspension of that right. But unless there is a just cause or a genuine business necessity, employers should refrain from e-mail surveillance and respect the right to e-mail privacy.

This dispute over e-mail privacy is fraught with many ambiguities and complexities, and it will probably never be resolved to the satisfaction of all the relevant stakeholders. As long as employers assert their property rights and as long as they worry about potential liabilities for what their employees do with the corporate e-mail system, they will be reluctant to recognize even a conditional right to e-mail privacy in the workplace.

Discussion Questions

1. In your estimation, could self-regulation be effective in protecting data privacy or does it need to be supplemented by laws and regulations? Is the European model worth emulating here in the United States?
2. What is your general assessment of cookie technology? Should there be some limits on how this technology is used?
3. Is it morally acceptable for an employer to intercept the e-mail of its employees? Under what circumstances should an ISP be permitted to tap into the electronic communications of its users?
4. Almost every major commercial Web site has a privacy policy. Visit one of these sites in order to read and evaluate that policy. Is the policy clear and comprehensible? Does it afford enough protection for that site's customers?
   For example, check out one of the following sites:
   http://privacy.yahoo.com/privacy/us
   http://legal.Web.aol.com/policy/aolpol/privpol.html

Cases

DoubleClick: The Ethics of Online Advertising

On February 23, 2000, Kevin Ryan, Chief Executive Officer of Double-Click, picked up a copy of the *Wall Street Journal* as he entered his office at the company headquarters in Manhattan. He saw the headline "A Privacy Firestorm at DoubleClick," and he knew the article would fuel the controversy surrounding the company's plans to use offline data to target its Web-based ads. The article described how he and other executives at DoubleClick had been blindsided by the backlash and were struggling to recover. This controversy was becoming a public relations nightmare and Ryan realized that he needed a quick resolution before things got out of hand.

Company Background

DoubleClick is the world's leading provider of Internet advertising and related marketing services. It is affiliated with over 11,000 Web publishers and it specializes in delivering targeted advertising to many of those Web sites. A core group of 1,500 Web sites comprise the "DoubleClick Network." These are frequently visited, branded sites where most of DoubleClick's ads appear. The company estimates that it sends out over one billion ads a day.[57]

How does the DoubleClick advertising service work? Many commercial Web sites rent out available space to other Web sites, which usually place "hotlink" banner advertisements in that space so that when the user clicks on the ad, he or she is linked to the advertiser's Web site. Double-Click functions as a broker in these transactions. The company seeks to place the advertiser's banner ad in front of an audience composed of individuals who match its demographic target. For example, an online bookstore trying to get its banner ad in front of an upper income, intellectual audience might find that DoubleClick places its ad on the Web site for a classical music radio station such as WQXR in New York City.

In addition, DoubleClick builds profiles of those users who traffic its affiliated Web sites. Whenever a user visits a DoubleClick affiliated Web site, the company deposits a cookie (an electronic file) on that user's hard drive. Each cookie has a unique ID number that links it to a particular computer user. Cookies collect information such as username and password (this makes it easier for those accessing Web sites that require authentication), items purchased online, Web sites visited, IP address, browser version, and so forth. DoubleClick uses the information collected by these cookies to build its profile.

But how precisely does DoubleClick succeed in targeting its banner advertisements? The first time a user visits a DoubleClick-affiliated Web site, the company deposits a cookie file with an identifying code (such as 7890) on the user's computer. After that, every time that user visits any DoubleClick-affiliated site, the visit is recorded and that user can be sent a targeted banner ad. That targeting occurs in the following manner. Let's assume that the user seeks to access a DoubleClick-affiliated Web site called Books.com, which happens to rent out ads to other Web sites. When Books.com receives the user's request, it returns its Web page, but with a blank space where the banner ad is supposed to appear. It also transmits an "IP-address link," which instructs the user's computer to automatically send a message to the DoubleClick server using the DoubleClick cookie. That message essentially says "This is cookie #7890—send me a banner ad to fill in the blank space on the Books.com Web page." After receiving this message, DoubleClick locates the user's profile (thanks to the cookie ID), initiates certain proprietary algorithms and sends along a targeted ad based on the information in that profile and other factors. The user's profile is also updated with the information that the Books.com Web page has been requested. Of course, DoubleClick is working behind the scenes, as the user only sees the Books.com Web page with a customied banner ad.[58]

The DoubleClick cookie is hard at work collecting information throughout this process. For example, it collects information through GET submissions, that is, from the query string entered by a user. A request for novelist John Grisham's books might look something like this:

http://www.books.com/search?terms=John Grisham

The cookie would capture the information that this user has entered a query for information about John Grisham. Users sometimes submit what is known as POST information when they fill in empty fields on a Web page such as their name and e-mail address. This information is also gathered by DoubleClick. Lastly, DoubleClick cookies collect information through invisible GIF tags placed on their affiliated Web sites, which "record the user's movements throughout the affiliated Web site, enabling DoubleClick to learn what information the user sought and viewed."[59] DoubleClick aggregates this information in its voluminous user profile database.

The Abacus Acquisition

On June 13, 1999, DoubleClick entered into an agreement to purchase a direct-marketing company called Abacus Direct Corp. for a little over one billion dollars. Abacus maintained its own database with names, addresses, telephone numbers, retail purchasing records, and other related data, which it sold to direct marketing companies. It is estimated that the Abacus database contained over 88 million buyer profiles compiled from records such as retail catalog purchases. In 1998 Abacus began to add some online data such as e-mail addresses, phone numbers, and click data to its database.

In November, 1999, DoubleClick completed the acquisition process. Almost immediately the company changed its privacy policy. That privacy policy displayed on Web site in 1998 stated the following:

> All users who receive an ad targeted by DoubleClick's technology remain completely anonymous. We do not sell or rent any information to third parties. Because of our efforts to keep users anonymous, the information DoubleClick has is useful only across sites using the DoubleClick technology and only in the context of ad selection.

However, DoubleClick announced plans to combine the online information in its customer profiles with the offline data in the Abacus database so that users would no longer retain their anonymity. DoubleClick asserted that "personally identifiable information (including user's name, address, retail, catalog and online purchase history, and demographic data)" would be linked up with "non-personally-identifiable information collected by DoubleClick from Web sites on the DoubleClick network."[60] For example, assume that a hypothetical user, let's call her Katie Miller, had given her name and address at a DoubleClick-affiliated Web site and that Double Click had collected this POST information by means of the cookie assigned to her. DoubleClick would now try to match her name with the name and address in the Abacus database. It could thereby extend its consumer profile of Katie Miller with the other offline data in the Abacus files. DoubleClick would know that she buys luggage from Coach and clothing from Talbot's. DoubleClick was convinced that the possession of this offline data would make its online ads much more effective. In Katie's case it could now send her online ads from upscale clothing companies. By mid-February, 2000, DoubleClick had already constructed "between 50,000 and 100,000 online-offline profiles."[61]

DoubleClick's plans caused a small furor. According to Anderson and Perine, privacy experts were nervous "over the idea that a firm most consumers never heard of can track their moves online and share that information with companies that can hit them with direct-mail, telemarketing calls, and targeted Web ads."[62] There were apprehensions that DoubleClick would know too much about its consumers, who would not have the wherewithal to block the company's surveillance techniques.

In response to this criticism, the FTC launched an investigation of the company's privacy policies and practices. The State of Michigan filed a lawsuit. And some irate consumers joined together in a class action lawsuit against the company, alleging that DoubleClick's collection and use of Internet data was "improper."

DoubleClick's defense was that it had done nothing wrong aside from "failing to communicate to the public just what it does and what it plans to do."[63] The company pointed out that it gave users adequate information about how to disable its cookies so they would not receive its targeted online ads and have their surfing habits included in the DoubleClick consumer profile. Nonetheless, the company was being pilloried in the press —according to Petersen, DoubleClick had gone from being a "dot-com darling with an inside track on e-commerce to an Internet privacy pariah."[64]

As Ryan and other DoubleClick executives pondered their next move, they expressed concern about the company's tarnished image. But Ryan was also convinced that targeted online advertising was the future. The banner ad might become a commodity, but targeted advertising based on previous purchasing behavior could easily give the company a strong competitive edge for years to come.

Discussion Questions

1. Does DoubleClick's new privacy policy infringe on consumer's privacy rights? Is there anything wrong with combining online and offline data as long as the user can opt out?
2. How do you assess the company's defense of its actions? Are they only guilty of miscommunication or something more serious?
3. What should Kevin Ryan do at this point?

Amazon's New Privacy Policy

After reading about the travails of an online company called Toysmart.com, Amazon executives wanted to avoid making the same mistakes. Toysmart specialized in selling educational toys for children over the Internet, but it went bankrupt in June 2000 along with many other "dot com" companies. Toysmart's privacy policy had made the following reassuring assertion: "You can rest assured that your information will never be shared with a third party." But during bankruptcy proceedings, Toysmart attempted to sell its customer information, since that information was considered to be a legitimate asset eligible for liquidation under the U.S. bankruptcy code. The company was strongly criticized, however, by privacy advocates and politicians for going back on its word. The Federal Trade Commission (FTC) accused the company of "unfair and deceptive" practices, and eventually a settlement was reached.

In the wake of this controversy, Amazon.com, the leading online bookseller, decided to modify its privacy policy so that it could avoid similar problems with the fate of data it had assembled on its 23 million customers. Here is the essential statement of Amazon's old privacy policy:

> We are committed to protecting your privacy. We use the information we collect on the site to make shopping at Amazon.com possible and to enhance your overall shopping experience. We do not sell, trade, or rent your personal information to others.

But Amazon announced a change to that policy in early September, 2000. Customers were essentially told that their information was now being regarded as a company asset. Here is an excerpt from the new Amazon policy:

> **Business Transfers**: As we continue to develop our business, we might sell or buy stores or assets. In such transactions, customer information generally is one of the transferred business assets. Also, in the unlikely event that Amazon.com, Inc., or substantially all of its assets are acquired, customer information will of course be one of the transferred assets.

On its current Web site, http://www.amazon.com, that same policy is still clearly stipulated. The company is also at pains to indicate the types of personally identifiable consumer data it collects. That data includes transaction information that consumers voluntarily provide when making a purchase: name, address, phone number, e-mail address, credit card number, and so forth. It also includes information collected automatically by architectures such as cookies. According to Amazon's current privacy policy,

> **Automatic Information**: Examples of the information we collect and analyze include the Internet protocol (IP) address used to connect your computer to the Internet; login; e-mail address; password; computer and connection information such as browser type and version, operating system, and platform; purchase history; the full Uniform Resource Locators (URL) clickstream to, through, and from our Web site, including date and time; cookie number; products you viewed or searched for; zShops you visited; your Auction history, and phone number used to call our 800 number.

In addition, at the same time Amazon announced that it would no longer allow new customers to opt out of arrangements that shared their data with other companies or third parties. Under the old policy customers could send e-mail to never@amazon.com to make the opt-out request. Amazon will honor requests made prior to this policy change and will continue to honor requests from European customers (out of a desire to comply with European privacy laws), but it will no longer honor this request from new American customers. According to Borrus, "Amazon says such restrictions on data-sharing would impede its budding partnerships with outfits such as toy merchant Toys 'R' Us and Drugstore.com."[65]

There is, of course, nothing illegal about this policy modification so it did not cause much of a stir with the FTC or with other government agencies. Even Amazon's customers, who received e-mail notification of the policy change, seemed to take the new policy in stride. Privacy experts were less forgiving, however, pointing out that this amendment in policy has significant ramifications because "it shifts the balance by taking control of information from the individual and giving it to Amazon."[66] Some legal experts, however, cited the importance of protecting creditors during bankruptcy proceedings, and they contend that this should include the right to sell one of the defunct company's most valuable assets, that is, consumer data. Also, a refusal to liquidate this asset might run afoul of bankruptcy laws. According to Borrus, "there are few legal protections against Chapter 11 transfers."[67]

Discussion Questions

1. Do you agree with the change in policy developed by Amazon.com? Should the company be allowed to treat this consumer data as an asset in the case of bankruptcy?
2. Should users be allowed to "opt out" of this practice, that is, prevent their data from being sold off if the company slides into bankruptcy?

Newport Electronics[68]

Until three weeks ago Julie Weber couldn't imagine herself out of a job. She had been one of Newport Electronics' leading salespersons and just last month she was promoted to associate sales manager for the U.S. western region. But a few days after her promotion, her career at Newport began to unravel. It had been a long day and Julie found herself alone in her office late one evening after learning that one of her best friends at the company had been fired for inappropriate behavior. Julie's friend, a secretary for the marketing department, had become entangled in a relationship with one of the corporation's senior executives and company officials felt that things were getting out of hand. The new human resources vice president, Roger Williams, was primarily responsible for this decision, and Julie decided to write him a letter indicating her dismay at how things were being handled. She was particularly upset that nothing happened to the executive and that her friend was given little severance pay and had no opportunity for a transfer. Julie was tired and emotionally distraught and her agitated state was reflected in the tone of the letter. She called the corporation "sexist" and accused Williams of being "unfair and unreasonable." She explained that several other women at Newport were equally perturbed by his unjust decision and that there would be "unpleasant consequences" if the decision was not reconsidered.

It was late when Julie finished the draft of her letter and she decided to leave it on her computer overnight before printing and sending it to Mr. Williams. She saved the Microsoft Word document, shut off her computer, and left the office. When she returned to work the next day, she reread the letter and came to the sobering conclusion that it was too incendiary and controversial. So she decided not to send it. She deleted the letter and set out for an overnight sales trip. Julie assumed that her deletion of this unread letter was the end of this unpleasant matter. But when she returned from her trip the next day, her boss summoned her to his office. Unbeknownst to Julie, Newport had recently installed a software monitoring package called **iNVESTIGATE** on all of the company's desktop computer systems. Among other things **iNVESTIGATE** surreptitiously logs the keystrokes of all employees; every keystroke entered in applications such as Microsoft Word, e-mail, PowerPoint, etc. is intercepted by this software. As a result, even though Julie deleted her letter, all of the keystrokes she entered that night were tracked and saved by the Newport computer system.

Since Julie's writings contained several key "alert" words like "protest" this document was automatically e-mailed overnight to the systems administrator. She turned it over to the Human Resources department and to Julie's manager as required by an updated corporate policy. The following is an excerpt from that document:

Logon 08/19/02 20:12:53 PM
Open Microsoft Word 20:14:03 PM
Initiate Microsoft Word Session 20:14:46 PM

To: Roger Williams
Vice President, Human Resources

From: Julie Weber

Date: August 19, 2002

I am writing to protest your recent handling of the Patricia C. situation. She has been shabbily treated in a one-sided and sexist decision making process. You should be ashamed of your conduct in this matter. How can you justify firing her and letting Mr. X remain in his position . . .

End Microsoft Word Session 20:33:12 PM

Logoff 08/19/02 20:35:08 PM

When Williams read the accusatory letter, he wanted Julie fired for her insubordinate attitude. Julie's boss disagreed, arguing that Julie should not be punished for a letter she never sent. But this plea fell on deaf ears, and he did not have the clout to take on the vice president of human resources, who had strong support among the management hierarchy. When Julie was informed of this unfortunate decision that afternoon, she was given an hour to pack her things and leave the premises.

Julie knew that she had little recourse. But several days later she sought out a lawyer. She wanted to sue the company for wrongful termination. She explained to her attorney that although Newport warned its employees that all of their computer activities (including e-mail, and Web access) were monitored, it never explained that *every keystroke*, including deletions, was logged and recorded for corporate scrutiny. This was only a draft of a letter she *thought* about sending, but never did. Isn't she entitled to some measure of privacy? Shouldn't her thought patterns and feelings expressed in this unsent missive be off limits? Her lawyer was sympathetic but not optimistic—there is no law that protects communications written on company-owned computer systems, and there is no legal requirement to inform employees of which monitoring devices have been installed on their computer systems and which activities are subject to such monitoring.

Discussion Questions

1. Has Julie been treated fairly in this case? Why or why not? Is this a case of "wrongful termination"?
2. How do you assess software programs like iNVESTIGATE? Is there something inherently unethical about using such a program? Is there a way in which such a program could be used responsibly?

References

1. Quoted in James Gleick, "Big Brother is Us," *New York Times Magazine*, Sept. 29, 1996, p. 130.
2. Louis Brandeis and Samuel Warren, "The Right to Privacy," 4 *Harvard Law Review* 193, 1890.
3. Ruth Gavison, "Privacy and the Limits of the Law," 89 *The Yale Law Journal*, 421, 1984.
4. Richard Spinello and Herman Tavani, "Introduction to Chapter Four: Privacy in Cyberspace," *Readings in CyberEthics* (Sudbury, MA: Jones & Bartlett, 2001), pp. 339–348. See also Charles Fried, "Privacy," in F.D. Schoeman, ed. *Philosophical Dimensions of Privacy* (New York: Cambridge University Press, 1984).
5. James Reiman, "Driving to the Panopticon: A Philosophical Exploration of the Risks to Privacy Posed by the Highway Technology of the Future," 11 *Santa Clara Computer and High Technology Law Journal* 27, 1996.
6. Carol Gould, *The Information Web: Ethical and Social Implications of Computer Networking* (Boulder, CO: Westview Press, 1989), p. 44.
7. Shoshana Zuboff, *In the Age of the Smart Machine: The Future of Work and Power* (New York: Basic Books, 1988), p. 344.
8. Richard Wassestrom, "Privacy: Some Arguments and Assumptions" in *Philosophical Dimensions of Privacy*, ed. Ferdinand Schoeman (New York: Cambridge University Press, 1984), p. 328.
9. Michel Foucault, *Discipline and Punish: The Birth of the Prison* (New York: Vintage Books, 1979), p. 200.
10. James Moor, "Towards a Theory of Privacy in the Information Age," *Computers and Society*, September, 1997, p. 29.
11. Jerry Markon, "Curbs Debated as Court Records go Public on Net," *The Wall Street Journal*, February 27, 2002, p. B1.
12. For a detailed account, see William M. Bulkeley, "Prescriptions, Toll Free Numbers Yield a Gold Mine for Marketers," *The Wall Street Journal*, April 17, 1998, p. B1.
13. Elizabeth Wasserman, "Internet Industry Fails Government's Test," *The Industry Standard*, June 8, 1998, p. 19.
14. Mark Gimein, "The Peculiar Business of One-to-One Marketing," *The Industry Standard*, August 24, 1998, p. 19.

15. Amy Harmon, "Software to Track E-Mail Raises Privacy Concerns," *The New York Times*, November 22, 2000, pp. A1 and C4.

16. Karl Belgium, "Who Leads at Half Time? Three Conflicting Versions of Internet Privacy Policy," 6 *Richmond Journal of Law and Technology* 8, 1999.

17. Jeffrey Pollock, "A Tangled Web—Thoughts for a Law Firm Using the Web, " 198 *AUG-N.J. Law*. 18, 1999.

18. Joel Reidenberg, "Resolving Conflicting International Data Privacy Rules in Cyberspace," 52 *Stanford Law Review* 1315, 2000.

19. Jerry Kang, "Information Privacy in Cyberspace Transactions, " 50 *Stanford Law Review* 1193, 1998.

20. Thomas Weber, "As Pendulum Swings, Protecting Privacy May Start to Pay Off," *The Wall Street Journal*, June 12, 2000, p. B1.

21. Larry Lessig, *Code and Other Laws of Cyberspace* (New York: Basic Books, 1999), p. 152.

22. Solveig Singleton, "Privacy as Censorship: A Skeptical View of Proposals to Regulate Privacy in the Private Sector," Cato Institute, Washington D.C., 1998.

23. Ibid.

24. Oscar Gandy, "Coming to Terms with the Panoptic Sort," in ed. D. Lyon, *Computers, Surveillance, & Privacy* (Minneapolis: University of Minnesota Press, 1996), pp. 132–158.

25. Immanuel Kant, *Foundations of the Metaphysic of Morals* (Indianapolis: Hacket Publishing Company, 1981), p. 47.

26. See John Finnis, *Fundamentals of Ethics* (Washington, D.C.: Georgetown University Press, 1983), pp. 124–126.

27. Jeffrey Rosen, *The Unwanted Gaze* (New York: Random House, 2000), p. 166.

28. Elizabeth Wasserman, "Save the Children," *The Industry Standard*, August 28, 2000, p. 110.

29. To *opt-in* is to accept some condition such as the sale of one's personal data ahead of time.

30. Eileen Colkin, "Privacy Law Requires Hard Work," *Information Week*, August 20, 2001, p. 54.

31. Robert Smith, *Ben Franklin's Web Site: Privacy and Curiosity from Plymouth Rock to the Internet* (Providence: Sheridan Books, 2000), p. 333.

32. Richard Spinello and Herman Tavani, "Introduction to Chapter Four: Privacy in Cyberspace," *Readings in CyberEthics* (Sudbury, MA: Jones & Bartlett, 2001), pp. 339–348.

33. Victor Mayer-Schonberger, "Generational Development of Data Protection in Europe," in P. Agre and M. Rotenberg, eds., *Technology and Privacy: The New Landscape* (Cambridge: The MIT Press, 1997), pp. 219–242.

34. Ibid.

35. Edmund Andrews, "European Law Aims to Protect Privacy of Data," *The New York Times*, October 26, 1998, p. A1.

36. Dag Elgesem, "The Structure of Rights in Directive 95/46/EC on the Protection of Individuals with Regard to the Processing of Personal Data and the Free Movement of Such Data," in *Readings in Cyberethics*, edited by R. Spinello and H. Tavani. (Sudbury, MA: Jones & Bartlett, 2001), pp. 360–377.

37. Ibid.

38. Ibid.

39. Joel Reidenberg, "E-Commerce and Trans-Atlantic Privacy," 38 *Houston Law Review* 717, 2001.

40. Patrick Thibodeau, "Europe's Privacy Laws May Become Global Standard," *Computerworld*, March 12, 2001, p. 77.

41. Glenn Simpson, "The Battle over Web Privacy," *The Wall Street Journal*, March 21, 2001, p. B1.

42. See the CoolCatalog Web page at http://www.CoolCatalog.com/catalogue/.

43. Ronald Coase, "Comment on 'The Muted Voice of the Consumer in Regulatory Agencies,'" in W. Samuels and H. Trebing (eds.), *A Critique of Administrative Regulation of Public Utilities* (East Lansing, MI: Institute of Public Utilities, Michigan State University, 1972).

44. See "Introduction: Privacy in the Workplace;" available at: http://eon.law.harvard.edu/privacy.

45. Neil Lewis, "Plan for Web Monitoring in Courts Dropped," *The New York Times*, September 9, 2001, p. A20.

46. Graham Sewell and James Barker, "Neither Good nor Bad, but Dangerous: Surveillance as an Ethical Paradox," *Ethics and Information Technology*, Vol 3, no. 3, 2001, p. 194.

47. Ibid.

48. Smith, p. 188.

49. 18 U.S. C. § 2511 (2)(a).

50. Lawrence Rothstein, "Privacy or Diginty?: Electronic Monitoring in the Workplace," 19 *New York Law School Journal of International and Comparative Law* 379, 2000.

51. Ibid.

52. Ibid.

53. Patricia Werhane, *Persons, Rights and Corporations* (Englewood Cliffs, NJ: Prentice-Hall, Inc., 1985), p. 103.

54. Manuel Velasquez, *Business Ethics: Concepts and Cases*, 3rd ed. (Englewood Cliffs, NJ: Prentice-Hall, Inc., 1992), p. 400.

55. Joseph Des Jardins, *Contemporary Issues in Business Ethics* (Belmont, CA: Wadsworth, 1985), p. 226.

56. Robert Clarke, "Information Technology and Dataveillance," *Communications of the ACM*, May, 1988, p. 499.

57. Diane Anderson and Keith Perine, "Marketing the DoubleClick Way," *The Industry Standard*, March 13, 2000, pp. 174–182.

58. This description has been adapted from *In re Double Click Inc. Privacy Litigation*, U.S. District Ct., N.Y., 00 Civ. 0641, [2000].

59. Ibid.

60. "FTC Complaint against DoubleClick, Inc. Re Privacy Practices," February 10, 2000, available at http://www.techlawjournal.com/privacy/20000210.com.htm

61. Anderson and Perine.

62. Ibid.

63. Andrea Petersen, "A Privacy Firestorm at DoubleClick," *The Wall Street Journal*, February 23, 2000, p. B1.

64. Ibid.

65. Amy Borrus, "Online Privacy: Congress Has No Time to Waste," *Business Week*, September 18, 2000, p. 54.

66. Keith Regan, "Amazon's Tough Love Privacy Policy, " *E-Commerce Times*, September 6, 2000.

67. Ibid.; Filing for bankruptcy under Chapter 11 allows the debtor to restructure and reorganize their debt while temporarily protecting assets from creditors' claims.

68. Although this is a fictitious case, the software functionality described in this case is readily available.

CHAPTER SIX

Securing the Electronic Frontier

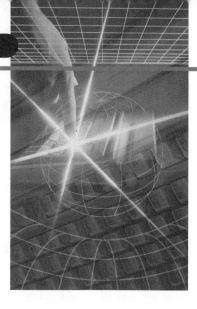

▶ Vulnerabilities of the Net

If there is any obstacle to the explosive growth of electronic commerce, it has to be the public's apprehension about the Net's security flaws. Stories appear frequently in the press exposing new problems and underscoring the Internet's fragile infrastructure. Despite the use of firewalls, security scanners, intrusion prevention products, and other security devices, Web sites have been the latest target for hackers. Hacking popular Web pages seems to be one of the most fashionable and costly forms of electronic intrusion.

One of the more notorious and widely publicized security breaches happened to the *New York Times* on September 13, 1998. Their Web site server was invaded by a group of belligerent hackers who posted pornographic material and printed this threatening message for all to see:

> FIRST OFF, WE HAVE TO SAY . . .WE OWN YOUR DUMB ASS.
> S3COND, TH3R3 AR3 SO MANY LOS3ERS H3R3. ITZ HARD TO PICK
> WHICH TO INSULT THE MOST.

The site had to be closed for nine hours while IT personnel cleaned up the offensive messages and plugged the hole.[1]

Of course, security breaches on the Internet can go well beyond attacks on a solitary commercial Web site. In testimony before Congress in May, 1998, several current and former hackers, members of a watchdog group called Lopht Heavy Industries, boasted that they would have no trouble in bringing the Internet to its knees in less than 30 minutes! They asserted that the Internet is so vulnerable that "it would be possible to terminate communications between the United States and all other countries and to prevent major backbone providers such as MCI and AT&T from routing network traffic to each other."[2] The group agreed to testify out of concern that business and government officials are too naive and nonchalant about security matters. According to these hackers, these officials do not seem to appreciate the risks associated with managing net-centric organizations. One hopes that this group's worst fears will never be realized. The Internet's insecurity may prove to have devastating consequences one day, and yet this issue still does not receive the serious attention and the financial support that it deserves.

Thanks to its open architecture, the Net is particularly susceptible to viruses, self-replicating programs usually hidden away in another host program or file. Macroviruses, which exploit programs called macros included in many applications like Microsoft Word, are particularly insidious. The macrovirus Melissa unleashed in 1999 caused a great deal of damage to many major corporations such as Lucent Technologies.

A 2001 survey by ICSA labs of 300 North American companies revealed that those companies had a monthly average of 103 virus infections per 1,000 computers; this is up from 91 infections per 1,000 computer systems in 2000. The report also blames the Internet and e-mail for "accelerating the spread of viruses and related programs known as worms."[3] *Worms* are also malicious pieces of code, which differ from viruses because they can run independently. They can travel from one computer to another across network connections. One other popular form of "malware" is the *trojan horse*, used to insert corrupt information into a program. There has been a rise in the use of backdoor trojan horses that are sent covertly through e-mail. According to one description, "You run the program and that opens a door, which people on the outside can use to steal your passwords, destroy files, and so on."[4]

One of the first cases that brought the public's attention to the Internet's inherent vulnerability was the "Internet Worm" developed by Robert Morris, a student at Cornell University. In November, 1988, Morris released this worm, a concise, self-replicating C program, from Cornells host computer system so it would quickly spread to other systems on the Internet. This worm's progress was facilitated by a fatal security hole in the UNIX operating system software of the infected machines. Once these computers were invaded, the program reproduced itself incessantly, consuming large volumes of memory. It did not modify system files or destroy any information, but the performance of systems infected by the worm deteriorated rapidly, causing many of them to crash.

Approximately 12 hours after the first system was infected, the Computer Systems Research Group at Berkeley developed a program to halt the worm's rapid spread. All of these disabled computer systems had to be taken offline in order to apply the remedial and preventive measures necessary to destroy the worm and prevent its recurrence. The final toll: 2,500 computers infected in some way and a clean up cost of over $1 million.[5]

Morris claimed that he was only running an experiment in order to expose security gaps on the network but that the worm duplicated itself much faster than he had anticipated. Nonetheless he was convicted under the Computer Fraud and Abuse Act. He was sentenced to a term of three years probation and fined $10,000.

Fortunately incidents on this scale are not an everyday occurrence, but in the years since this event occurred, it does not appear that enough progress has been made in securing the electronic frontier. As more and more organizations begin heavily relying on the Internet for electronic commerce or other networking applications, they are discovering that implementing strong security measures is a complex challenge. The fundamental problem is familiar: the Net's underlying architecture is a radically open one, designed to share information and not to conceal it. It *is* possible to develop an adequate level of security with an acceptable degree of risk, but this requires an investment of time and money that many government agencies and corporations have been reluctant to make.

Computer system security is a massive topic and we cannot possibly do it justice here. We will dwell in this chapter on just four basic issues that are intimately connected with some of the other themes that have been articulated in this book. We will first examine the topic of *cybercrime*: how it is defined, what sorts of activities can be categorized as cybercrime, and whether or not hardware companies should incorporate antipiracy technologies as an appropriate antidote. Second, in this context we will consider the issue of *trespass*, or unauthorized access, perhaps the most common and persistent security problem on the Internet. Trespass may seem like a simple matter, but it is characterized by some unusual ethical and legal conflicts. Is "trespass" an appropriate metaphor for electronic intrusion? What constitutes trespass in cyberspace? Why is it so wrong even if no damage is done, and what are the appropriate legal remedies for its victims?

Third, we will review the most salient security measures that should be adopted to protect electronic commerce and online communications against unauthorized access and other abuses. This discussion will include some treatment of digital certificates and other protocols that are designed to safeguard the integrity of information being transmitted to and from Web sites.

Finally, we will devote some attention to the matter of encryption and the public policy debate it has stirred up in the United States. One way to achieve information security is by encrypting one's communications.

This makes the data undecipherable to anyone who does not have a key to the encrypted data. The U.S. government has sought some control over this technology since it fears that in the hands of criminals and terrorists, encryption can be used to develop unbreakable codes. Export controls had been in effect until 2000 when President Clinton reversed his policy. However, immediately after the terrible events of September 11, 2001, there were calls to reinstate those controls so that strong encryption technology is less likely to be used by terrorists. Is it now necessary to recalibrate the balance between liberty and security? If so, what implications does this have for encryption policy?

Our purpose here is not to provide an exhaustive account of the Internets security deficiencies or a primer about proper preventative security measures. Rather, it is to explore several ethical dimensions of this important problem, to illustrate how the critical goal of information security can sometimes collide with other worthy objectives (such as the preservation of privacy rights), and to ponder how these competing objectives can be effectively balanced.

▶ Cybercrime

It is no secret that the Internet has become a breeding ground for certain forms of cybercrime—there are unfortunately many criminals lurking in the virtual world of cyberspace. The term *cybercrime* is rather nebulous, so some clarification of its precise meaning is essential. We will define cybercrime as a special category of criminal acts that can only be executed through the utilization of computer and network technologies. Cybercrime then includes three basic categories: 1) software piracy, 2) computer sabotage, and 3) electronic break-ins.[6] What all of these crimes have in common is that they require the use of a computer, which is the target and/or the tool of the crime. Obviously these crimes can be committed with an isolated, unconnected computer system, but the locus of most of these crimes today is the network, since connectivity enables creative variations of rogue activities like piracy and sabotage.

The first category, software piracy, involves the unauthorized duplication of proprietary software and the distribution or making available of those copies over the network. The unauthorized copying and distribution of proprietary operating system software, applications software programs, or MP3 files would fall under this category. The No Electronic Theft Act of 1997 forbids the willful infringement of a copyright for purposes of commercial advantage or for some financial gain. This act and other laws protecting copyrighted material are often flouted by those who subscribe to the philosophy that "content on the Internet wants to be free." The copying of music and video software files has become rampant. As discussed in Chapter 4, what the music industry sometimes regards as piracy, Web sites like Napster see as fair use. Although Napster is no longer a threat, other music-sharing networks such as Morpheus and Kaaza are quickly emerging to take its place.

Software piracy remains a high profile problem, especially on university campuses in the United States. In December, 2001, federal law enforcement authorities shut down computer networks at MIT and the University of California at Los Angeles (UCLA). Students at these and other universities were operating a piracy ring called "DrinkorDie" with their own public Web site. According to Shenon, that network "had distributed things like the latest copy of Windows software and digital copies of the hit film 'Harry Potter and the Sorcerer's Stone.'"[7] This ring was targeted because it operated a global network that facilitated the movement of large volumes of pirated material.

The second category of cybercrime, *computer sabotage,* implies interference with computer systems, such as the disruption of operations by means of a virus, a worm, or a logic bomb. According to Tavani, computer sabotage also involves using computer technology to "destroy data resident in a computer or damage a computer system's resources."[8] As noted, the spread of viruses has been particularly troublesome. Latest surveys from the Computer Security Institute indicate that ten to fifteen new viruses are launched each day. Some of the more successful viruses have also been quite promiscuous and expensive. The infamous ILoveYou virus infected tens of thousands of computers and caused an estimated $11 billion in damage.

Another popular form of computer sabotage in recent years has been the Denial of Service (DoS) attack, which attacks a Web site with mock requests from multiple computers until the server crashes and service is disrupted. The software to send the mock requests can be easily and surreptitiously implanted in computers all over the world. When signaled, those PCs spring into action and begin bombarding a chosen Web site with requests, unbeknownst to the PCs' owner. According to Sager, "It's a deceptively diabolical trick that has temporarily halted commerce on some of the biggest Web sites, raising the question, how soft is the underbelly of the Internet?"[9] In 2000 there were a number of high profile attacks on Web sites such as Yahoo and eBay, and there is evidence that the DoS remains a popular weapon of hackers. According to a University of California (San Diego) study, "During a three-week period in mid-2001 [researchers] detected 12,800 DoS attacks against more than 5,000 targets."[10] When these attacks are executed on a massive scale they can have devastating consequences for a Web site, which becomes inaccessible to legitimate users. The end result is lost revenues and diminished customer loyalty.

The final category, electronic break-ins and unauthorized access, raises some complex issues that will be covered later in this chapter. There is a long tradition of unauthorized access by curious hackers but sometimes the accusation of "trespass" is unwarranted. In order to demonstrate physical trespass, one must focus on the trespasser's intent to enter into a forbidden property without permission. But proving cybertrespass using this criterion is much more challenging. For example, spam has been labeled as a form of trespass, but does a user have implicit permission to send out thousands of unwanted e-mail messages to destinations on the Internet, which, after all, is a public network?

Not included in this definition of cybercrime are crimes that are facilitated thanks to the use of computer and network technologies. These crimes do not require computer technology, that is, the use of a computer to commit the crime is not necessary, but it may aid the commission of that crime. In most cases these crimes have been going on long before the arrival of the Internet. One might include in this category stalking, theft (including fraud, swindling, or embezzlement), and the distribution of illegal material. Computer and network technology can make some these crimes easier to commit.

Some argue, for example, that while stalking is not a new crime, the electronic version of stalking is on the rise because stalking is easier to do over the Internet. The stalker can use the Net to learn about his or her target, has a better chance of remaining anonymous in cyberspace, and can accomplish these objectives from the confines of his or her own home. Hence, according to Grodzinsky and Tavani, "Internet technology has made possible certain modes of stalking that would not have been possible in the pre-Internet era."[11]

Finally, in addition to cybercrime and crime facilitated by computer technology, law enforcement officials must deal with the use of the Internet as a communications medium to plan crimes in the physical world. For example, some traditional crimes like bank robbery might be coordinated by e-mail instead of the telephone. We might refer to these last two categories, crimes facilitated by the Internet or crimes planned and carried out with the help of the Internet and related technologies, as *computer-related crimes.*

▶ Antipiracy Architectures

In Chapter 4 we discussed digital rights architectures as a means of safeguarding intellectual property rights. It is worth revisiting that topic in light of this discussion on the crime of piracy. Laws have been ineffectual in combating software piracy, as users seem to have few qualms in bootlegging music and videos. As a result, Hollywood and the content industry have become increasingly frustrated with the constant pilfering of digital music and videos. So the fact that there are requests for more reliance on code is not surprising. What is alarming to some, however, is that those requests are turning into persistent demands from the content industry, which now insists that hardware manufacturers help solve their problem. In testimony before Congress in March, 2002, Michael Eisner, CEO of Disney, accused companies such as Apple, Dell, and Microsoft of failing to develop secure systems because piracy actually helped them sell more computers. He cited Apple's slogan, "Rip, Mix, Burn" as a signal to consumers that an Apple computer facilitates theft.

The broader goal of the entertainment industry is to incorporate a copy-protection mechanism not only into personal computers but also into DVD players and other digital media devices. But are these techno-logical mechanisms the best method of fighting the crime of piracy and securing content? Whose role is it to stop the illicit copying of software? Is it the responsibility of hardware manufacturers to assume this role, to make systems that afford maximum protection for fluid digital media? Why should hardware technology become the enforcer for ineffectual copyright laws? According to Harmon, "Telling technology companies to build devices that prevent copyright infringement . . . is like telling auto makers to build cars that cannot exceed the speed limit."[12]

Many in Congress, however, are sympathetic with Hollywood's plight and might be willing to mandate the use of such a copy-protection mech-anism. During the hearings in which Eisner testified, one senator referred to the Internet as a "haven for thievery." In response, a new law called the Security Standards and Certification Act has been proposed by Senator Ernest Hollings. It would forbid the creation, sale, or distribution of "any interactive device that does not include and utilize certified security tech-nologies."[13]

This potent combination of law and code might finally solve the prob-lem that law could not solve on its own—the tight enclosure of content and the end of file-sharing without permission of the copyright holder. But some would argue that this combination is too lethal and that the need for security, the need to address a costly cybercrime, cannot come at the expense of other critical values such as openness. The PC as an open platform has spurred innovation for years, and that could change if this system is rearchitected to stop all forms of piracy. The larger question, of course, is who should have a say in the future functionality of technol-ogy? Should Hollywood dictate what components will be included in the next generation of personal computer systems?

As we noted in Chapter 4, it should be possible to build feasible Digi-tal Rights Management (DRM) systems that allow users to make copies of music or video files for their own personal use. If consumer rights and in-terests along with broader values like fair use and first sale are accorded due respect, it may be possible to achieve security through means of DRM without causing great collateral damage. Once again the process of solving social problems with technology must be tempered and guided by ethical awareness, in this case an awareness of the consumer's right to make backup copies, to time shift, and to use a piece of content on diverse platforms (a Macintosh, DVD player, etc.).

▶Trespass and Unauthorized Access in Cyberspace

Unauthorized access to computer systems is a widespread problem on the Internet. Despite the efforts of legal authorities to clamp down on cyberspace trespassers, there is still an unfortunate tendency to avoid taking these transgressions all that seriously. The culprits are often recreational hackers who thrive on breaking into supposedly "secure" systems. Indeed, according to Dorothy Denning, the hacker ethic is predicated on this transcendent principle: "Access to computers—and anything which might teach you something about the way the world works—should be unlimited and total."[14]

As far back as 1983, when Neil Patrick and six other Milwaukee teenagers were convicted of computer trespassing, their response was that "we were just playing a game." The so-called game involved alleged break-ins to institutions with extremely sensitive data such as the Los Alamos National Laboratory and the Sloan Kettering Cancer Center in New York. And consider the advertising for the popular Hollywood movie *Hackers* that boldly proclaimed, "Their only crime was curiosity." The message implicit in both the advertising and the movie itself was that these high school computer nerds really hadn't done anything so terribly wrong by breaking into secured computer systems all over the United States. Unfortunately, this movie typifies the distorted perspective of the media, which has sometimes tended to sensationalize hacking and to elevate hackers to celebrity status.

The problem is that many people do not see an exact parallel between trespassing on a computer system and physical trespass. They regard the former as more abstract, rationalizing that networked computer systems are something to be "borrowed" and returned with no harm done. But is unauthorized access the same as physical trespass despite the fact that the Internet's architecture is such an open and unstructured environment?

Even if one answers this question affirmatively, the notion of trespass in cyberspace still raises some intriguing questions partly due to the fact that we are dealing with virtual boundaries instead of physical ones. For example, if someone releases a worm or virus, does that virus trespass on the computer system that it infects? Is unsolicited e-mail or spam a form of trespass, especially if it is forced upon another's virtual mailbox, which is part of that individual's personal space? Or does linking to other Web sites without permission constitute trespassing? If these actions do meet the legal standard of trespass, a criminal offense, it will give their victims a viable cause of action.

The 1986 Computer Fraud and Abuse Act (CFAA), which was last amended in late 1996, is evidence that the United States legal system has begun to take this issue more seriously. The provisions of this act protect the confidentiality of proprietary information and make it a crime to "knowingly access a computer without or in excess of authority to obtain classified information." The statute also makes it a crime to access any "protected computer" without authorization, and as a result of such access, to defraud victims of property or to recklessly cause damage. Thanks to the 1996 amendment, protected computers include those used by the government, financial institutions, or any business engaged in interstate or international commerce, or anyone involved in interstate communications. The category of "protected computer," therefore, includes virtually any computer connected to the Internet. According to the CFAA, trespass is a federal crime if one does so to pilfer classified information, to perpetrate fraud, or to cause damage (for example, to destroy files or disable an operating system).[15] It is also a federal crime to cause the transmission of a program or piece of code (such as a virus) that intentionally causes damage to a protected computer. In addition, the CFAA "prohibits unauthorized access that causes damage regardless of whether or not the damage was 'recklessly caused.'"[16]

All U.S. states, with the exception of Vermont, have also enacted their own computer crime statutes, which in some cases go well beyond the scope of the Computer Fraud and Abuse Act. Specifically, most state laws (such as New York) make unauthorized use of computers a crime even if the motive is just curiosity and one is merely sniffing around. There are harsher penalties for computer trespass where the entry has occurred to commit another crime such as the theft of material.

Some have argued that law enforcement officials should not be taking such a hard line against purely recreational hacking, that is, incidents of trespassing that do not involve damage to property or theft of data. There have been numerous arguments put forth to defend break-ins by hackers, especially when there is no deliberate destruction of property. Among these arguments are that break-ins actually serve a valuable purpose because they uncover security flaws that would otherwise go unnoticed, and the intruder is probably only utilizing idle resources so there is really no cost for the victim. There is also what Eugene Spafford calls the student hacker argument—"some trespassers claim that they are doing no harm and changing nothing—they are simply learning about how computer systems operate."[17] Still others might say that a little digital graffiti on a World Wide Web site is merely a prank, and should be treated accordingly.

On the surface it might appear that some of these arguments are defensible and that there is little or no harm to most forms of electronic intrusion. If, for example, a hacker is able to penetrate a secure environment and search through a few programs but does no damage, where is the harm? This might be analogous to walking through someone's property while leaving everything perfectly intact. Thus, one could argue that unauthorized access that leaves the environment undisturbed is only a minor ethical transgression and not worth much of a fuss. And digital graffiti is not much worse since it can be cleaned up more easily than the graffiti that comes from spray paint.

If we examine the problem through the lens of Lessig's framework, it is apparent that the strongest constraints on this deviant behavior are technology and the law. There are numerous technologies designed to deter hackers, along with laws like the CFAA that prescribe strict punishment for electronic trespassing. On the other hand, social norms are ambivalent, since we do find some cultural acceptance of hacking in cyberspace. Society sends mixed signals about hackers who are seen as rogues and villains but also as modern day Robin Hoods and adventurers, who are admired for their skill and ingenuity.

This ambivalence is not found, however, when we apply ethical norms to hacking. To begin with, it is generally recognized that it is simply wrong to trespass even if no direct damage is caused. When one trespasses, one violates respect for property rights, which is an important ethical and social value. Property rights buttress the moral good of autonomy since they allow individuals to control what they own, which is essential for their commercial and personal well-being. Breaking into a private corporate headquarters after hours just to look around the lobby is still trespassing even if one does not pilfer any files or cause any damage. There is no basis to treat a hacker who breaks into a secured computer site only to "look around" any differently. Individuals should not go where they do not belong, either in real space or in cyberspace—this is a fundamental rule of law and basic tenet of morality.

Furthermore, the hacker may intrude into a system and not intend to do any harm, but he or she may inadvertently cause damage to a file or program. The more complex the system, the more likely the occurrence of accidental damage. In addition, unauthorized use of a computer system wastes the victim's valuable CPU resources, which does amount to a more tangible form of theft. Moreover, even if there is no malicious intent or destruction of Web pages, a trespasser's activities can still be disruptive and costly since any unwarranted intrusion must be inspected by system administrators. They must spend time verifying and checking their systems and software to make sure that no damage has been done. As Johnson points out, "Those who attempt to gain unauthorized access, plant worms and viruses, and so on, force the computing community to put energies and resources into protecting systems and files when they could be using their energy and resources to improve the technology in other ways. . . ."[18]

Thus, as Spafford and others have illustrated, most of the arguments that support hackers are spurious ones that do not stand up to objective scrutiny. Intruders who insist that they are doing us a favor when they hack into sensitive networks and expose lax security are merely rationalizing illegal and immoral behavior. The case against hacking is even stronger when property is stolen or Web pages are defaced, since greater harm is inflicted upon the victim, who must expend even more resources to fix these problems.

There are at least two ways in which property rights of Web site owners can be transgressed. The first occurs when the Web page is hacked by intruders. The content is usually damaged by adding files to the Web server. The second is much less serious but certainly not inconsequential, and it involves unauthorized visits to a Web page. This might take place if one cracks a password code to an online seminar and participates without permission. While most Web sites are open to the general public, some are accessible only to authorized users and require a password and username before entry. In rare cases Web site owners have limited access to their sites by means of the honor system. Several law firms, for example, indicate on their home pages that anyone may browse through their sites as long as they are not using a commercial computer service that charges for every minute of use. Those who defied this instruction and continued reading would technically be guilty of trespassing.

If any of these acts *are* equivalent to trespass, the implication is that Web sites are property. Property is usually understood to be physical property or chattel of some sort. But does a Web site also qualify as real private property? Despite the fact that the World Wide Web is an open and public environment where users are invited to participate, the notion that a Web site is the property of its owner does have some plausibility.

Trotter Hardy relies on some of the familiar philosophical arguments we invoked in Chapter 4 to demonstrate that a Web site should indeed be classified as property. As a result, both unwanted visitors and Web page hackers could be culpable of trespassing under certain conditions. He cites Locke's "labor-desert" theory and utilitarianism to justify his claim. From a Lockean perspective, there ought to be property rights in Web sites because "their value and even their existence derive entirely from someone else's labor in setting up the site."[19] The production of a Web site is often a labor-intensive activity and this effort should confer a property right for those who made the investment of time and effort to build that site. Likewise, the utilitarian argument that ownership rights are justified because they maximize social utility and provide an incentive to build future Web sites is less compelling but still somewhat germane. To some extent, a recognition of private property rights in a Web site does provide an incentive to develop new sites, since developers are motivated by the rights to manage and earn income from that site.

Hardy therefore concludes that a common law "cause of action for 'trespass to Web sites' should exist as a means of controlling access to Web sites."[20] Although Web page hacking is the more serious offense, users must respect Web sites that are off limits as long as a Web site properly signals the restriction. Right now almost all Web sites are publicly accessible and encourage visitors. The Internet should be a public place, an open forum for the exchange of ideas and information. That does not imply, however, that Web sites are common property, fair game for users and hackers. Web site operators have the prerogative to set the terms of access, albeit within certain moral limits such as respect for the common good. While we must encourage an open World Wide Web that does not impede a user's navigation or constrain information flows, there is a strong moral imperative to respect properly demarcated borders even in cyberspace.

▶ Questionable Forms of Trespass

Before we move on to other matters, it would be instructive to revisit the issue of spam and to consider other deviant activities that have been labeled as forms of trespass. As we pointed out in Chapter 3, spam has imposed significant costs on its recipients and especially on the Internet Service Providers (ISPs) that serve as a means for the spammer to deliver those messages to their ultimate destination. Some of those ISPs have retaliated by suing spammers for "trespass to chattels," and they have sought injunctive relief to protect their "property."

Trespass to chattels is a tort action based on the unauthorized use or interference with another's property. For the claim to stick, there must be some kind of damage, debilitation, or removal of that property.[21] But how can an allegation of trespass to chattels make any sense in a virtual world where the property is intangible? And how could spammers be guilty of such an offense? Recall that spam is transmitted from the sender through multiple servers to the recipient's mail server where it may reside for some length of time before it is opened by the recipient. Spam therefore affects both the property of the ISP, whose server space is occupied in this process, and the property of the final recipient.

The case of *CompuServe Inc. v. CyberPromotions, Inc.* is indicative of the dangers underlying the claim that spam transmitted through an ISP violates property rights. This case was triggered when the ISP CompuServe notified CyberPromotions that it was prohibited from using its mail servers to transmit its unsolicited bulk e-mail (or spam). CyberPromotions refused to comply with this request, and CompuServe filed suit contending that the defendant was trespassing on its property. The specific legal claim was trespass to chattels. CyberPromotions argued that because CompuServe invited others to enter its property for business purposes, it could not later restrict access to that property. In other words, when CompuServe put its mail server on the Internet, implicit permission was granted for any of its paying customers to use that server. They also argued that CompuServe had assumed the role of postmaster, to whom all the strictures of the First Amendment applied, and that to allow CompuServe to enjoy a legally protected interest in its computer equipment in this context is to license a form of censorship that violates the First Amendment.

In a decision handed down in February, 1997, Judge Graham of the U.S. District Court in Ohio ruled against CyberPromotions, rejecting its claims as groundless. Judge Graham fully recognized the burdens imposed by spam on mail servers, concluding that "the property rights of the private owner could not be overwhelmed by the First Amendment."[22] Moreover, reasoned the judge, CompuServe is a private actor and not a government agency seeking to stifle CyberPromotions right to communicate. The court also found that there was interference and impairment of CompuServe's property since the volumes of spam sent by the defendant were clearly a burden on its equipment, using up computer memory and bandwidth. According to Judge Graham, "To the extent that defendants' multitudinous electronic mailings demand the disk space and drain the processing power of plaintiff's computer equipment, those resources are not available to serve CompuServe subscribers. Therefore, the value of that equipment to CompuServe is diminished even though it is not physically damaged by defendants' conduct."[23] As a result, he granted an injunction prohibiting CyberPromotions from sending unsolicited electronic mail to any e-mail addresses maintained by CompuServe.

The court's reasoning in this case has been met with mixed reviews. For some, the decision to side with this ISP was clearly based on an analogy to physical trespass, which does seem to fit here. The burden imposed on this ISP cannot be denied: CompuServe's physical computer system and mail server were being used by CyberPromotions to send messages at a significant cost to CompuServe's resources.

Recall that one of the elements in the definition of property is the right to exclude others from use. A corollary of that right is the need to seek permission of the owner to use his or her property. CyberPromotions assumed that it had permission to use CompuServe's mail servers without any restrictions. And one could argue that by placing a mail server on the public Internet, permission to receive volumes of mail from multiple sources is strongly implied. CompuServe, however, says that it grants "permission" to use its mail servers with a caveat: one cannot overwhelm the mail server and thereby debilitate the system. The question is whether CompuServe has a right to limit its permission to receive electronic mail. Those who agree with this decision say that CompuServe does have that right as part of its overall property right in its equipment or mail servers.

Other legal scholars, however, believe that this court erred in its judgment and that trespass to chattels is being wrongly applied in this case. They advance arguments that the ruling bestows upon CompuServe a new proprietary right that enables it to draw its own borders in cyberspace by excluding unwelcome content. But as Reeves argues, cyberspace property rights should encourage open, not closed, boundaries.[24]

This case also leaves unanswered a larger question that concerns the ultimate target of spam: does spam constitute trespass at the user level as well? If a company sends me unsolicited, unwanted e-mails are they trespassing on my property in some way? This is a much more complicated question and deserves further elaboration.

Some antispammers have asserted that all Internet communications should be consensual. But this is an extreme position that would be difficult to justify from any ethical or practical standpoint. The heavy costs of such an exclusionary policy would far outweigh any benefits. Do the majority of Internet users really want to preclude any communications to which they have not given their consent? Wouldn't they be impoverished by such a restriction? The open communications and democratic expression enabled by the Internet would be seriously undermined if we insisted that all exchanges had to be consensual.

Furthermore, the right to free speech is sufficiently broad in most countries to include the right to commercial speech. This implies that vendors and other organizations should have the right to send their promotional material to prospective online customers just as they have a right to send out advertisements and flyers through the regular mail.

However, although advertisers do have a right to send this mail, they do not have a right to force it upon someone. If that were to occur, spam could rightfully be construed as a form of trespass, at least from a moral perspective. The right to communicate must be balanced with the rights of property and privacy, that is, the right to be left alone within one's own personal domain. In order to effect some compromise in this situation, individuals must be allowed to maintain some measure of control over this unwanted mail. Each individual should have the right to control his or her domain or private space. This should include the prerogative to protect it from unwanted mail, whether it be regular mail sent to one's house or electronic mail sent to one's electronic mailboxes, which should also be regarded as an extension of one's private space or property. This is derived from the more basic right of autonomy over one's person and possessions, which is violated by the coercive activity of making someone a captive audience to another's communications. Of course, the user can exercise control simply by deleting the unwanted message. It also seems reasonable, however, that the user should be able to go a step further and tell the sender to stop sending any more messages or mailings. Failure to comply with that request would constitute trespassing on one's personal space. The right to communicate must be limited by the preferences of an unreceptive consumer. At a minimum, then, unsolicited electronic mail does amount to trespassing when it is intentionally forced upon individuals against their will.

Trespass is also being used as a pretext to prevent other forms of unwelcome speech and to stifle socially beneficial activities that might be perceived as problematic for a particular Web site. Recall the case of *Intel v. Hamidi*, for example, where Mr. Hamidi was enjoined from sending any e-mail messages to Intel employees critical of the company's human resources policies. Although he sent only five or six messages over a two year period, the court considered his unflattering missives as a form of trespass and Hamidi has been enjoined from sending additional e-mail messages to Intel employees. Similarly, in the case of *eBay v. Bidder's Edge*, a court sided with eBay in its quest for an injunction to prevent a Bidder's Edge spider from crawling its Web site in order to aggregate comparative auction data. eBay's lawyers also relied on this ancient doctrine of trespass to chattels, which "lies where an intentional interference with the possession of personal property has proximately caused injury" (*Thrifty-Tel v. Beznik* 1996).

There might be a problem, however, in labeling all unwelcome activity or communication as trespass. Companies such as eBay and Intel reap the benefits of open connectivity but are unwilling to internalize the costs of that connectivity including unwanted speech or unwanted spiders. Also, invoking exclusionary laws such as trespass has the detrimental effect of fragmenting the network, "allowing sites that have been physically connected to segregate themselves . . . from the network."[25] On the other hand, if we concede that a Web site is property, shouldn't the Web site owner enjoy the most basic aspect of that right, which is the right to exclude others and to set the conditions for entry, particularly when there is a *bona fide* threat of impairment?

▶ Security Measures in Cyberspace

What can be done to guard against the threats of trespassers or other cybercriminals, to safeguard the Internet and make it a more secure environment? A sound security scheme should begin with protecting the perimeter, usually by means of a *firewall*. The firewall is the first line of defense since it should prevent intruders from gaining access into the internal network. A firewall consists of hardware and/or software that is positioned between an organization's internal network and the Internet. Its goal is to insulate an organization's private network from intrusions by trapping any external threat such as a virus before it can penetrate and damage an information system. The simplest form of firewall is the packet filter, which relies on a piece of hardware known as a router to filter packets between the internal network and an outside connection such as the Internet. It operates by examining the source address of each individual packet along with its destination address within the firewall. If something is suspicious or the source address is considered to be untrustworthy, it can refuse the packet's entry. According to Garfinkel and Spafford, "Ideally, firewalls are configured so that all connections to an internal network go through relatively few well-monitored locations."[26] The goal of the firewall is to allow legitimate interactions between computers inside and outside the organization, while turning away unauthorized and potentially harmful interactions.

In the wake of costly DoS attacks, some companies began implementing specialized firewalls in order to handle DoS filtering. According to Yasin, "router-based filtering has emerged as one method of stemming DoS attacks, since most routers can filter incoming and outgoing packets."[27] But these firewalls are much more expensive than general purpose firewalls and they also tend to degrade performance.

Of course, a firewall is not always effective, and in those cases where a break-in has occurred, an intrusion detection system can be quite helpful. This software monitors the network to look for signs of an intrusion, takes steps to stop the intrusion, and highlights the security hole so that it can be repaired at a later date.

Antivirus software is obviously another critical element of any sound security architecture. This software is programmed to scan a computer system for malicious code and deletes that code once it has been found. This software works pretty well against known viruses, but new viruses evolve all the time and this requires the constant updating of antivirus programs. Even the more conservative estimates claim that there are about 300 new viruses introduced each month. For example, antivirus programs now screen for macroviruses, but they must be continually updated to detect new variations of these viruses.

Filtering systems can also be a helpful security mechanism. Software such as MIMESweeper can scan incoming mail for spam or for viruses while searching outgoing mail for sensitive corporate data that should not leave the confines of the organization. This software may increase security but it also diminishes employee privacy, and these tradeoffs need to be carefully weighed.

A more complicated problem is securing information that is being sent from one Internet user to another over this open network. The optimal way to secure this data is through encryption, encoding the transmitted information so it can only be read by an authorized recipient with a proper key that decodes the information. Through the use of encryption, this information can be protected against interception and tampering and its integrity can be assured. Data encryption has its roots in the ancient science of cryptography, that is, the use of ciphers or algorithms that allow someone to speak and to be understood through secret code. When a message is encrypted, it is translated from its original form or plain text into an encoded, unintelligible form called *cipher-text*. Decryption, which is usually accomplished with a key, is the process of translating cipher text back into plain text.

The first encryption systems were symmetric, that is, the same key is used to encrypt and decrypt the data. This is sometimes referred to as a *single key encryption system*. In a simple encoding pattern, the numbers 1–26 might represent the letters of the alphabet (1=A, 2=B, 3=C, and so forth) so that the message 7-18-5-5-20-7-19 means "Greetings." The "key" simply refers to the decoding pattern. In order for this method of encryption to work properly, both parties, the sender and receiver of the data, must have access to this key. The same key that scrambles the message is the one used to descramble it. The key itself then must be communicated and maintained in a secure fashion or it could be intercepted by a third party and fall into the wrong hands. Another disadvantage of private key cryptography is that if the key gets lost, it will be impossible to decrypt the messages encrypted with this key.

Private key encryption has been in widespread use since the 1960s. Although numerous encryption algorithms have been developed, the most popular commercial one is the DES or Data Encryption Standard, which the government has utilized as its standard since 1977. The DES was originally created in the 1960s by IBM researchers, but it was modified by the National Security Agency (NSA) before being adopted as a standard. The DES is currently used in many electronic mail and networking packages and was recently recertified by the government in 1993.

These keys are comprised of bits of data that can have a value of 1 or 0. DES keys are 56 bits long, so there are 2^{56} possible values. In 1998, the Electronic Frontier Foundation demonstrated that it could break a DES key in about two days using a $200,000 computer system. Hence, to ensure full confidentiality users need to rely on strong encryption, that is, a 128 bit (2^{128} possible values) algorithm, which is virtually unbreakable.

The other popular encryption technique is *public key encryption,* or the *dual key system,* considered to be one of the most critical innovations of this short network age. Data transmissions are even more secure using this method since even if one key is intercepted or stolen, it is impossible to derive the other key. With public key encryption, each party gets a pair of keys, one public and one private. The public key, which is usually kept in a directory or is posted on a Web site, is used to encrypt a message, while a secretive private key is used to decrypt the message. Messages encrypted with this public key can only be decrypted with the private key that is known only to the recipient of the message. Public key cryptography also provides a secure means of authenticating the sender of an electronic communication. The sender signs the message with his private key and the recipient uses the sender's public key to unlock that signature. The two most popular public key systems are RSA (Rivest-Shamir-Adelman) and PGP (Pretty Good Privacy).

The obvious advantage of public key cryptography is greater security. The sender and receiver of the message do not have to exchange a secret private key before they begin to communicate. The bottom line, according to Michael Baum, "is that public-key encryption creates trusted commerce for all parties doing business."[28]

In practice, the Secure Socket Layer (SSL) protocol is most often used in e-commerce transactions. SSL is used to encrypt data sent between Web browsers and Web servers. Thanks to SSL, data such as a credit card number can be exchanged through a secure conduit, which will prevent would-be intruders from seeing or tampering with that data. SSL also authenticates the server so that users know that they are at the Web site they intended to visit.

Why the need for protocols such as SSL? Consider what transpires in a typical online transaction. If someone decides to buy a book from an online bookstore, they must electronically submit a credit card number along with some personal information to complete this transaction. There is a danger that the credit card number or password will be "sniffed" by hackers. Sniffers are automated programs used to seek out security lapses and to intercept vulnerable communications travelling over a network. In order to avoid this, SSL relies on encryption so that data travelling between the customer's Web browser and the online book store cannot be sniffed out or monitored while it is in transit. SSL also supports digital identification so that each party can verify the other's identity. This helps prevent *impersonation*, criminals using phony identities to purchase goods.

Online transactions can also be made more secure if identification of both parties is authenticated. Authentication refers to the process whereby a security system establishes the validity of an identification. In this way, if George sends a message to Nancy, Nancy can be sure that the message is really from George and not from an impostor. The best way to verify identity is through the use of *digital signatures*, which are made possible by public key encryption. In this case a private key is used to sign one's signature to some message or piece of data and a public key is used to verify a signature after it has been sent. Assume that Nancy is sending an important request to her lawyer, George, regarding a transfer of funds. Nancy will sign the request with her private key and then encrypt the contents of the signed message with George's public key that she finds on his Web site. When George receives this encrypted request, he applies his private key to descramble that message. He then uses Nancy's public key to authenticate that the message is really from Nancy; with that public key he unlocks a signature that could only have come from her. As Levy observes, "This nonrepudiation feature is the electronic equivalent of a notary public seal."[29]

There are, of course, many reasons why companies should be motivated to implement these and other security techniques in order to ensure information integrity and system reliability. There are certainly market pressures at work that encourage corporations to pay attention to security. Customers will punish vendors who have a cavalier attitude about their personal data and credit card numbers by shunning their Web sites. Sound security mechanisms, on the other hand, will bolster consumer confidence that the Internet is a safe place to do business.

In addition, there is a moral imperative to ensure that the level of on-line security is adequate. When customers make purchases online, they are placing their trust in the hands of these e-commerce companies. If those companies are negligent or lack the proper security consciousness, the end result could be calamitous for customers who may find themselves as victims of credit card fraud if their credit card number is intercepted or their personal data is misappropriated. Therefore, there is a moral duty to take reasonable precautions and to implement feasible security measures that will provide for the integrity of online transactions and prevent the risk of harm to unsuspecting consumers. "Bad faith" efforts to secure the data of e-commerce customers cannot meet the standards of morality or the sometimes tougher standard of the marketplace.

▶ The Encryption Controversy: A Public Policy Perspective

As we have seen, the optimal means of achieving the elusive goal of information security is through the use of encryption. This technology enables users to transmit sensitive data over an insecure network like the Internet. Public key encryption, however, has been a problematic means of achieving "trusted commerce" thanks to the reluctance of government regulators to fully support this technology. The government has been apprehensive about the export of sophisticated encryption systems (e.g., 128 bit keys) and as a result it has sought to regulate exports by demanding "back door access," that is, some form of control over all public and private keys. The government worries that international terrorists or bands of criminals will get their hands on an encryption system to which law enforcement authorities do not have the key and which cannot be decoded. It is concerned, therefore, that the proliferation of these systems will diminish its capacity for wire taps and surveillance and perhaps in the long run imperil national security. There are no restrictions on the domestic uses of encryption and after a decade of squabbling, the export restrictions on encryption systems have been greatly relaxed.

Giving the government the key to all encryption systems was never well received by privacy advocates or the software industry since it seems to be too obtrusive and conjures up certain Orwellian overtones. Companies also consistently argued that the widespread use and export of strong encryption without restrictions is essential for the growth of e-commerce. Thus, these long-standing concerns about public safety collided with protection for civil liberties and the demands of international commerce.

Over the past few years the government has offered a number of proposals to resolve this problem and deal with the tensions between preserving personal privacy while not compromising national security. As Markoff points out, "The goal of a national voice- and data-security standard is intended to provide privacy for government, civilian and corporate users of telephone and computer communications, while also assuring that law enforcement agencies can continue to eavesdrop on or wiretap voice and data conversations after obtaining warrants."[30] It is worthwhile to review these proposals along with the criticisms that they have provoked.

The Clipper Chip

The Clipper system was originally designed by the National Security Authority (NSA) as an encryption device for the telephone, but the plan was to quickly extend its use for computer data and communications. The *Clipper Chip* was a specialized computer chip with an encoded algorithm known as Skipjack, which would give law enforcement authorities access to all encrypted data communications. It was introduced in 1993 as a voluntary plan, but the government indicated that it would only purchase Clipper phones, and these phones would not interoperate with non-Clipper phones. The government's goal was to have this encryption chip become the industry standard for encryption.

The Clipper chip was a key escrow system with a back door key that was to be split between two government agencies. Each agency would hold half of a binary decryption key that could be used to decode encrypted communications. With a proper court order, law enforcement authorities could access these two halves so that this key could be used to eavesdrop on conversations of criminal suspects.

The technology behind Clipper was complicated but worked as follows. When two individuals using phones (or computers) equipped with these Clipper Chip encryption devices activate the encryption functionality, a symmetrical key is generated known as a *session key*. That session key encodes the sounds of the speaker as they leave one end of the phone and decodes those sounds at the other end. The phone also automatically transmits a packet of information called a LEAF (Law Enforcement Access Field). The LEAF included an encrypted version of the session key and a unique chip identifier. The FBI would have a universal family key that would give it access to the LEAF. Whenever the FBI (or other authorized law enforcement agency) was granted a legal warrant to wiretap, it could then extract from the LEAF the unique chip identifier. Once the FBI had this identifier, it could request the two portions of the unique key from the respective government agencies holding them in escrow; each agency looks up the unique identifier provided by the FBI and provides its portion of the key corresponding to that number. The FBI combines the two halves of the key, thereby enabling it to decode the session key and to listen in on the encrypted communication.[31]

The NSA and other law enforcement authorities saw Clipper as an ideal solution that balanced the conflicting goals of privacy and public safety. According to an FBI white paper on the issue, this encryption chip "provides extra privacy protection but one that can be read by U.S. government officials when authorized by law. . . . This 'key escrow' system would protect U.S. citizens and companies from invasion of their privacy by hackers, competitors, and foreign governments. At the same time, it would allow law enforcement to conduct wiretaps in precisely the same circumstances as are currently permitted under the law."[32]

The Clipper Chip proposal, however, was not met with the same enthusiasm outside of the federal government. It engendered enormous criticism and touched off a spirited and sometimes divisive debate. Security experts were quick to point out its many technical flaws: the Skipjack algorithm was classified and the scrambling was done by circuits hardwired on a tamper-proof computer chip rather than by software. This would make it more difficult to change or upgrade this technology in the future. It also had the effect of making products with these devices more expensive since tailor-made chips are costly.

But most of the criticism was based on ideology and not on the absence of sound technology. Many believed that key escrow plans like Clipper Chip are flawed because they rely on trusted third parties, that is the escrow agents holding the keys. According to this logic, the more parties involved in a cryptography scheme, the weaker it is. Civil libertarians saw this scheme as a massive assault on privacy rights that raised the specter of government officials routinely prying into the affairs of private citizens. According to the ACLU, the Clipper Chip plan was "the equivalent of the government requiring all homebuilders to embed micro-phones in the walls of homes and apartments."[33] John Perry Barlow's polemic against the Clipper Chip sounded like a call to arms:

> Clipper is a last ditch attempt by the United States, the last great power from the old Industrial Era, to establish imperial control over cyberspace. If they win, the most liberating development in the history of humankind could be-come, instead, the surveillance system which will monitor our grandchildren's morality. We can be better ancestors than that.[34]

The Clipper did have its supporters who feared what might happen if wiretapping became impossible thanks to hard-to-crack encryption tech-nologies without any back door entry. They appreciated the legitimacy of the government's goal to prevent the spread of uncrackable encryption code. According to Stewart Baker, the strident and exaggerated opposi-tion to Clipper reflected a "wide . . . streak of romantic high-tech anar-chism that crops up throughout the computer world."[35]

To be sure, there is some merit to these arguments. The exploitation of encryption by terrorists or computer-literate criminals is a valid public safety issue. When the FBI recently broke up a child pornography net-work, it had to contend with encrypted computer files. And encryption was also a factor in the covert communications about an assassination attempt on Pope John Paul II during his trip to the Philippines. As crim-inals become more heavily reliant on computer systems to plan and execute their crimes, they will most likely turn to encryption in order to conceal these illicit activities.

Rhetoric aside, however, Barlow and his colleagues also had a con-vincing claim about the potential intrusiveness of the Clipper Chip. In its efforts to balance national security needs and privacy, this technology might have put too much emphasis on national security by creating a system where the risks to privacy invasions were unacceptably and un-necessarily high.

Clipper II

Vice President Al Gore signaled the first signs of the government's retreat from this plan when he promised to negotiate a compromise with indus-try leaders. As the negative publicity mounted, the original Clipper Chip proposal soon became defunct. Federal officials abandoned the effort to install a government-designed chip in all telephones and computers in order to control encryption. The Clinton Administration responded with a new version of regulations for data encryption in the fall of 1995, which earned "the sobriquet of Clipper II."[36] The bottom line, however, was that export restrictions would remain. This revised plan would permit the export of products with strong algorithms (up to a 56-bit DES), but the government still wanted back door access so decryption keys would be held in escrow by government-approved escrow agents. One concession made later by the Clinton Administration was to give users a choice of escrow agencies (they could be "trusted third parties" from the private sector). Law enforcement authorities seeking out the escrowed keys would have to follow the same procedures used to get authorization for a wiretap. This proposal was seen as less intrusive than the ill-fated Clipper Chip but it too failed to win industry support, since there was widespread sentiment that 56-bit DES was not strong enough. Also, privacy advocates were still uneasy about giving any government agency (or private escrow agent) the key to these communications, no matter what safeguards against abuse were put in place.

In May, 1996, the National Research Council (NRC) issued a major report on this complex issue entitled "Cryptography's Role in Securing the Information Society." The report argued that the export control should gradually be relaxed but not completely eliminated, that the federal government should drop export restrictions on encryption software already available abroad, and that the government should invest more heavily in programs to strengthen the FBI and the CIA's ability to crack private encryption codes. It reasoned that those steps would improve communications security without jeopardizing confidentiality.

Key Management Infrastructure (KMI) or Clipper III

At the same time the NRC report was released, the government issued its third encryption plan in as many years. It was called Key Management Infrastructure or KMI, and it authorized a government infrastructure with key recovery services. KMI was based on the premise that there must be a duly authorized certificate for all public keys. This would be achieved by registering the keys with a key escrow agent and having them digitally signed by Certification Authorities (or CAs). These CAs would function as "digital notaries public" who would verify the identity of the individual associated with a given key.

Under this plan, encryption products with keys of any length could be exported as long as they included a sound key escrow (which the government now preferred to call "key recovery") plan. The plan had to show how trusted third parties or escrow agents would hold the decryption key and be prepared to turn it over to federal authorities if presented with a warrant.

Companies could immediately begin exporting 56-bit keys (up from 40 bits) provided that they complied with this plan for handling keys that exceeded 56 bits and filed a plan within two years for installing key recovery in new 56-bit products.

This proposal met with the same recalcitrant opposition from privacy advocates and software firms, since the U.S. Government would not abandon the requirement of key recovery. But some companies supported the new plan. Others grew tired of waiting for the magic solution, and began working out compromises with the government. In early 1996, Lotus Development Corp. announced that it had won government approval to export a version of Notes 4.0 with high-end 64-bit encryption. But it consented to giving a secret master key to the government so that law enforcement agencies could decode documents or messages encrypted in Notes. This meant that Lotus foreign customers were vulnerable since their encrypted communications could be exposed to U.S. government officials without their knowledge. Lotus saw this as a compromise since it gave the government access to only 24 of the 64 bits. The government agreed to this since 40 bit keys are weak and can be easily cracked if necessary.

In summary, the KMI proposal included the following policy guidelines, which were adopted in the fall of 1996:

- Jurisdiction over cryptography exports was shifted from the State Department to the Commerce Department.

- Companies could apply for approval to export encryption products using 56-bit DES immediately with the proviso that they must present their plans to implement key recovery in 56-bit products within a two year period.

- Finally, high-end encryption products (such as 128-bit DES) could be exported but only if they included key recovery.

The shift of control for encryption products to the Commerce Department was seen as quite significant since this action signaled that the government no longer regarded encryption products as weapons to be managed by the state department. Nonetheless, in his executive order authorizing this change, President Clinton reiterated the need for firm government control over this technology:

> I have determined that the export of encryption products . . . could harm national security and foreign policy interests even where comparable products are or appear to be available from sources outside the United States, and that facts and questions concerning the foreign availability of such encryption products cannot be made subject to public disclosure or judicial review without revealing or implicating classified information that could harm the United States national security and foreign policy interests.[37]

Policy Reversal

In January, 2000, the Clinton Administration finally reversed its stand on tight export controls. It issued a set of new encryption regulations that represented a fundamental change in U.S. policy. In the U.S. government's view, these revised principles would help achieve the balance of competing interests between electronic commerce and national security. The specific policy changes included the following: any encryption commodity or software of any key length can now be exported to any non-government end user in any country (except the seven countries that support terrorism: Cuba, Iran, Iraq, Libya, North Korea, Sudan, and Syria); it must first undergo an initial technical review; a new product category has been established called "retail encryption commodities and software" for encryption software that is most widely available; these retail encryption products of any key length can be exported to any end user (except in the seven states that support terrorism); finally, postexport reporting is required for exports of products with keys above 64 bits (unless they are finance specific).[38] The new policy does not allow the export of strong encryption to government end users without a license.

Shortly after the United States changed its policy, the European Union followed suit. Data encryption exports had been encumbered by licensing reviews and technical checks, but the new EU regulation will allow "almost free circulation of encryption software in the 15 EU countries and in 10 other countries, which together make up over 80% of the world market."[39]

Because of the events of September 11, however, the encryption debate is likely to be reopened. While there is no evidence at the present time that the terrorist group called Al Queda relied on encrypted messages to plan the September 11th attack, there are indications that this group has used encryption for certain communications. As a result, some members of Congress have been calling for a reexamination of the country's encryption export policy in order to give government greater access to encrypted data. They are apprehensive that future terrorist plans may remain shrouded in secrecy due to this technology. Senator Gregg of New Hampshire, for example, has resurrected the key escrow approach; his proposal "would create a quasijudical agency to hold 'keys' that could be used to unscramble encrypted communications."[40]

▶ Encryption Code, Privacy, and Free Speech

The heated encryption debate is closely interconnected with several of the other major themes that have been treated in this book, specifically privacy and free speech. The encryption controversy is yet another example of how technology or "code" affects and controls behavior. The purpose of encryption code is to help guarantee the privacy and security of online communications. This code gives individuals the power to scramble their communication in a way that makes it quite difficult for law enforcement authorities or anyone else to decrypt it. Once again, however, the radically decentralized network technology is empowering the individual in a way that threatens the state. The United States has retreated from its impulse to regulate encryption but there is no guarantee that it will not impose new regulations. The government has seen fit to recalibrate the balance between security and privacy and the freedom to use strong encryption may be an early victim of that recalibration.

According to Michael Godwin, cryptography is central to free speech on an insecure medium such as the Internet since it allows us to "speak with the assurance of confidentiality."[41] Without encryption, users cannot speak with that confidence. It is important for people to feel that they can reveal "secrets" and speak freely without fear that the government may be listening. Encryption code has been regarded by libertarians as a way to promote the value of free speech in cyberspace. Hence their visceral reaction to intrusive plans such as Clipper or even the more modest KMI plan.

Furthermore, allowing government to have back door access to encryption programs is an infringement of privacy rights, since it opens up the possibility for general government surveillance. Once a person's encryption key is uncovered, all of the individuals who electronically communicate with that person become the subjects of that surveillance. A warrant is required before such surveillance begins, but as Kang points out, "electronic eavesdropping cannot be regulated by a warrant precisely because of its dragnet quality; the object to be seized or the premises to be searched cannot be limited or even specified, because it is the very nature of the technology to capture everything."[42]

As we have seen, strong cryptography is important for protecting the information infrastructure. But the government's key escrow plans might have actually *diminished* security. How could escrow agents guarantee that those repositories of escrowed keys would be safe from security breaches? Wouldn't those facilities come under attack from criminals or terrorists? And how could escrow agents guarantee that only authorized law enforcement officials would get access to the escrowed keys? Government is not known for its efficiency in these matters—just look at the recent problem of in-house spies at the FBI. Any failure or security lapse by government officials or trusted third parties could lead to cataclysmic consequences.

Export controls were probably futile anyway, since encryption was already widely dispersed. As a result, the government's liberalized export policies were long overdue. Any attempt to curtail the proliferation of strong encryption would be like trying to put the crypto genie back in the bottle. Critics of these export restrictions had frequently pointed out that high end 128-bit encryption was widely available from non-U.S. software vendors.

Nonetheless, we must also acknowledge that the debate about encryption restrictions and the government's role in managing this technology has sometimes been a bit one-sided. The government has the awesome responsibility to enforce the laws and to ensure order and stability. It is understandably threatened when terrorists or criminals use strong encryption to communicate. The government's formidable challenge has also become more acute in the aftermath of the September 11th terrorist attack. As U.S. national security strategy is revised in the light of these events, there is more sympathy for giving the government greater latitude to monitor suspicious activities in order to prevent future terrorist attacks. However, any plans to enhance security must be implemented in a way that reflects the new realities of our post September 11th world, while remaining sensitive to the centrality of privacy and free speech rights in the lives of Americans.

Discussion Questions

1. Do you agree with the conclusion that spam is a form of electronic trespass? If so, what are the implications for how it should be regulated?
2. Should a Web site be considered private property? In what ways should it be treated differently from physical property?
3. Where do you stand on the controversial encryption issue? Should governments like the United States be allowed to have an escrowed key to all encrypted communications? Is unfettered encryption a good thing for cyberspace?

Cases

The Case of the Pretty Good Privacy (PGP) Encryption Program

In June, 1991, Philip Zimmerman completed a complex and elaborate encryption program that he called "Pretty Good Privacy" or PGP. The program, based on public key cryptography, offered users strong, virtually unbreakable 128-bit encryption. It allowed ordinary users to encrypt their messages so that they could not be deciphered by unauthorized individuals, including law enforcement authorities. Zimmerman believed that people using the Net would need unbreakable encryption for the security of their daily communications.

To the dismay of government officials, the program was made available free of charge to the general public. Zimmerman handed PGP over to an unidentified "friend" in the summer of 1991. That individual subsequently placed the program on a bulletin board system on the Internet for anyone to access, with no fees to pay, registration forms to fill out, or questions to answer.

Since Zimmerman has distributed this user-friendly program it has become the most widely used encryption program in cyberspace. Zimmerman himself never shipped the product to other countries (in violation of U.S. export laws) but there is no doubt that others have taken this free program and made it available to users all over the globe. According to Zimmerman, PGP was dispersed through cyberspace "like thousands of dandelion seeds blowing in the wind."[43]

While Zimmerman is admired by many civil libertarians and those who opposed U. S. export controls on encryption products, he does not enjoy the same status with law enforcement officials. They have contended for years that PGP has interfered with their efforts to apprehend criminals and stop crime. The problem is that PGP makes it possible for terrorists or criminals to protect their communications with extremely strong encryption code, thereby making them off limits for surveillance.

According to the government's perspective, PGP has undermined U.S. export controls of encryption software and efforts to prevent uncrackable encryption programs from falling into the wrong hands, such as the seven countries still off limits for the U.S.'s liberalized encryption policy thanks to their support of terrorism. PGP has also caused difficulties on the domestic front. Several years ago, California police reported that PGP encryption prevented them from reading the electronic diary of a pedophile, which would have helped them crack an expanding ring of child pornographers.

Zimmerman has been investigated by the FBI and by a federal grand jury, but he has never been indicted or convicted of any wrongdoing. He has explained and justified his actions in many forums. In an essay written when the PGP software had just been completed, he cited the need for privacy protection for all citizens as his primary motivation for writing this program:

> If privacy is outlawed, only outlaws will have privacy. Intelligence agencies have access to good cryptographic technology. So do the big arms and drug traffickers. So do defense contractors, oil companies, and other corporate giants. But ordinary people and grassroots political organizations mostly have not had access to affordable "military grade" public-key cryptographic technology. Until now.

> PGP empowers people to take their privacy into their own hands. There's a growing social need for it. That's why I wrote it.[44]

In 1997, Zimmerman sold his popular PGP program to a corporation called Network Associates, Inc. (NAI), a leading United States software company. Soon thereafter, in 1998, NAI announced that it would be selling PGP through its Dutch subsidiary. According to Burns, "NAI had contracted with a Swiss computer company to sell a product that was 'functionally equivalent' to its Pretty Good Privacy; under this arrangement NAI customers outside the United States could purchase the Swiss software and expect it to be fully compatible with NAI's own U.S. version."[45] In a purely technical sense, NAI was not violating U.S. export laws in force at the time since it wasn't exporting any products. But in the eyes of the Commerce Department, NAI was surely violating the spirit of those laws by making 128-bit encryption available outside U.S. boundaries. Some saw the NAI as a personification of Zimmerman's heroism for defying United States export controls. But others saw the NAI as a villain, willing to evade the law for the sake of profits.

According to Petreley, Zimmerman says that he still has no regrets about creating the Pretty Good Privacy strong encryption program "even though terrorists may use it." In his view, strong encryption is essential to protect our "Internet transactions and routine communications," and its occasional use by terrorists or criminals is not enough to discredit the worth of this program.[46]

Questions:

1. From a moral standpoint, do you agree with Zimmerman's decision to release PGP so freely on the Internet given the restrictions at the time?
2. How do you assess NAI's strategy to sell this software abroad in spite of U.S. export restrictions?

eBay v. Bidder's Edge: Trespass or Legitimate Access?

eBay is the largest online auction service in the United States. Founded in 1995, eBay is one of the true pioneers of e-commerce. The eBay model allows sellers to list items for sale so that buyers can bid on those items. The online auctions have been one of the fastest growing business models on the Net, appealing mostly to hobbyists and collectors. According to Porter, despite the fact "that between 98 percent and 99.8 percent of all the people in the world had never attended an auction—for real or in cyberspace, eBay believed that by acting as a cross between auctions, classified advertisements, collectible shows, garage sales, and flea markets, it could take a substantial slice of the market for traditional person-to-person trading in the US."[47]

Unlike physical auction houses, eBay is able to exploit scale economies—its one Web site serves the entire world. eBay has also been able to capitalize on its advantages as the first mover in this industry. According to *The Economist*, "Because eBay was the first and grew quickly enough in its early days, it was able to steamroller the local competition in every international market that it entered."[48] During the first quarter of 2002, eBay earned $46.7 million on revenues of $285 million. It expected to post revenue of $1.1 billion for all of 2002.[49]

Bidder's Edge, a small Massachusetts company, is an auction aggregation site, that is, it uses a bot (or spider) to search for items across different online auctions.[50] It then compiles these items in a list so that its customers can search through that list and realize what is available at different auction sites by only consulting one site. If a buyer, for example, is in the market for rare books, especially nineteenth century British novels, that individual could check the Bidder's Edge site and thereby ascertain all of these British novels available for auction, along with their initial asking price, across multiple online auction sites. Bidder's Edge essentially provides a price comparison service.

eBay, however, objected to the activities of Bidder's Edge and it attempted to block Bidder's Edge spiders through its robot exclusion header. eBay relied on a Robot Exclusion Standard, that is, a machine readable message in a robots.txt file that instructs the unwelcome robot to keep out. Further, the eBay user agreement forbids the use of "any robot, spider, other automatic device, or manual process to monitor or copy our Web pages or the content contained herein without our prior expressed written permission."[51]

eBay claimed that Bidder's Edge violated this agreement and that the company was guilty of trespass. Unable to stop the Bidder's Edge spider through electronic means, eBay filed suit, seeking an injunction against Bidder's Edge. The company's lawyers invoked the ancient doctrine of "trespass to chattels, " that is trespass that harms one's personal property. The argument is that Bidder's Edge has "intermeddled" or interfered with eBay's chattel (i.e., property). CompuServe used the same theory to keep spammers off its mail server in the *Compuserve v. CyberPromotions* case.

Why was eBay so opposed to the incursion of the Bidder's Edge spider? It objected to this practice for several reasons. First, it argued that the robots were a burden on the company's servers. Before the suit was filed the Bidder's Edge spider accounted for 100,000 server hits per day; approximately 1.5 percent of the traffic on the site was attributable to this spider's activities. Second, eBay cited its proprietary rights. According to the company's attorney, Jay Monahan, "Ultimately, the property owner of the $40 million computer system has the right to say when you can come in."[52]

Bidder's Edge had a simple defense. They maintained that there was no trespass since eBay's Web site is publicly accessible. They also contended that there was little evidence that eBay's site had been really damaged at all by the use of these spiders. Finally, Bidder's Edge maintained that they were providing a valuable resource to Web surfers who benefit from their price comparison service.

eBay has won the initial round of this legal struggle. The court rejected the Bidder's Edge defense and it issued a preliminary injunction barring Bidder's Edge "from using any automated query program, robot, Web crawler or other similar device, without written authorization, to access eBay's computer systems or networks, for the purpose of copying any part of eBay's auction database."[53]

Questions

1. Do you agree with the Court's decision in this case? Is Bidder's Edge really guilty of trespass? How strong a case has eBay presented regarding this claim?

2. Assume that you are a lawyer working on the appeal for Bidder's Edge. What arguments would you present on the company's behalf?

3. What are the possible ramifications for the Net if this ruling is not overturned?

References

1. Jason Krause, "You've Been Hacked," *The Industry Standard*, September 28, 1998, p. 50.
2. Rutrell Yasin, "Hackers: Users, Feds Vulnerable," *InternetWeek*, May 25, 1998, p.1.
3. Don Clark, "Computer Viruses Still Proliferating," *The Wall Street Journal*, March 4, 2002, p. B5.
4. Gary Anthes, "Malware's Destructive Appetite Grows," *Computerworld*, April 1, 2002, p. 46.
5. For more background on this see "The Internet Worm," in Richard A. Spinello, *Ethical Aspects of Information Technology* (Englewood Cliffs, NJ: Prentice-Hall, 1995), pp. 208–212.
6. This definition is derived from Tavani's definition of computer crime. See "Defining the Boundaries of Computer Crime: Piracy, Break-ins, and Sabotage in Cyberspace," in R. Spinello and H. Tavani, eds., *Readings in CyberEthics* (Sudbury, MA: Jones & Bartlett, 2001), pp. 451–462.
7. Philip Shenon, "Internet Piracy is Suspected as Agents Raid Campuses," *The New York Times*, December 12, 2001, p. C1.
8. Tavani, "Defining the Boundaries of Computer Crime."
9. Ira Sager, "CyberCrime," *Business Week*, February 21, 2000, p. 38.
10. Jaikumar Vijayan, "Denial-of-Service Attacks Still a Threat," *Computerworld*, April 8, 2002, p. 8.
11. Frances Grodzinsky and Herman Tavani, "Some Ethical Reflections on Cyberstalking," *Computers and Society*, March 2002, p. 22.
12. Amy Harmon, "Piracy or Innovation? It's Hollywood vs. High Tech," *The New York Times*, March 14, 2002, p. C1.
13. Ibid.

14. Dorothy Denning, "Concerning Hackers Who Break into Computer Systems," in ed. Peter Ludlow, *High Noon on the Electronic Frontier* (Cambridge, MA: MIT Press, 1996), p. 141.
15. *The Computer Fraud and Abuse Act*, Section 1030 (a), (1)–(9).
16. Eric Blackwell, "Computer Crimes," 38 *American Criminal Law Review* 481, 2001.
17. Eugene Spafford, "Are Computer Hacker Break-ins Ethical?," *Journal of Systems Software*, January, 1992, p. 45.
18. Deborah Johnson, *Computer Ethics*, 2nd ed. (Englewood Cliffs, NJ: Prentice-Hall, 1994), p.116.
19. I. Trotter Hardy, "The Ancient Doctrine of Trespass to Web Sites," 1996 *Journal of Online Law* art. 7, par. 29.
20. Ibid., par. 53.
21. *Restatement (Second) of Torts*, §§ 217–218.
22. *CompuServe, Inc. v. CyberPromotions, Inc.*, 962 F. Supp. 1015 (S.D. Ohio. [1997]).
23. Ibid.
24. See Harold Reeves, "Property in Cyberspace," 63 *University of Chicago Law Review* 761, 1996.
25. Dan Burk, "The Trouble with Trespass," 4 *Journal of Small and Emerging Business Law* 27, 2000.
26. Simson Garfinkel (with Gene Spafford), *Web Security and Commerce* (Cambridge: O'Reilly & Associates, 1997), p. 21.
27. Rutrell Yasin, "The Cost of Security," *InternetWeek*, February 21, 2000, p. 12.
28. Quoted in Laura DiDio, "Internet Boosts Cryptography," *Computerworld*, March 16, 1998, p. 32.
29. Steven Levy, *CRYPO* (New York: Viking, 2001), p. 73.
30. John Markoff, "U.S. as Big Brother of Computer Age," *The New York Times*, May 6, 1993, p. D7.
31. See Steven Levy, *CRYPO*, pp. 232–233.
32. Quoted in Levy, pp. 240–241.
33. See Dan Froomkin, "Deciphering Encryption," *The Washington Post*, May 8, 1998, p. A4.
34. John Perry Barlow, "Jackboots on the Infobahn," *Wired*, April, 1994, p. 87.
35. Stewart Baker, "Don't Worry Be Happy: Why Clipper is Good For You," *Wired*, June 1994, p. 91.
36. Levy, p. 294.
37. President William Clinton, Executive Order 13026, 61 F.R. 224, 1996.
38. Fact Sheet: Administration Implements Updated Encryption Export Policy, Center for Democracy and Technology, (2000) available online at http://www.cdt.org/crypto/admin
39. Geoff Winestock, "EU to Relax Rules on Data-Encryption Exports," *The Wall Street Journal*, April 28, 2000, p. A 17.
40. J. Rendleman, "Mixed Messages," *InformationWeek*, October 1, 2001, pp. 18–19.
41. Mike Godwin, *CyberRights* (New York: Random House, 1998), p. 156.
42. Teddy Kang, "Cryptography," 2002; available at http://eon.law.harvard.edu/privacy/Encryption%20Description.html
43. Quoted in Steven Levy, "Crypto Rebels," *High Noon on the Electronic Frontier*, p. 192.
44. Philip Zimmerman, "How PGP Works/Why Do You Need PGP?" in *High Noon on the Electronic Frontier*, p. 184.
45. Jennifer Burns, "Network Associates: Securing the Internet," Boston: Harvard Business School Publications, 1999.
46. Nicholas Petreley, "Secrecy is an Illusion," *Computerworld*, March 25, 2002, p. 43.
47. Kelly Porter, "eBay, Inc." Boston: Harvard Business School Publications, 1999.

48. "Internet Pioneers," *The Economist*, February 3, 2001, pp. 69-71.

49. Saul Hansell, "eBay's Rapid Growth Beats Expectations," *The New York Times*, April 19, 2002, p. C4.

50. A bot (or spider) is a software device that enters a Web site and compiles information at superhuman speed.

51. *eBay, Inc. v. Bidder's Edge, Inc.*, 100 F. Supp. 2d 1058 [N.D. Cal. 2000].

52. Oscar Cisneros, "eBay Fights Spiders on the Web," *Wired News*, July 31, 2000.

53. Ibid.

Glossary
The Language
of the Internet

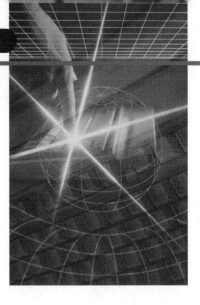

Bot: a software device that enters a Web site and gathers information at superhuman speed.

Browser: a software tool enabling users to navigate the Web, download data, and link from one Web site to another.

Cache: storing information so that the end user can access it more quickly; a Web browser cache stores previously visited Web pages on the user's hard drive.

Clipper Chip: a system developed by the National Security Authority (NSA) of the United States for the encryption of telephone and computer communications; this system was never implemented due to concerns about privacy.

Cookie: a small file deposited on a user's hard drive from a Web server that often contains concise data about what that user examined at the Web site.

Cybersquatting: the practice of registering popular trademark names for ransom, that is, selling them at an exorbitant price to the trademark holder.

Data Encryption Standard (DES): a symmetric private key cryptography system approved by the U.S. government; the same secret binary key is used for encryption and decryption.

Data Mining: the process of sifting through large amounts of data in order to uncover new correlations and patterns to better guage consumer behavior.

This is not an exhaustive list of Internet terminology, but it does provide definitions for the new and unfamiliar terms that are introduced in this book.

Deep Linking: the practice of linking to subordinate pages within the Web site to which one is linking instead of that site's home page (some Web sites object when their home page is bypassed).

Digital Certificate: provides electronic validation of the identity of someone sending a message or transmitting other data in cyberspace.

Digital Versatile Disk (DVD): optical media storage devices designed to store movies in digital format.

Domain Name: a worldwide naming convention that permits each Web site to have a unique, identifiable name, which is linked to a URL address.

Eavesdropping: electronic snooping of Internet data as it is transmitted through multiple computer systems to its final destination.

E-Commerce (Electronic Commerce): refers to business models for generating revenues by taking advantage of the Internet and technology-mediated relationships.

Encryption: process whereby data is encoded or scrambled to make it unintelligible to eavesdroppers; the data is decoded or converted back to its original form by means of a key available only to the intended recipient of that data.

Filter: software program used to censor Internet content.

Firewall: security mechanism that positions hardware/software between an organization's networked server and the Internet.

Framing: occurs when a Web page author includes within that Web page material from another Web page in a "frame" or block on the screen, usually with its own advertising and promotional material.

Hypertext Markup Language (HTML): a language of formatting commands used to create multimedia hypertext documents or Web pages.

Internet Protocol (IP) Address: a unique four part numeric address identifying any computer system connected to the Internet so that information being transmitted over the network can be sent to its proper destination.

Internet Service Provider (ISP): worldwide computer networks that enable individual subscribers or organizations to link to the Internet, usually for a monthly fee.

Key: used in cryptography to encrypt and decrypt data.

Link: a connection between two different Web pages or between two different locations within the same Web page; a "hyperlink" within a Web page contains the address for another Web site, which appears in the form of an icon and is activated with the click of a mouse.

MP3 (stands for MPEG-1, Layer 3): a compression standard that allows music to be stored on a computer hard drive without any degradation of sound quality.

Macrovirus: rogue software that exploits programs called "macros" found in applications such as Microsoft Word.

Metatag: concise description of Web pages' contents embedded into the heading of an HTML Web page, which remain invisible to the user but can be recognized by search engines.

Open Source Code Movement: the source code of application or operating system software is made freely available for modification, corrections, and redistribution; (source code consists of a computer program's statements written in a high level language such as Java or C++).

Opt-in: an approach to privacy based on informed consent; it requires vendors to seek permission before selling or reusing someone's personal information.

Opt-out: similar to opt-in, but in this case users are notified that their personal data will be used for secondary purposes unless they disapprove and the notify the vendor.

Panoptic Sort: term coined by Oscar Gandy that represents the use of personal data for discriminatory purposes.

Peer-to-Peer Network: a network that enables two or more personal computers to share files directly without access to a separate server.

Platform for Internet Content Selection (PICS): a labeling standard that provides a way of rating and blocking online material such as hate speech or pornography.

Platform for Privacy Preferences Project (P3P): a technological framework that relies on predefined standards set by the user to negotiate with Web sites about how that user's information will be utilized and disseminated to third parties.

Portal: a Web-based interface that gives users access to online content such as news services, links to commercial Web sites, and e-mail facility all through one main screen; portals also provide for search functionality.

Pretty Good Privacy (PGP): a 128-bit public key encryption method developed by Philip Zimmerman and made available over the Internet to interested users.

Private Key Encryption: a symmetric encryption scheme that uses the same secret binary key to encode and decode data.

Proxy Server: an Internet server that controls client computer systems' access to the Internet.

Public Key Encryption: an asymmetric encryption scheme in which one of the two keys used in the encryption process is published in a directory or otherwise made public and the other is kept private.

RSA: a standard public key encryption system available from RSA Data Security Inc.

Secure Sockets Layer (SSL): a security protocol that protects data sent between Web browsers and Web servers.

Spam: electronic junk mail sent in bulk form from an individual or organization promoting their goods or services to potential customers on the Internet.

Spider: robotic software that explores the Web by retrieving and examining documents by following its hyperlinks.

TCP/IP: the network protocols that enable data to be transferred on the Internet from one computer to another.

TLD (Top Level Domain): the last extension on a domain name that identifies a Web site; examples include .edu and .com.

Trusted System: a system consisting of hardware and/or software programmed to enforce copyright protection by enforcing usage rights that dictate how and when a digital work can be used.

Universal Resource Locator (URL): the unique electronic address for a Web site.

Web Server: the hardware system on which a Web site resides.

World Wide Web: a location within the Internet that provides for the multimedia presentation of information in the form of Web sites.

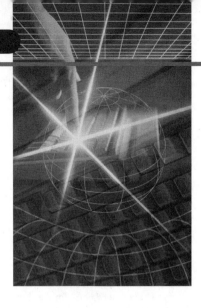

Bibliography

Internet and Society

Borgmann, Christine. *From Gutenberg to the Global Information Infrastructure: Access to Information in the Networked World*. Cambridge: MIT Press, 2000.

Camp, Jean. *Trust and Risk in Internet Commerce*. Cambridge: MIT Press, 2001.

Castells, Manuel. *The Internet Galaxy*. New York: Oxford University Press, 2001.

Dyson, Esther. *Release 2.1*. New York: Broadway Books, 1998.

Gibson, William. *Neuromancer*. New York: Ace Books, 1984.

Grossman, Wendy. *Net.wars*. New York: New York University Press, 1997.

Hance, Oliver. *Business and Law on the Internet*. New York: McGraw Hill, 1996.

Huber, Peter. *Law and Disorder in Cyberspace*. New York: Oxford University Press, 1997.

Kahin, Brian and James Keller, eds. *Public Access to the Internet*. Cambridge: MIT Press, 1995.

Kahin, Brian and Charles Nesson, eds. *Borders in Cyberspace: Information Policy and Global Information Infrastructure*. Cambridge: MIT Press, 1997.

Langford, Duncan, ed. *Internet Ethics*. London: MacMillan. Ltd., 2000.

Lessig, Larry. *Code and Other Values of Cyberspace*. New York: Basic Books, 1999.

Lessig, Larry. "The Code is Law," *The Industry Standard*, April 19–26, 1999, p. 18.

Ludlow, Peter, ed. *High Noon on the Electronic Frontier: Conceptual Issues in Cyberspace*. Cambridge: MIT Press, 1996.

Mandel, Michael and Robert Hof. "Rethinking the Internet," *Business Week*, March 26, 2001, pp. 117–122.

Miller, Steven. *Civilizing Cyberspace: Policy, Power, and the Information Superhighway*. Reading, MA: Addison-Wesley, 1996.

Naughton, John. *A Brief History of the Future*. New York: The Overlook Press, 1999.

Negroponte, Nicholas. *Being Digital*. New York: Knopf, 1995.

Post, David. "Of Horses, Black Holes, and Decentralized Law-Making in Cyberspace." Paper delivered at Private Censorship/Perfect Choice conference at Yale Law School, April 9–11, 1998.

Rheingold, Howard. *The Virtual Community: Homesteading on the Electronic Frontier*. Reading, MA: Addison-Wesley, 1993.

Samuelson, Pamela and Hal Varian. "The 'New Economy' and Information Technology Policy," Working Paper, University of California, Berkeley, July 18, 2001.

Shapiro, Andrew. *The Control Revolution*. New York: Century Foundation Books, 1999.

Shenk, David. *Data Smog: Surviving the Information Glut*. New York: Harper Collins, 1997.

Simon, Leslie. *NetPolicy.Com*. Baltimore: John Hopkins University Press, 2000.

Spinello, Richard. *Regulating Cyberspace: The Policies and Technologies of Control*. Westport, CN: Quorum Books, 2002.

Stefik, Mark. *Internet Dreams*. Cambridge: MIT Press, 1996.

Information Technology Ethics

Baase, Sara. *A Gift of Fire: Social, Legal and Ethical Issues in Computing*. Upper Saddle River, NJ: Prentice-Hall, Inc., 1997.

Bynum, Terrell Ward. *Information Ethics: An Introduction*. Cambridge, MA: Blackwell Publishers, 1998.

Collste, Goran, ed. *Ethics in the Age of Information Technology*. Linkoping, Sweden: Linkopings Universitet Centre for Applied Ethics, 2000.

Edgar, Stacey. *Morality and Machines*. Sudbury, MA: Jones & Bartlett, 1997.

Ermann, M. David, Mary Williams, and Michele Shauf, eds. *Computers, Ethics, and Society*, 2nd ed. New York: Oxford University Press, 1997.

Forrester, Tom and Perry Morrison. *Computer Ethics: Cautionary Tales and Ethical Dilemmas in Computing*, 2nd ed. Cambridge, Ma: MIT Press, 1990.

Gotterbarn, Don, Keith Miller, and Simon Rogerson. "Software Engineering Code of Ethics." *Communications of the ACM*. V. 40, No. 11, November 1997, pp., 110–118.

Gould, Carol, ed. *The Information Web: Ethical and Social Implications of Computers*. Boulder, CO: Westview Press, 1989.

Hester, D. Micah and Paul Ford, eds. *Computers and Ethics in the Cyberage*. Upper Saddle River, NJ: Prentice-Hall, 2001.

Johnson, Deborah. *Computer Ethics*, 3rd ed. Upper Saddle River, NJ: Prentice-Hall, 2001.

Johnson, Deborah and Helen Nissenbaum, eds. *Computers, Ethics and Social Values*. Englewood Cliffs, NJ: Prentice-Hall, 1995.

Kling, Rob, ed. *Computerization and Controversy*, 2nd ed. San Diego, CA: Academic Press, Inc., 1996.

Rogerson, Simon and Terrell Ward Bynum. *Information Ethics: A Reader*. Cambridge, MA: Blackwell Publishers, 1998.

Rosenberg, Richard. *The Social Impact of Computers*, 2nd ed. San Diego, CA: Academic Press, 1997.

Severson, Richard. *The Principles of Information Ethics*. Armonk, NY: M.E. Sharpe, 1997.

Spinello, Richard. *Case Studies in Information Technology Ethics*. Upper Saddle River, NJ: Prentice-Hall, Inc., 2002.

Spinello, Richard and Herman Tavani. *Readings in Cyberethics*. Sudbury, MA: Jones & Bartlett, 2001.

Tavani, Herman. "The State of Computer Ethics as a Philosophical Field of Inquiry." *Ethics and Information Technology*. V. 3, No. 2, 2001, pp. 97–108.

Free Speech and Content Control

Branscomb, Ann. "Anonymity, Autonomy, and Accountability: Challenges to the First Amendment in Cyberspace." 104 *Yale Law Journal* 1628, 1995.

Elmer-Dewitt, Phillip. "Cyberporn." *Time*. July 3, 1995, pp. 37–41.

Electronic Privacy Information Center. *Filters & Freedom*. Washington, D.C.: EPIC, 1999.

Froomkin, Michael. "Flood Control on the Information Ocean: Living with Anonymity,

Digtial Cash, and Distributed Data Bases." 39 *University of Pittsburgh Journal of Law and Commerce* 245, 1996.

Godwin, Michael. *CyberRights*. New York: Random House, 1998.

Katz, Jon. *Virtuous Reality*. New York: Random House, 1997.

Lessig, Larry. "Tyranny in the Infrastructure." *Wired*. July, 1997, p. 96.

Pool, Ithiel de Sola. *Technologies of Freedom*. Cambridge, MA: Belknap Press, 1983.

Resnick, Paul and James Miller. "PICS: Internet Access Controls without Censorship." *Communications of the ACM*. V. 39, No. 10, October 1996, pp. 87–93.

Rosenberg, Richard. "Free Speech, Pornography, Sexual Harassment, and Electronic Networks." *The Information Society*. V. 9, 1993.

Rosenberg, Richard. "Controlling Access to the Internet: The Role of Filtering." *Ethics and Information Technology*. V. 3, No. 1, 2001, pp. 35–54.

Sopinka, John. "Freedom of Speech and Privacy in the Information Age." *The Information Society*. V. 13, 1997, pp. 171–184.

Spinello, Richard. "Ethical Reflections on the Problem of Spam," *Ethics and Information Technology*, V. 1, No. 3, 1999, pp. 185–191.

Sunstein, Cass. "The First Amendment in Cyberspace." *Yale Law Journal* 104 (1995).

Sunstein, Cass. *Republic.com*. Princeton, NJ: Princeton University Press, 2001.

Turner, William Bennet. "What Part of 'No Law' Don't You Understand? A Primer on the First Amendment and the Internet." *Wired*. March, 1996, pp. 104–112.

Wallace, Jonathan and Mark Mangan. *Sex, Laws, and Cyberspace*. New York: Henry Holt Books, 1996.

Weckert, John. "What is so Bad about Internet Content Regulation." *Ethics and Information Technology*. V. 2, No. 2, 2000, pp. 105–111.

Intellectual Property

Alderman, John. *Sonic Boom: Napster, MP3 and the New Pioneers of Music*. Cambridge, MA: Perseus Books, 2001.

Barlow, John. "The Economy of Ideas: A Framework for Rethinking Copyrights and Patents." *Wired*, March, 1994, pp. 47–50.

Bettig, Ronald. *Copyrighting Culture*. Boulder, CO: Westview Press, 1996.

Boyle, James. *Shamans, Software and Spleens*. Cambridge, MA: Harvard University Press, 1996.

Clapes, Anthony Lawrence. *Softwars: The Legal Battles for Control of the Global Software Industry*. Westport, CT: Quorum Books, 1993.

Ginsburg, Jane. "Copyright Legislation for the 'Digital Millennium.'" 23 *Columbia-VLA Journal of Law and the Arts* 137, 1999.

Goldstein, Paul. *Copyright's Highway*. New York: Hill & Wang, 1994.

Greene, Stephanie. "Reconciling Napster with the Sony Decision and Recent Amendments to Copyright Law." 39 *American Business Law Journal* 57, 2001.

Littman, Jessica. *Digital Copyright*. New York: Prometheus Books, 2001.

McCuaig, David. "Halve the Baby: An Obvious Solution to the Troubling Use of Trademarks as Metatags." *John Marshall Journal of Computer and Information Law*, 18: 643, 2000.

Moore, Adam, ed. *Intellectual Property: Moral, Legal and Intellectual Dilemmas*. Lanham, MD: Rowman & Littlefield, 1997.

National Research Council. *The Digital Dilemma: Intellectual Property in the Information Age*. Washington, DC: National Research Council, 2000.

Raymond, Eric. "The Cathedral and the Bazaar," 1998. www.tuxedo.org/~esr/writings/cathedral-bazaar/cathedral.

Samuelson, Pamela et al. "A New View of Intellectual Property and Software." *Communications of the ACM*. V. 39, No. 3, March, 1996, pp. 21–30.

Spinello, Richard. "The Use and Abuse of Metatags," *Ethics and Information Technology*, V. 4, No. 1, 2002, pp. 23–30.

Stallman, Richard. "GNU Manifesto." 1985. www.gnu.org/gnu/manifesto.html

Stefik, Mark. "Trusted Systems." *Scientific American*, March, 1997.

Privacy Issues

Agre, Philip and Marc Rotenberg, eds. *Technology and Privacy: The New Landscape.* Cambridge: MIT Press, 1997.

Behar, Richard. "Who's Reading Your E-mail?" *Fortune*, February 3, 1997, pp. 57–61.

Bennett, Colin. "Cookies, Web Bugs, Webcams, and Cue Cats: Patterns of Surveillance on the World Wide Web." *Ethics and Information Technology*, V. 3, No. 3, 2001, pp. 197–210.

Branscomb, Anne. *Who Owns Information?* New York: Basic Books, 1994.

Brin, William. *The Transparent Society.* Reading, MA: Addison-Wesley, 1998.

Cohen, Julie. "Examined Lives: Informational Privacy and the Subject as Object." 52 *Stanford Law Review* 1373, 2000.

DeCew, Judith. *In Pursuit of Privacy: Law, Ethics, and the Rise of Technology.* Ithaca, NY: Cornell University Press, 1997.

Elgesem, Dag. "The Structure of Rights in Directive 95/46/EC on the Protection of Individuals with Regard to the Processing of Personal Data and the Free Movement of Such Data," in ed. R. Spinello and H. Tavani. *Readings in Cyberethics.* Sudbury, MA: Jones & Bartlett, 2001, pp. 360–377.

Etzioni, Amitai. *The Limits of Privacy.* New York: Basic Books, 1999.

Flaherty, David. *Protecting Privacy in Surveillance Societies.* Chapel Hill, NC: University of North Carolina Press, 1989.

Gandy, Oscar. *The Panoptic Sort: A Political Economy of Personal Information.* Boulder, CO: Westview Press, 1993.

Gandy, Oscar. "Coming to Terms with the Panoptic Sort," in ed. D. Lyon, *Computers, Surveillance & Privacy.* Minneapolis: University of Minnesota Press, 1996, pp. 132–158.

Gavison, Ruth. "Privacy and the Limits of the Law." *Yale Law Journal.* V. 89, pp. 421–471, 1984.

Gurak, Laura. *Persuasion and Privacy in Cyberspace.* New Haven: Yale University Press, 1997.

Kang, Jerry. "Information Privacy in Cyberspace Transactions, " 50 *Stanford Law Review* 1193, 1998.

Lyon, David and Elia Zureik, eds. *Computers, Surveillance, & Privacy.* Minneapolis: University of Minnesota Press, 1996.

Moor, James. "Towards a Theory of Privacy in the Information Age." *Computers and Society*, September, 1997, pp. 27–32.

Reidenberg, Joel. "Resolving Conflicting International Data Privacy Rules in Cyberspace." 52 *Stanford Law Review* 1315, 2000.

Reidenberg, Joel. "E-Commerce and Trans-Atlantic Privacy." 38 *Houston Law Review* 717, 2001.

Rosen, Jonathan. *The Unwanted Gaze.* New York: Random House, 2000.

Rothstein, Lawrence. "Privacy or Dignity?: Electronic Monitoring in the Workplace." 19 *New York Law School Journal of International and Comparative Law* 379, 2000.

Schwartz, Paul. "Privacy and Democracy in Cyberspace." 52 *Vanderbilt Law Review* 1609, 1999.

Sewell, Graham and James Barker. "Neither Good nor Bad, but Dangerous: Surveillance as an Ethical Paradox." *Ethics and Information Technology*, V. 3, No. 3, 2001, pp. 183–196.

Singleton, Solveig. "Privacy as Censorship: A Skeptical View of Proposals to Regulate Privacy in the Private Sector." Cato Institute, Washington DC, 1998.

Sipior, Janice and Burke Ward. "The Ethical and Legal Quandary of Email Privacy." *Communications of the ACM*, December, 1995, pp. 48–54.

Smith, Robert Ellis. *Ben Franklin's Web Site: Privacy and Curiosity from Plymouth Rock to the Internet.* Providence, RI: Sheridan Books, 2000.

Spinello, Richard. "E-Mail and Panoptic Power in the Workplace," in ed. L. Hartmann, *Perspectives on Business Ethics.* New York: McGraw Hill, 2002.

Tavani, Herman. "Internet Search Engines and Personal Privacy," in ed. J. van den Hoven, *Proceedings of Conference on Computer Ethics: Philosophical Enquiry.* Rotterdam, The Netherlands: Erasmus University Press, 1997, pp. 169–178.

Westin, Alan. *Privacy and Freedom.* New York: Atheneum, 1967.

Wright, Marie and John Kahalik. "The Erosion of Privacy." *Computers and Society*, V. 27, No. 4, December, 1997, pp. 22–26.

Encryption, Trespass, and Security Issues

Barlow, John Perry. "Jackboots on the Infobahn." *Wired.* April, 1994, pp. 87–88.

Burk, Dan, "The Trouble with Trespass." 4 *The Journal of Small and Emerging Business Law*, 27, 1999.

Denning, Dorothy and Peter Denning. *Internet Besieged.* Reading, MA: Addison-Wesley, 1998.

Diffie, Whitfield. "The First Ten Years of Public Key Cryptography." *Proceedings of the IEEE.* May, 1998, pp. 560–577.

Froomkin, Michael. "The Metaphor is the Key: Cryptography, the Clipper Chip, and the Constitution." *University of Pennsylvania Law Review.* V. 143, 1995, pp. 709–897.

Garfinkel, S. and Gene Spafford. *Web Security and Commerce.* New York: O'Reilly Publishing, 1997.

Grodzinsky, Frances and Herman Tavani, "Some Ethical Reflections on Cyberstalking." *Computers and Society*, March 2002, pp. 22–32.

Hardy, Trotter. "The Ancient Doctrine of Trespass to Web Sites." *Journal of Online Law*, Art. 7, 1996.

Hoffman, Lance. *Rogue Programs: Viruses, Worms, and Trojan Horses.* New York: Van Nostrand Reinhold, 1990.

Levy, Steven. *CRYPTO.* New York: Viking, 2001.

Levy, Steven. *Hackers.* New York: Dell Publishing, 1984.

Levy, Steven. "Wisecrackers." *Wired*, March, 1996, pp. 128–134.

Siponen, Mikko. "Five Dimensions of Information Security Analysis." *Computers & Society*, June, 2001, pp. 24–29.

Spafford, Eugene. "Are Computer Hacker Break-ins Ethical?" *Journal of Systems Software*, January, 1992, pp. 41–47.

Tavani, Herman. "Defining Computer Crime: Piracy, Break-Ins, and Sabotage in Cyberspace" in R. Spinello and H. Tavani, eds. *Readings in CyberEthics.* Sudbury, MA: Jones & Bartlett, 2001.

Whitfield, Diffie and Susan Landau. *Privacy on the Line: The Politics of Wiretapping and Encryption.* Cambridge: MIT Press, 1998.

Legal Cases Cited

A&M Records, Inc. et al. v. Napster, Inc.

ACLU v. Reno

Amazon.com, Inc. v. BarnesandNoble.com

American Banana Co. v. United Fruit Co.

American Library Association v. Pataki

Aschcroft v. ACLU, et al.

Brookfield Communications Inc. v. West Coast Entertainment Corp.

CompuServe Inc. v. CyberPromotions, Inc.
Diamond v. Diehr
eBay v. Bidder's Edge
Eldred v. Ashcroft
Ginsberg v. New York
Griswold v. Connecticut
Harper & Row Publishers, Inc. v. Nation/Enters
Intel Corp. v. Hamidi
Mainstream Loudon v. Board of Trustees of Loudon County Library
Mazer v. Stein
Metro-Goldwyn-Mayer Studios Inc., et al. v. Grokster, Ltd., et al.
Miller v. California
Multnomah Public Library et al. v. U.S.
Priceline.Com, Inc. v. Microsoft Corporation and Expedia, Inc.
Planned Parenthood v. American Coalition of Life Activists
Playboy v. Terri Welles
Reno v. American Civil Liberties Union
Smyth v. Pillsbury Co.
State Street Bank and Trust Co. v. Signature Financial Group, Inc
Thrifty-Tel v. Bezenek
United Christian Scientists v. Christian Science Board of Directors
Universal City Studios, Inc. v. Remeirdes
Washington v. Heckel
Yahoo, Inc. v. La Ligne Contre Le Racisme et L'Antisemitisme, et al.

INDEX